W9-CKI-897

To Neesa Sweet —
All good wishes,

Bill Reutebuchler
6/13/88

THE
PAPER SWORD
of Bill Rentschler

THE
Paper Sword
of Bill Rentschler

Chicago Review Press, Incorporated, Chicago

Copyright © 1987 by William H. Rentschler

All rights reserved

Manufactured in the United States of America

First Edition

First Printing

Book design and typography by Claire J. Mahoney

Library of Congress Cataloging-in-Publication Data

Rentschler, William H.
    The paper sword of Bill Rentschler.

1. United States — Social life and customs — 1971-
2. United States — Politics and government — 1981-
I. Title.
E169.02.R47   1986   973.9   86-26827
ISBN 0-914091-98-0

The columns and editorials in *The Paper Sword* appeared originally during the years 1983 through 1986 in these Illinois newspapers on Chicago's North Shore:
  Highland Park News/Voice
  Lake Forest News /Voice
  Deerfield News/Voice
  Winnetka News/Voice
  Northbrook News/Voice
  Glencoe News/Voice
  Wilmette News/Voice
  Glenview News/Voice
  Evanston News/Voice

Published by Chicago Review Press, Incorporated

To Martha, with love

CONTENTS

'You've got to be taught to hate . . .'

Once over lightly

If we care about justice . . .

PART TWO

The stuff of fantasy: Being a boy again

Hope for the 'Hopelost' . . .

Footprints across my mind

The predatory sharks of big banking

PART THREE

PART FOUR

Unsigned News/Voice *editorials by the author*

A gentler side

PREFACE

I write because I'm bursting with things to say and share. I treasure my patch of turf.

I write to make people think, to test another view, to explore a new idea, to express a deep-etched conviction, to vent my outrage, to cry out against injustice, to poke a little fun and prick a lot of pomp, to share visions of beauty and tranquility and a better world, to expose perfidy and venality.

I've never believed in "going along to get along." It's cost me dearly on occasion, but lets me feel good about myself.

If everybody's for something or somebody, whether a piece of legislation, a national fad, or a popular politician, I take a very hard look. I often wind up on the other side.

I respect the readers of my column.

I have the notion they're looking for something more than predictable pap or ideology masquerading as principle.

I assume they enjoy being challenged.

I know they are bright, educated, opinionated, accomplished, involved, influential.

Being editor of my own newspaper in my own adopted hometown fulfills a dream. Aside from my family, the *News/ Voice* newspapers are my first love, and they have given me both the goad and the opportunity to write each week the little essays which comprise this book.

— WHR

ACKNOWLEDGMENTS

My profound thanks and appreciation go especially to Jerry E. Kramer, executive editor of *News/Voice Newspapers,* and Sarah Wimmer, my good left arm and associate, who have been the "expediters" of these columns week after week.

Together, they put up with my tangled, tortured manuscripts, water-spotted and coffee-stained; inattention to deadlines, and helter-skelter, eleventh-hour revisions and corrections. Without them, who can say what might have emerged?

Sid Cato nursed this book from its inception and ultimately put the pieces together. Edward Robert Brooks inspired the jacket design.

My lifelong gratitude goes to the late Stella Weiler Taylor, a remarkable lady who made reading and writing for me a special pleasure at an early age. She was my second grade teacher at Madison School in Hamilton, Ohio. Her gentle prodding and constant encouragement got me started writing and made it impossible for me to stop.

The credit to my dear wife, Martha, is of a different sort. She is a loving, well-meaning obstacle to my writing, and I thank her for stimulating my fierce discipline as a writer. When I bury myself in my back room bent on writing, it is she who beguiles me with countless tempting distractions: the beauty of a spring (or summer or fall or winter) day beckons outside, or I simply must get some exercise, or I must do anything but stay chained to my writing machine. She is hard to resist, but resist her I must, or I would rarely write.

So I steel myself against her blandishments, and this is the discipline she imparts by indirection. I think I do better because she lets me think she can barely get along without me.

Finally, thanks are due the special and expanding breed who read our nine hometown newspapers on Chicago's North Shore. They *are* very special. They are my inspiration, for I know they are smart, tough, demanding, selective, critical — and warm, sensitive, and appreciative, possibly more so than any "audience" anywhere in America. I know they will not accept, nor would I ever intentionally serve them, less than my best. Even though I infuriate them on occasion, most come back. They know I'll be honest with them, that I won't succumb to the tyranny of one ideology or another, that I write from deep-etched conviction with which they may not agree. I think they take a certain comfort from knowing I won't change to accommodate the winds of the moment. Some doubtless suffer me largely for that reason. It is these readers who keep me "up" and goad me to do better and stay on course.

Thank you all.

— BILL RENTSCHLER

INTRODUCTION

This is no ordinary book.

Some of America's foremost figures in journalism and public life testify that it is, in fact, quite extraordinary.

It is a series of newspaper columns — call them essays — written by a largely undiscovered writer and editor who is uncommonly literate, graceful, strong-minded, deeply-committed, passionate, tough, tender, irreverent, sometimes downright funny.

At a time when we literally are drowning in overblown potboilers and how-to-do-almost-anything-without-really-trying manuals, *The Paper Sword* offers a refreshing contrast.

It is well worth keeping at your bedside table and reading in fits and starts, browsing, tasting. Open this book to any page — front, back, middle — and find writing that grips, pulls, wrenches, brings tears and smiles, makes you mad, makes you cry. You will come back again and again, each time discovering fresh insights, new perspectives, common-sense alternatives, sensitive, precise, often elegant prose.

This book is often buoyant and uplifting, for Bill Rentschler is to many who know him the ultimate, incorrigible, dauntless optimist. But it is by no means always so, for he is acutely conscious of the dark underside, of the price we pay for man's follies, of sinister intrusions on personal freedom, of hallowed institutions which aren't working.

Through this book, he expresses his deep-felt sense of outrage and indignation as he blisters those who abuse high office and high obligation in both public and private sectors.

It is an eclectic collection by a writer of great sweep and scope who reflects a homely, earthy wisdom and perspective.

Bill Rentschler's writings strike a chord as much with top journalists and national leaders as with his foremost fans, the regular readers of his weekly column.

It would be impossible for me to characterize Bill's essays and columns more generously and unreservedly than some of those.

On reading a selection of the columns which make up this book, Walter Cronkite put them in the front rank of U. S. journalism:

> This collection of Bill Rentschler's columns reminds us forcefully and sadly of what we are missing in much of today's journalism — those tough no-holds-barred, no-quarter-given, first person editorial voices that once blessed our newspapers. Rentschler reminds us of the greats such as William Allen White and H. L. Mencken who frequently reflected the common wisdom but did not shrink from trumpeting outrageous opinion when they felt their cause was just.

Hodding Carter III, Public Broadcasting's media commentator, was blunt in his acclaim:

> Bill Rentschler's work is what journalism is supposed to be all about: committed, outspoken, tough-minded and caring. In a nation whose newspapers suffer from the blands, he reminds us all why the Bill of Rights begins with the First Amendment.

Both clearly recognize the unique qualities of Bill Rentschler's mind and prose and guts, which transcend the "blands" of today's press, according to Carter, and summon for Cronkite memories of two of America's legendary journalists.

In his terse appraisal, nationally-syndicated columnist and investigative reporter Jack Anderson uses only four disparate words to characterize *The Paper Sword:* "Stabbing, provocative, original, and literate."

"In the currency of public opinion," U. S. Senator Mark O. Hatfield (Republican, Oregon) writes, *"The Paper Sword is fresh mint.* Whether the issues are struck in global, national, or local colors, Bill Rentschler calls it like he sees it with refreshing candor and valuable insight."

The old curmudgeon of the U. S. Senate, Barry Goldwater (Republican, Arizona) retiring after thirty years and a GOP Presidential nomination, says of the author, "I wish more Americans could read Bill Rentschler's works. They are pithy, to the point, and they get that point across."

Illinois' two U. S. Senators, both Democrats, chime in with perceptive praise. Writes Paul Simon, a former weekly newspaper publisher himself, increasingly mentioned as a Presidential prospect:

> Bill Rentschler's columns are candid, fresh, sensitive and tough. He has the common touch but has an uncommon feel for the big picture and he portrays that big picture in a down-to-earth style that is distinctively Bill Rentschler.

Senior Senator Alan Dixon, reelected by a landslide in 1986 to his second term, says of Rentschler: ". . . a thoughtful and thought-provoking writer. This collection is a pleasure to read."

Nationally-syndicated *Baltimore Sun* columnist Roger Simon sums up: "You may swear at him or you may swear by him, but you've got to admit William Rentschler is not afraid to speak his mind."

Perhaps this is what elicits strong response — including high praise and unbridled fury — from Rentschler's grass roots readers, such as these excerpts from Letters to the Editor of *News/Voice:*

O   Ione D. Cole, Wilmette, Illinois:

"Praise the Lord that we have Bill Rentschler to write the opinions many of us feel. . . . Keep on speaking out, Bill Rentschler. Your articles may help some of our population see the light. Praise God we still have freedom of speech. . . ."

O   Phyllis Santullano, Highland Park:

"Bill Rentschler's column on hunger was an eloquent and timely reminder of how fortunate most of us who live on the North Shore are . . . how fortunate most Americans are . . . We do not often feel the pangs of hunger, thank God, nor do we see the 'hollow-eyed children with bloated bellies' and pipe-stem legs. . . ."

O   Martin C. Hausman, Chicago:

"Your courage as expressed in your column entitled, "The Conscience of a Lifelong Republican" really bowled me over. I dropped everything else in order to get this letter of commendation and admiration to you promptly. Boy-oh-boy, how this country needs more gutsy guys like you."

O   Arthur Shay, Deerfield:

"Your column on Chuck Percy's night of defeat was a classic. It must have been difficult for an old friend to retain clear, insightful perspective, but you did it, and you did it concisely. It is not always easy to write about a fine ship going down, but you managed to convey the atmosphere, the sadness."

O   Anonymous, Lake Forest:

"Your editorial today leaves me appalled. . . . If you don't realize it by now, you have just committed political and business suicide, not to mention a drastic curtailment in social life. In this short time I could name for you more than a score of subscribers who either will call and stop their subscriptions immediately or fail to renew. And already I know there is a proposed boycott being organized to demand that your present advertisers get out or suffer a serious drop in business. . . ."

○   Aaron Adler, Wilmette:

"I was appalled at a recent letter in the *Wilmette News/ Voice* which threatened you with social ostracism and a business boycott because of your column on President Reagan. . . . My congratulations on your willingness to take what might be an unpopular position. I hope you will continue to speak your mind and your convictions."

○   Mrs. Ruth Lustig, Highland Park:

"In the past few weeks I have been anxiously searching for a clear, definable analysis of our political situation. I have found threats, lies, insinuations, and dissembling, but nowhere, until your column of Oct. 25, an accurate presentation of the facts. Thank you. I'm relieved to know that others are paying attention in the real world."

○   Sharon Rudnick, Northbrook:

"I was sincerely moved by your column. . . . Your analysis and conclusions required and displayed a rare courage in publicly announcing and explaining an obviously unpopular position on the North Shore, particularly among lifelong Republicans. When a person of your stature, reputation and background would willingly and unselfishly evaluate the issues involved and announce unpopular conclusions on a public forum, it would indicate a unique heroism that few of us possess.

"You must realize that when an intelligent, thinking, staunch Republican like William Rentschler admits to having arrived at what he must consider a painful conclusion, he should surely be admired by both friend and foe."

○   Gene Leherissey, Lake Bluff:

"This time you have stuck your neck out a mile. . . . We are sure *Your/Voice* will hear from a lot of straight thinking and better informed readers who, like us, are deeply hurt and disappointed. . . ."

○   John D. Daniels

"You bit your lower lip and did a hard thing. Your courage is obvious to me and I thought someone ought to tell you so."

Bill Rentschler is more than a very good writer, commentator, and outspoken editor of community newspapers. Much more.

He is also the innovative, hands-on Chief Executive Officer of a group of expanding "low tech" manufacturing companies with sales around $75,000,000, employees numbering more than 900, and 13 acres of plant under roof in Illinois, Mississippi, and Michigan.

Rentschler has stitched together his group of privately-owned companies in little more than five years, starting June 15, 1981, with sales just over $6 million and 151 employees, this while the Fortune 500 was showing a net loss of jobs and the economy was relatively listless and uncertain.

Increasingly known as "an apostle (or champion) of low tech," even as the futurists, economists, and media tout high tech and services, Rentschler's contrary approach was noted as long ago as February 22, 1983, in a front-page article in the *Wall Street Journal:*

William H. Rentschler is driving happily in the low-tech lane at a time when most ambitious entrepreneurs are trying to get up speed in the high-tech lane. . . .

"The battlefields of video games, robots and computers will be littered with casualties," he says. "High tech is already overcrowded. They can have it."

In July 1986, Rentschler's common-sense approach to badly-needed job growth in Illinois and the Midwest prompted Democratic U. S. Senators Alan Dixon and Paul Simon to appoint him to head a Low Tech/High Return campaign to nurture, expand, and revitalize basic manufacturing companies.

"My father earned a pretty good living over 55 years running two iron foundries in Ohio and Indiana," Rentschler said. "I'm convinced this nation's future preeminence and our envied standard of living are dependent on an industrial renaissance."

A lifelong Republican activist and self-described "citizen politician," who eschews what he considers "today's kneejerk ultra-conservative ideology," Rentschler twice ran strong primary races for the U. S. Senate from Illinois, losing to candidates hand-picked by incumbent GOP governors. He notes dryly that both his foes lost overwhelmingly, as he had predicted, in general elections, and that their patrons likewise were unseated.

President Eisenhower made him the youngest member of the Republican Committee on Program and Progress in 1960. He guided political strategy for Charles Percy's first winning campaign for the U. S. Senate in 1966 and served as chairman of Richard Nixon's successful Illinois campaign for President in 1968.

"That was when Nixon was resurrected from the political dead. Remember that 1968 started his *good* term," Rentschler has said.

For William H. Rentschler, acquiring his very own group of "hometown" newspapers in 1983 was, in his words, "a lifelong dream come true." His father used to say ink ran in his eldest son's veins.

Bill Rentschler was on the editorial staff of every newspaper at every school he ever attended — junior high, high school, prep school — as reporter, sports editor, associate editor, columnist. He wrote a "light" column while in the U. S. Navy, for Yale's wartime campus paper, later founded and edited a weekly newspaper called *Transition* at a Navy separation center in Toledo, Ohio. At Princeton, he was chairman (editor-in-chief) of the *Daily Princetonian,* an early proving ground for the likes of the elder Adlai Stevenson, first U. S. Secretary of Defense James V. Forrestal, and respected *New York Times* pundit Arthur Krock. He later became a byline reporter for the *Cincinnati Times-Star* and *Minneapolis Star & Tribune.*

He wrote a column — entitled "Viewpoint from Mid-America" — for some 100 Midwest newspapers, did commentary for the National Public Radio outlet in Chicago, and authored a monthly column — "Capitalist Curmudgeon" — for *North Shore Magazine.*

In mid-1983, Rentschler took over a group of bland, raggedy, aimless weekly newspapers, renamed them *News/Voice,* and has guided them to substance and significance in the influential, demanding, affluent North Shore market they serve on Chicago's North Shore. He cherishes his "patch of turf," filling it each week with the diverse essays that make up this book.

Consistently, week in, week out, he has produced a most personal work entitled, somewhat understatedly, "Bill Rentschler's Column," which appears in his newspapers, illustrated with a head-on, no-frills photograph of the author.

In a similar direct and unflinching style, he has produced what many of his wordsmith friends and writers of national stature agree is some of the finest writing, criticism, and commentary found anywhere . . . among newspapers large and small, daily and (as in his case) weekly.

Sometimes abrasive, usually free-wheeling, carefully researched, wide-ranging, learned, somewhat obtuse, I consider him the ultimate "pamphleteer" in the truest sense of that nearly extinct breed of journalist.

Others' descriptions of him include words like "articulate, tart, provocative, witty, wise. Committed, outspoken, caring."

He sees himself as "a good and literate writer, a competent observer of the contemporary scene with a viewpoint leavened by a sense of humor, an educated man with strong, supportable opinions."

"I have seen cynicism, arrogance and venality in the press," he has written. "I also have seen idealism, devotion, great courage, and an unsurpassed level of craftsmanship. . . . We want to be known and respected for fairness, balance, good sense, and independence of thought. No advocates of whatever persuasion need fear that their voices will be stilled or buried in these newspapers."

He is invited by the likes of the U. S. Senate Foreign Relations Committee to testify against import curbs on steel. He speaks to DePaul University's Institute for Business Ethics on the "grandeur and majesty of work." He unabashedly champions basic low tech manufacturing over the high tech and service crazes.

His ear for a memorable quote is as facile as his mind. To support his assumptions and positions, he quotes the likes of Aristotle, Archibald MacLeish, U. S. Supreme Court Justices William O. Douglas, Oliver Wendell Holmes, and Louis D. Brandeis; Goethe, even J. Edgar Hoover, former President James Madison, patriot Tom Paine — all in one carefully researched column.

He also relies on the words and thoughts of such a varied cast as English poet William Wordsworth, French writer Voltaire, Father Theodore Hesburgh, Euripides and Plato, personal heroes like Teddy Roosevelt and Churchill — and, frequently, his perceptive, supportive wife Martha, and daughter Hope, now 14, his "latter-day baby" among ten children and stepchildren.

About the Pulitzer Prize he unabashedly covets for his weekly newspapers: "I'll be disappointed if we don't bring home a Pulitzer within five years. If the jury doesn't see fit to give us one, I want to feel we've earned it anyway." He personally has been nominated twice for a Pulitzer for "distinguished commentary."

This, you will discover for yourself, is something special, a remarkable collection of columns, essays, exhortations — call them what you will.

All I can do is commend it to you.

— SID CATO

**THE
PAPER SWORD
of Bill Rentschler**

Part One

Hamilton, Ohio:
roots, memories of my hometown

Until now, you very likely weren't aware that Hamilton, Ohio, is the center of the universe.

Well, it is. That's been my unshakable theory ever since I grew up there, and nobody's ever disproved it to my satisfaction. I guess most people feel that way about *their* hometown.

MARTHA SAYS I could stop at a fast food place on the moon and run across a cashier from Hamilton.

I phoned recently to make a reservation at a restaurant in Naples, Florida.

When I gave my name, the lady asked, "You don't happen to come from Hamilton, Ohio, do you?

"I sure do."

It turns out we were classmates at Hamilton High a few decades back.

I've lived twice as long in Lake Forest, Ill., as in Hamilton, but there's something about one's origins you never shake off.

Somehow the events of childhood and growing up are both memorable and indelible.

1

I REMEMBER vividly all my grade school teachers in Hamilton, but most of my college professors are blurred and indistinct.

I can picture the exact route I walked to school as a boy, right down to the cracks in the sidewalk and broken copings, the spreading "buckeye" trees and slightly leaning, rich brown telephone poles, the house with the frilly lampshade in the front window, the little store that sold bubble gum, pretzel rods and suckers for a penny.

The lot across from school where we played hardball is still etched in my mind, with its clumps of tough weeds which slowed a triple into a single, the jagged, hazardous rocks and broken bottles, the downhill slope of the terrain.

I can see the muddy Great Miami River which divides Hamilton, meandering purposelessly on its path to nowhere in particular. I remember my father's tales of that docile river rampaging 13 feet above its banks in 1913 and inundating the first floor of the family homestead, which was more than two miles away. He was 16 then and raising ducks in the backyard, and they took refuge from the flood atop the family piano, floating in the living room.

I've never doubted for a minute that Hamilton was America's quintessential, made-to-order hometown. I give thanks often for growing up in that grimy, prosaic milltown surrounded by lush farms, which was a microcosm of the nation, rather than the pristine suburbs of the North Shore, where we have raised our 10 children in a kind of improbable fairyland.

FOR ME, HAMILTON was indeed a "A Boy's Town," — *the* boy's town, in fact, of American author William Dean Howells' warm and gentle book by that name.

"My Boy's Town," he wrote in 1890, "was a town peculiarly adapted for a boy to be a boy in . . ." He described Hamilton as "a town appears to a boy from his third to his eleventh year, when he seldom if ever catches a glimpse of life much higher than the middle of a man, and has the most distorted and mistaken views of most things . . ."

2

A book of the 1980s confirms my lifelong prejudices about the place of my growing up. Its title: "Hometown."* Its setting: Hamilton, Ohio, of course.

MY HOMETOWN WAS singled out by New York author and Academy Award recipient Peter Davis, after an exhaustive pilgrimage to dozens of hometowns all across this broad land, as the prototype American hometown.

He relied on these parameters as he embarked on his search: "The town should be northern enough to be industrial, southern enough to have a gently rural aspect, western enough to have once been on the frontier, eastern enough to have a past."

A Census Bureau researcher told Davis, "You have to find a place big enough to have everything its people need and small enough so you can figure out what the hell is going on.

"You could do worse than go to Hamilton, Ohio."

And so, Peter Davis went there.

I don't mean to be smug, but I knew it all along.

I'll never go back for more than a visit, and I love this part of America where I've lived virtually all my adult life, but to my last breath I shall cherish the roots and memories, the good friends and solid underpinnings, of my hometown.

Howells ended his book with sentiments which mirror my thoughts and feelings to this very day:

". . . He is glad to have had a boyhood fully rounded out with all a boy's interests and pleasures, and he is glad that his lines were cast in the Boy's Town; but he knows, or believes he knows, that whatever is good in him now came from what was good in him then and he is sure that the town was delightful chiefly because his home in it was happy. The town was small and the boys there were hemmed in by their inexperience and ignorance; but the simple home was large with vistas that stretched to the ends of the earth, and it was serenely bright with a father's reason and warm with a mother's love."

---

* Copyright, 1982, Simon & Schuster.

Believing in heroes, from Lindy and TR to Pete Rose

I believe in heroes. They're good for the soul.
I did as a boy. I do today.

If we have no heroes, who's to stir us to greater glory and summon the best that's in us?

CHARLES A. LINDBERGH was foremost among my childhood heroes.

He flew alone across the Atlantic in 1927, before the days of radar, pressurized cabins, and sophisticated electronic gear, in the *Spirit of St. Louis,* a tiny craft that looked like an "amusement park" plane suspended from chains and going roundabout to nowhere.

It hangs today in the Smithsonian in Washington, D.C., and, if you haven't already, you ought to have a look at it sometime. It seems so much the toy, and yet it carried Lindbergh, the tall, slim, boyish pilot of 25, some 3,500 miles across the treacherous Atlantic from New York to Paris in just 33 hours.

No co-pilot, no voices, no bathroom, no hot food, no modern technology. Only the hum of a single, simple engine, the excruciating pressure of staying alert and awake, the total blackness of that night over the inky ocean, the perfect solitude, the buffeting by winds and weather, the total reliance on God and self and a flimsy, primitive machine.

When I first saw the *Spirit of St. Louis,* dangling by wires, as if in a toy-store window, I wondered how the lanky Lindy, about my height and dimensions, even possibly managed to fit into the cockpit of that very small plane. How could he have handled a severe leg cramp or sharp, sudden stomach pains, or any of the demons which sometimes torture human beings totally alone, enshrouded by darkness, in strange surroundings?

LINDBERGH TO ME was the consummate hero, whose personal courage and incredible solo feat exceed those of the brave astronauts. They by comparison are more like robots entombed in capsules controlled by vast crews of technicians and scientists and other-worldly, futuristic equipment. It is the wide gulf between the bold entrepreneur, whose daring mission cost $15,000, and the combined federal/corporate colossus, whose conquest of space requires many billions.

"In an age of corporations and committees he had acted alone," writes Ludovic Kennedy in his new book, *The Airman and the Carpenter*. I guess that explains it best for me.

Kennedy captures with these words the epic quality of Lindbergh's 1927 flight:

"First the boldness of it, the sheer effrontery of this boy of twenty-five who looked eighteen, relying on his skills, the endurance of his frail craft to take him where no one had been before. It was an odyssey like that of the heroes of antiquity, a voyage into the uncharted — into a tunnel of darkness and storm, cold and turbulence, hallucinations and exhaustion — all of which he overcame to emerge into a daylight that was both real and metaphorical, purified and strengthened by the ordeal."

BECAUSE BASEBALL was the game I loved, and first base my position, the fabled **Lou Gehrig** became the sports hero of my boyhood. Except that both were prodigious, feared hitters, Gehrig and his legendary New York Yankee teammate, Babe Ruth, were complete opposites.

The Babe was an uncouth, unlettered brawler and beery woman-chaser. Gehrig, by contrast, was quiet, earnest, "laid back" in today's vernacular, circumspect, educated at Columbia, respected, and as "straight" as Ruth was wild. He set a major league record for 2,130 consecutive games played until a fatal illness cut him down.

5

When I was 12 or 13, and baseball was supremely important in my life, my grandfather met Yankee manager Joe
McCarthy during spring training in St. Petersburg, Florida,
and they became fast friends. Grandpa let it be known that
Lou Gehrig was his grandson's idol, and McCarthy arranged
to introduce Grandpa to the great Gehrig. It wasn't long before Gehrig had parted with a favorite bat — one he actually
used to blast towering home runs — and sent it with a gracious
note to an awe-struck kid in Hamilton, Ohio.

That hero's bat was the proudest possession of my youth.

THERE WERE others who became my heroes along the
path of life:

• The maverick, boisterous, outspoken patrician, **Teddy
Roosevelt,** ever willing to take on powerful forces which
threatened the public interest and summon others to bold
deeds with words like these: "Far better it is to dare mighty
things to win glorious triumphs, even though checkered by
failure, than to take rank with those poor spirits who neither
enjoy much nor suffer much, because they live in the gray
twilight that knows not victory nor defeat."

• Indomitable, intrepid, unsurpassably eloquent **Winston
Churchill,** who seemed at times bent on defending his proud
and tiny island nation with his own bare hands if need be.
"We have not journeyed all this way across the centuries,
across the oceans, across the mountains, across the prairies,"
he said, jaw thrust forward belligerently, shortly after Pearl
Harbor Day in 1941, "because we are made of sugar candy."

• **Everett McKinley Dirksen** of downstate Pekin, foremost
parliamentarian of our time, Republican minority leader of
the U.S. Senate, a righteous, earthy plainsman who radiated
both grandeur and a certain homely vision. "No, you can't eat
freedom," I heard him purr one chill night in 1966, "or buy
anything with it. You can't hock it downtown for the things
you need. When a baby curls a chubby arm around your neck,
you can't eat that feeling either, or buy anything with it. But

6

what in this life means more to you than that feeling, or your freedom? We must glue our eyes on the cause of freedom. It's the one thing that counts. . . ."

• Kindly, tough, at times irascible **General Ike, Dwight David Eisenhower,** hero of World War II, the last President to lead us through eight years of uninterrupted "good feeling" and steady progress as a nation during the decade of the '50s.

• And, of course, **Abe Lincoln,** the stringy country boy from the heartland with the good heart and gentle, profound wisdom.

A WRITER/EDITOR like myself, after all, surely would have heroes in that realm.

Few of you will know the name of **Henry Jarvis Raymond.** Nor did I until Jeter A. Isely, professor of Civil War era history at Princeton and my advisor there, urged me to "find out" about Raymond and make him the subject of my senior thesis. I dug deep, foraging in his birthplace, Geneseo in upstate New York, and in libraries and dusty newspaper files, and found a remarkable, oddly obscure figure of historic importance. Raymond, a protégé of Horace Greeley, founded the *New York Times* in 1851, bestowed on it the character it retains to this day, served as speaker of the New York House of Representatives, became a confidant and campaign manager for Lincoln in 1864, and died at the tender age of 49. He properly may be celebrated as the "inventor" of fair, balanced, objective coverage of the news in a time of raucous, unreliable, personal journalism. Before or since, there have been few — there are even fewer now — of his journalistic persuasion.

Another hero is the defiantly irreverent, ceaselessly bellicose muckraker and savant, **H. L. Mencken,** editor of the *Baltimore Sun* and its most famous writer.

Such simple brilliance as this from Mencken qualifies as heroic in its way: "The public demands certainties; it must be told definitely and a bit raucously that this is true and that is false. But there *are* no certainties."

7

OR, STILL BETTER, this: "It takes no more actual sagacity to carry on the everyday hawking and haggling of the world, or to ladle out its normal doses of bad medicine and worse law, than it takes to operate a taxicab or fry a pan of fish." Amen!

From my childhood, I remember the gentle, hopeful lilt of the poems of **Robert Louis Stevenson.** They mean more to me now than then.

"The world is so full of a number of things, I'm sure we should all be as happy as kings," he wrote.

Another time, he gave us this, which I read first as an adult: "So long as we love we serve; so long as we are loved by others, I would almost say that we are indispensable; and no man is useless while he has a friend."

AND THIS: "If your morals make you dreary, depend upon it, they are wrong. I do not say give them up, for they may be all you have, but conceal them like a vice lest they should spoil the lives of better and simpler people."

Perhaps you can see why those are heroes of a sort to me.

Today, in an era of precious few heroes, mine are **Lee Iacocca** and **Pete Rose,** two of a kind in so many ways.

Many Americans of both parties make the very political, yet non-political, Iacocca their choice for President, ahead of all others, except Ronald Reagan, who can't run again, and Sen. Ted Kennedy, sentimental bearer of the flame for his fallen brothers. Iacocca mirrors the quintessential American success story of the immigrant who bends to no man, who battles giant competitors, bureaucrats, bankers, and the conventional wisdom in restoring his battered company to respectability, profits, and innovative product leadership at a time when much of America's industrial might is declining, withering, surrendering.

LEE IACOCCA IS the reincarnation of the ordinary man from simpler times who struggles against impossible odds, against entrenched, fossilized greed, power, and privilege, against the bureaucrats of commerce and government and their suffocating, constipated ways.

As for Pete Rose, I'd give anything to have him on my team . . . business, baseball, newspaper, whatever. The sprint to first base after drawing four balls, the headlong slide, the feisty, chesty ways, the infectious zest for *his* business, are the qualities that make any enterprise soar.

Sometime soon, probably midway through September, Pete Rose, a ballplayer of middling natural talents and few of the gifts of great hitters like Ted Williams, Stan Musial, and Gehrig, will surpass the previously unassailable record of Ty Cobb and become the all-time leader in base hits among all those who have played professional baseball since its origin in 1869.

This incredible personal accomplishment is a tribute to the man himself, to his sheer grit, durability, and an inner quality no one can understand or assess from the outside looking in.

These are heroes from among the famous. But all heroes do not by any means bear instantly recognizable names.

THERE ARE THOSE of humble beginnings — immigrant, black, poor, handicapped — who achieve a measure of success, which may not be recognized or publicized. These heroes must walk through fields of broken glass, and often suffer endless indignities, to reach their grail. Surely, too, those public figures are heroes who fashion their own resounding, inspiring words and ideas, who stand tall and unbending against the forces of temptation and corruption, who adhere to principle, who shun easy solutions and keep faith with the people.

It is cynics who deride heroes, who point to their feet of clay.

My heroes are not without blemish. Nor are yours.

Nor are we.

But I am better for having embraced some heroes along the way.

What more can I, or anyone, ask?

A hunger tour for Mr. Meese

This is a personal invitation to Edwin Meese, the White House expert on hunger in America, to come here as my guest anytime between now and Christmas to do some firsthand research on the true extent of poverty, homelessness, unemployment, and especially hunger in these parts.

Mr. Meese recently made some asinine, offensive, insensitive remarks suggesting that hunger is a mythical problem dreamed up by "liberals," freeloaders, and worse to embarrass the Reagan Administration.

LET ME SAY flatly that this lifelong Republican — many others, too — was embarrassed and appalled by Mr. Meese's comment that people who don't really need help "go to soup kitchens because the food is free." He added, "I don't know of any authoritative figures that there are hungry children."

Sadly, I think Mr. Meese's callous remarks probably are more a mirror of his personal bias than anything else. I suspect he is so insulated in that Ivory Tower on Pennsylvania Avenue he really isn't aware of the grim plight of many Americans.

He was, after all, a local prosecutor in California, and he has carried all the way to the White House the characteristic, one-dimensional prosecutorial assumption that there are crooks under every bed and that most strangers are trying to rip somebody off.

This is an unfortunate mentality for anybody with substantial power, but a calamity when it involves a high Presidential advisor with substantial input into national policy.

IF MR. MEESE should accept my invitation to come here, I'll meet him at O'Hare and propose the following itinerary:

• We'll drive directly to the grimy West Side ghetto of Chicago, where my friend Primus Mootry, the devoted, knowledgeable executive vice president of the Better Boys Founda-

10

tion, will give him a terse, factual rundown on hunger and introduce him to a half-dozen — hundreds, if Mr. Meese prefers — decent citizens who know hunger and struggle each day to put a little food in their children's bellies.

• From there, in contrast, we'll head to a somewhat more opulent setting in Chicago's Loop, where Mr. Meese will meet Franklin A. Cole, chairman of Walter E. Heller International, the financial giant, who has just led the enormously successful United Way/Crusade of Mercy campaign, which raised more than $70 million to support a range of overburdened private social agencies throughout Chicagoland. A tough-minded businessman, and surely no "bleeding heart," Mr. Cole, a Highland Park resident, wrote just two weeks ago in *News/Voice,* "There are literally thousands of hungry people in the Chicago area, people without enough food to eat on the basic level." I'm fairly sure Mr. Cole could enlighten Mr. Meese on the depressing facts of hunger right here in mid-America.

• We proceed along the North Shore to meet the Rev. William Wilcox, Executive Director of Interfaith Community Services, Inc. He'd welcome a visit with Mr. Meese and tell him of the growing pressure on churches and private agencies in north Lake County, especially Waukegan and North Chicago, to provide food, housing, and heat for the needy, moreso as winter descends. Together, we'd visit a Catholic soup kitchen in Waukegan. Says Rev. Wilcox, "People, and that means poor people as much as any others, have a lot of pride. It's not easy for people to admit they're hungry. So it's not easy to get exact statistics. But we see the need growing. This will be a very hard winter for many."

• Good politicians know how their constituents are faring, and I'd take Mr. Meese to see State Sen. Adeline Geo-Karis, a Republican from Zion, and State Rep. John Matijevich, a Democrat from North Chicago. I'm quite sure each would acknowledge bluntly and without dramatics the local dimensions of a national problem to which Mr. Meese seems oblivious. They would tell him of misery and despair in their districts.

11

I DOUBT I'll be hearing from Mr. Meese.

But this I say to my fellow Americans, including President Reagan: If in this most richly blest of all nations, there is a single hungry child, that is one too many and none of us should rest easy until that child is fed.

Imperfect as we mortals are, that nonetheless must be our national objective and certainly the goal of any who claim now or aspire to national leadership.

Thursday, July 26, 1984

Uninvited 'guest' stirs tears, sympathy

Hope and I were hitting tennis balls against the garage door one recent summer evening when our small black dog, Nipper, began barking on the other side of the house with the kind of high-pitched urgency that suggested he had cornered a raccoon or, heaven help us, another skunk.

Hope dropped her racquet and went after him, and I ambled along a minute or so later.

Martha, standing on the back porch with wide eyes, said in a kind of stage whisper, "I think someone's in the playhouse."

When Hope, now 11, was three and four and five, she practically lived in that playhouse, nestled in a corner of our yard behind the house, but ramshackle and abandoned at this point.

NIPPER SEEMED to be barking "at" the playhouse; oddly, the front door was propped shut and the rickety shutters were closed.

Somewhat gingerly, I walked over and tapped my racquet on the side of the tiny house and then pulled open one of the shutters.

A black and white dog with pointed ears appeared in the window, front paws holding him up on his hind legs. So that's what Nipper was barking at . . .

12

But how in the dickens, I puzzled vaguely to myself, could that little dog close the door and shutters?

I peered into the darkish interior and saw a shape, a body, curled up on the floor. Good God.

"Hello," I said, not knowing what to expect.

THE FIGURE STIRRED, and a man pulled himself up on one elbow.

"What are you doing in there?" I asked.

"Catching a little sleep," he answered in a scratchy voice.

"Well, I'm asking you to leave," I said stiffly. "Right now."

He got partway up, rubbing his eyes, and I decided to back off, leaving him with a little dignity as he made his departure.

Martha, Hope and I went into the house, mused about our uninvited guest, waited about five minutes, and went back outside.

ONCE AGAIN, the door and shutters were closed. Apparently, our visitor, whose face we still hadn't seen, rolled over and went back to sleep the minute we retreated.

This time I was more insistent.

"Hey, I asked you to leave, and I *mean* it."

There was some rustling and scratching in the playhouse, and soon a bony, rumpled, old man emerged with his dog on a leash. Nipper, who had been taken inside but managed to push open the screen door, was beside himself, barking and doing half circles in front of the pair.

I felt a surge of sympathy for the old man. He smiled shyly and said he'd be going.

I walked behind him to the back gate, where he turned and said to me, "I'm not bad, mister. Honest, I needed a place to sleep. I'm a walker, and I don't mean nobody no harm."

HIS FACE WAS gaunt and gray, his eyes hollow. He had no front teeth. His dog was the picture of health.

From my childhood during the Great Depression, I conjured up memories of similarly ragged old men — they were

13

called hoboes then — who came regularly to our back door. The family rule was that we fed them if they weren't reeking of liquor.

About that time, Hope came up behind me and tugged at my shirt.

"Mom and I think you ought to give him some money," she whispered.

I looked down at her. Tears were staining her cheeks, and her eyes were red.

"Please."

I reached into my pocket and fished out nine or ten dollars, handed them to him across the gate, and said, "Maybe this will help a little."

He peered at the wadded bills in his hand, then directly at me.

"It sure will. Thanks, mister." He turned and walked off, limping a little, his dog straining at the leash, to God only knows where.

I stood for a moment thinking about the good fortune of some of us mortals and the crosses others bear.

MARTHA AND HOPE gave me a big, teary hug, and we went inside for a quiet, uncommonly thoughtful evening.

In this paranoid, suspicion-ridden society we live in, I might have called the police the minute we guessed someone was in the playhouse. Probably the police and some of our friends would have urged that course. I'm glad we didn't.

Or I might have approached the playhouse brandishing a gun, which quite a few people would have done — if indeed I owned a gun, which I don't. I'm glad I went with only my tennis racket, which was more than enough, thank you.

Finally, Martha and I treasured the tears that night.

We could feel Hope's concern and caring for a fellow human being, dirty and unkempt, the sort she doesn't encounter often in her North Shore habitat, but which are all too abundant across this affluent land of ours. Her tears were never far from flowing that night.

It gave us the good feeling we are doing something right with our children.

The FBI story: Freedom withers
where informers thrive

> The law is good, if a man use it lawfully.
> — 1 Timothy 1:8

You wouldn't invite Michael Raymond home for dinner. You wouldn't let Michael Burnett date your daughter.

You wouldn't trust George White across the street with your Irish setter.

You wouldn't touch this unholy "trio" with asbestos gloves and a surgeon's mask. Not if you knew the truth.

THE TRUTH is that Raymond, Burnett, and White are one and the same person, the user of a string of aliases to conceal his true identity, that of a repulsively sleazy, scheming, dangerous, oft-convicted swindler, congenital, out-and-out crook, and 30-year career criminal, who among other distinctions is a prime suspect in the "mysterious disappearance" (translation: probable murder) of two wealthy Florida women and a former business partner.

Why, you may logically ask, isn't this lifelong malefactor locked up for close to eternity in a grim bastille where law-and-order politicians tell us bad people must be incarcerated to protect society?

There is a shocking explanation for his freedom. You see, Michael Raymond — let's call him that for the moment — has a few impressive, even eyebrow-raising, references on his otherwise sordid resumé. It turns out he's the current darling

15

of the FBI here, of crime-busting U.S. Attorneys Anton Valukas and Rudolph Giuliani in Chicago and New York, and of
the ruling elite in the U.S. Justice Department.

These intrepid protectors of our morals, property, and safety literally embrace Michael Raymond with the warmth normally reserved for your huggable favorite uncle, shower him
with lucre and other goodies to sustain his luxurious lifestyle,
pamper and protect him like nobility, treat his sullied word
as gospel over that of hitherto respected citizens, brush aside
his 30-year record as disreputable con man and innate crook,
and let him off the hook as long as he does *their* bidding and
testifies to *their* liking against *their* targets — under oath,
mind you, in a court of law, which, more and more, means less
and less.

AND, OF COURSE, to stay outside the slammer, he'll tell
'em almost anything about almost anybody. Bet the next mortgage payment on that.

Informers like Michael Raymond are the tools of tyrants,
and where they flourish, they threaten our liberties, yours and
mine. They breed fear. It has been said through the centuries
that freedom withers where informers thrive.

But this is a nation ruled by law, you say. Why should this
practice trouble us as long as we ourselves obey the law and
informers are used only to convict genuine wrongdoers?

In theory, fine. The truth is, however, that the laws are applied selectively to fit the somewhat ignoble objectives of the
law enforcers and prosecutors.

This is a law-and-order administration in Washington, any
Reaganite will tell you, but the laws are bent for lawbreakers
like E. F. Hutton, General Dynamics, General Electric, and
Teamster boss Jackie Presser.

There is a law-and-order administration in Springfield, too,
headed by former federal prosecutor James R. Thompson, but
rich corrupters with names like Crown, Origer, Everett, and
Miller go free, and gray-flannel graft flourishes in Illinois.

16

IN THE FIRST century B.C., Julius Caesar, of all people, said wisely, "All bad precedents began as justifiable measures." He recognized the obvious then, which we so often overlook now. The rise of despots and their totalitarian regimes, all through the pages of history, started mildly, gradually, and logically, and the rationale for oppressive acts seemed always to be "justifiable" — until it was too late.

In this "land of the free," we quite indiscriminately applaud most politicians and prosecutors who trumpet their staunch advocacy of law and order. Often we do not demand, as we should, that they, too, adhere scrupulously to rule by law.

If you believe "law and order" are applied equally and equitably, fellow citizens, you surely believe as well in the Easter Bunny, busy this day in his hutch decorating eggs, and the Tooth Fairy, pirouetting at the foot of your six-year old's bed. It is my duty, sadly, to disabuse you of such quaint notions and shatter your innocence and idealism.

Our prisons overflow with mostly young, poor, powerless, often illiterate, mainly black and Hispanic inmates, many of whom are non-violent first offenders, while we arrange for a sinister creep like Raymond — and there are plenty more who fit that mold — to live in luxury's lap on your tax dollars, enticing politicians and others into criminal acts, rigging phony scenarios for entrapment, posing as legitimate businessmen and Arab sheiks, flashing and spending big money — all at the inspiration of the FBI to ensnare pols it has targeted, while others equally venal or worse are given a pass.

BY SHEER coincidence, we are told, the FBI turned loose the notorious Raymond to incriminate almost exclusively the black associates and employees of Chicago Mayor Harold Washington. When FBI chief Edward Hegarty was queried about this strange happenstance, he told the press with a straight face that Raymond, the FBI's house-pet, "was brought here by corrupt present and former political figures for corrupt purposes in violation of existing State of Illinois, City of Chicago and federal laws."

17

That's a blunt, declarative statement, which puts Mr. Hegarty in the role of investigator, prosecutor, judge, and jury. Whatever happened to the presumption of innocence, a forlorn casulty in this era of trial by press conference and prosecutorial arrogance?

Hegarty's statement is suspect in the light of what facts are known.

In July, 1984, according to newspaper accounts, Raymond and an accomplice named Varley, armed with a loaded machine gun and silencer, automatic pistol, and ammunition, were arrested in Nashville, Tennessee, on a tip from the FBI, which provided local police with meticulously-detailed information on the pair's plans to burglarize the homes of two prominent Nashville businessmen. Even though the arrests were made by Nashville police, the FBI immediately took custody of old pal Raymond and his associate. Raymond was able to "sell his services" to the FBI, providing damaging testimony against Chicago political figures close to Mayor Washington, in return for his freedom and other benefits.

The result was the long-running, highly-touted series of revelations, which started last Christmas, about alleged corruption in the Washington administration, based solely on leaks and statements originating from the offices of U.S. Attorney Valukas and FBI chief Hegarty, and eagerly lapped up by federal beat and City Hall reporters. The only basis for such charges was the word of this certified con man and tapes which he recorded on a body microphone he presumably wore constantly during his service in behalf of the FBI.

IS THIS SORT of conduct honorable? Ethical? Lawful? Reliable? Fair?

Former U.S. Attorney Thomas A. Foran, now a Loop lawyer, thinks emphatically not.

"I would never have used such testimony when I was U. S. Attorney. Some prosecutors will tell you they don't choose their witnesses. They take them where they find them. But they don't have to. Nobody puts a gun to their head. There is a thing called prosecutor's discretion," Foran said.

Foran gets highly emotional about the use of "corrupt bums" by federal prosecutors to nail high-visibility political targets. In his closing argument in defending the late Charles S. Bonk, a Cook County Commissioner who was acquitted, Foran assailed the prosecutor, then Assistant U. S. Attorney Valukas, a longtime Thompson protégé, for basing his entire case on the testimony of "a couple of diabolically evil guys."

In his successful tirade, Foran also branded the federal witnesses as "shysters, rotten thieves, whore lawyers, fake, phony, scum, and liars."

Patrick A. Tuite, one of Chicago's top defense lawyers, whose client, Judge John G. Laurie, is the only key figure acquitted thus far in the ongoing Greylord investigation of court corruption in Cook County, lashed out at the prosecutors for using immunized witnesses of dubious credibility:

"To make deals with scumbugs like (them) is an outrage. . . . They (the prosecutors) pick a defendant, then try to find the evidence. . . ."

IN THE GREYLORD cases, the FBI bugged judicial chambers to procure evidence. The Laurie tapes were barely audible and Tuite charged they were "doctored" to his client's disadvantage — by the FBI, a genuine shock and criminal offense if true.

The FBI used much the same technique in convicting previously-unblemished members of Congress in the so-called Abscam scandal, using as their prime witness a Raymond-like creep named Melvyn Weinberg, who was paid lavishly for his services and himself spared prison time to incriminate the congressmen.

U. S. Sen. Alan Dixon (D., Ill.) recently used the term "sewer-types" to describe the FBI's choice of informants.

All of this is fairly routine for the FBI, says Rob Warden, editor of *Chicago Lawyer,* and an astute, hard-nosed observer of prosecutorial techniques and criminal justice abuses.

"To anyone familiar with the FBI," says Warden, "he (Michael Raymond) is nothing out of the ordinary. . . . The FBI regularly fraternizes with swindlers and murderers, sex offenders, drug pushers, pimps and prostitutes. In fact, the FBI unabashedly *aids and abets* criminals for the avowed purpose of *fighting* criminals.

"It does that sometimes, when its agents have spare time — *when they're not fully occupied with their preferred role of creating rather than rooting.* (Italics mine).

THIS SHOULD make your blood run cold. It makes a farce of the noble canons of equal justice. It lays the groundwork for a national police force, ever ready to still the voices of dissent, cut down the political foe, render impotent those who challenge the status quo or the reigning administration.

The perceptive park-bench philosopher and advisor to presidents, Bernard Baruch, said three decades ago, "So efficient are the available instruments of slavery — fingerprints, lie detectors, brainwashings, gas chambers — that we shiver at the thought of political change which might put these instruments in the hands of men of hate."

Baruch might have added to his ominous list the highly sophisticated electronic eavesdropping gear which is used today by the FBI and others to penetrate the innermost sanctums of personal privacy and which, unchecked, surely infringe and threaten the freedoms we Americans are guaranteed.

Are we in truth a nation that is ruled by inviolable law, or a lawless nation whose laws may be broken with impunity by the forces sworn to uphold them?

"Nobody," said Jean Anouilh in *Antigone,* "has a more sacred obligation to obey the law than those who make the law."

If the enforcers are corrupt, if they use techniques which mock good faith, besmirch reputations, violate rules of decency, our liberties are diluted and gravely threatened.

"Wherever law ends," John Locke warned in 1690, "tyranny begins."

THIS IS AS true today as ever in our two centuries of constitutional government.

There are few checks and balances on our federal law enforcement apparatus. We have as Attorney General one whose understanding and devotion to the Constitution are at best thin. The FBI and U. S. Attorneys nationwide pursue their own agendas with little interference or oversight. We have good reason to be gravely concerned about their depredations and their assault on time-honored principles of equal justice and equal protection, with clear, unassailable safeguards for the rights of every citizen.

"The people should fight for their law as for their city wall," warned Heraclitus nearly 2500 years ago.

We must not be passive. Or we shall come to rue the day when we allowed our law enforcers, our presumed protectors, to rape and pillage the law without restraint.

September 29, 1983

There's profit and jobs in 'low tech'

The high tech shakeout is upon us. All of a sudden, many "get-rich quick" home computer and video game hotshots — darlings of a frenzied stock market — are in hot water and threatened with extinction.

One of the original stars, Osborne Computer Corp., filed earlier this month for bankruptcy protection. Atari, Texas Instruments, and others have recorded staggering losses. Even Apple's stock has plummeted. Some small copy-cat companies jumped in with public offerings and made big money for their founders even before they had a workable product to sell.

For months now, I've been cautioning against high tech euphoria. My column this week is a composite of articles I've had published over the past 18 months in Crain's Chicago Business, Enterprise, *and* Mississippi Business Journal.

Americans are so bedazzled today by the glitter of high technology that our basic industrial underpinnings are threatened.

High tech's lure is seductive. High tech is nirvana — the easy, glittering path to untold riches. Ask the money merchants and traders, the market analysts and quick-profit speculators who show little concern for U.S. longer-term interests. High tech whets the public appetite for futuristic stocks and meteoric price surges.

If we attract high tech research and industry to our aging cities, the politicians and media tell us, we will magically wipe out unemployment and other economic woes.

Not so fast. Pause for a moment and consider the flip side. Consider the virtues of low tech, which is nothing more or less than all those oft-overlooked and taken-for-granted basic products each of us uses every day of our lives.

We should not easily forget, despite our preoccupation with megatrends and robots, Jedi and genetics, that there's profit in the prosaic, the basic, the unglamorous, the tried-and-true. And jobs — many, many jobs. There's profit and jobs in toasters and toys, glassware and greeting cards, lockers and fasteners, corn flakes and cookies, farm machinery and machine tools.

There's profit and jobs in hundreds of low tech companies of every size and description, each more than a little removed from the fantasyland of high tech, companies that today may be struggling and recovering slowly from such body blows as outlandish interest rates, inflation and recession. They represent the bedrock strength of the American economy, and though I clash here with many self-styled futurists, forecasters, economists and consultants, I believe such companies will continue to provide us with a vital and solid, if unspectacular, foundation as far ahead as most of us can imagine.

Indeed, high tech is sexy and exciting. Home computers are the most visible example. Yet even this early in the heralded high tech boom, the field is cluttered. For every Apple, there will be 10,000 worms.

The high tech shakeout in fabled Silicon Valley, Calif., already is under way, and the odds of hitting it big are about as good as on the craps tables at Las Vegas. Consider the market downswing, ferocious price-cutting, and bankruptcies in such fairly recent high flyers as CB radios and pocket calculators. Consider the well-heeled, well-entrenched competition from the corporate giants.

How much of today's high tech is largely hype — a frenzy churned up by stock promoters, speculators, entrepreneurs, and others seeking short-term gain?

Newsweek reported recently on the breathless San Francisco lawyer who bought three high tech stocks "even though he has no real idea what products they make. All he knows or cares about is that each one has some connection with high technology."

He's made money, of course, in the recent frenetic run-up of "futuristic stocks," but there's a downside too, which for many will resemble the scariest ski run at Vail.

High tech almost invariably means high risk. Low tech usually means low risk — much lower risk.

For every gigantic, highly publicized payoff in genetics and home computers, there are literally hundreds of high tech failures — good ideas that die, ideas that sag or limp and fade because of myopic planning, unrealistic expectations, inept management, and threadbare funding.

High tech has an insatiable appetite for money. The big bottom-line payoff that gets the saliva flowing is unpredictable light years away, as distant and ephemeral as the Land of Oz.

My inclination is to forego the seductive dazzle of high tech and seek out basic low tech products with a reasonably consistent demand and growth cycle. Low tech is "out of season" right now, but to turn our backs on it would be a grevious mistake.

We still aren't at the threshold of cutting our grass with laser beams. People will continue to slice bananas over cold cereal at breakfast. Many low tech executives sleep well at night, confident some genius won't "invent" them out of business before morning with a substitute for lockers or casters or range hoods or whatever.

Of course high tech is critical to our progress and survival and quality of life. We must always encourage innovation and dramatic technological breakthroughs. But it is equally critical, as we gradually emerge from the economic depths, to restore a climate conducive to low tech resurgence.

Let it never be said that here in the 1980s the epitaph for low tech was writ. Let us understand, as National Association of Manufacturers Chairman Bernard O'Keefe has said, that "old ways of doing business, like old buildings, have their place." And let us give a damn about the less prestigious, less glamorous, slower-growing low tech companies that often are ignored by government, media and the public at large, but that, properly tended and cultivated, provide the solid undergirding for growth, jobs, great enterprises, and national prosperity and security.

February 9, 1984

'To soar freely with all the rest'

Ahead of me on the gulf beach at water's edge, a bevy of sandpipers, 200 or so, moved back and forth in unison, prodding the sand with long beaks for a seafood feast as the whitecaps broke gently and receded.

AS I CAME CLOSER, they skittered like so many wind-up toys in lockstep away from the shoreline to give me walking room. They moved in a kind of undulating wave, and as I passed, they rolled smoothly en masse back down to the lapping gulf waters.

All but one.

Of all those soft, gray-brown, feathered creatures which moved with such seeming discipline and precision, one did not. I paused to watch more closely.

He was left behind when his fellows quickstepped out of my way. He flopped awkwardly and looked dishevelled and disorganized and out-of-sync. By the time I had passed, and the others were returning with dainty precision to the lapping waves, the "loner" had barely arrived high on the beach at the place the others had just left.

HE SEEMED "out of it" and forlorn. The others ignored him. I wondered why. Then I saw.

The "outsider" had only one leg. One spindly, twig-like black leg. He was different. He was what we humans call "handicapped."

I mused to myself that he was being treated by his fellow sandpipers the way we humans so often treat our own "handicapped" — the crippled, misshapen, blind, deaf, mentally impaired, the eccentrics and dissenters, even those who merely move to the beat of a "different drummer."

We isolate them, ignore them, treat them deferentially, steer around them. We are ill at ease when we are with them. We sometimes consign them to a kind of human scrap heap.

I kept my eyes riveted on that one-legged sandpiper. He was a carbon copy of the rest — minus one leg. He had all their soft-gentle beauty. But one leg was missing, and that set him apart. He couldn't accomplish those graceful pirouettes on the beach. Nor could he keep up as the others danced lightly across the sand.

OTHERWISE, HE SEEMED like all the rest, able to cope, dig out his dinner, thrive in the clear salt air.

Without thinking I suddenly walked briskly into the flock, "aiming" directly at the outlander.

He hopped awkwardly on one leg while the others skittered away from me with quickening pace until my looming presence triggered their instinct to fly. They swooped off in a graceful arc out over the water and returned to land a hundred yards down the beach.

My "special" sandpiper was among them, every bit as accomplished in flight, as he soared and landed with all the rest.

I WAS PLEASED. I could feel my smile. He probably didn't even know he might be branded as "handicapped" by us civilized human beings.

I wonder if the time might ever come when we'll give our "handicapped" the same chance to soar freely with all the rest.

June 14, 1984

Fearsome monsters threaten safety, sanity

- Swaggering bullies that dominate the concrete ribbons linking our towns and great cities.
- Fearsome monsters hurtling through the inky darkness.
- Great looming beasts as much in command of their turf as maddened bull elephants.
- Arrogant potentates who rule our highways.
- Trucks.

What else?

Here comes another, zeroing in on me, passing within 30 inches or so on the narrow road, the suction pulling me toward its capacious jaws.

RAINING NOW, the roads are glassy. Three great trucks in a line coming at me. A blinding spray wiping out all visibility for a few seconds. Flying blind and praying hard.

Trucks are indeed the swaggering bullies of America's highways.

They used to be good samaritans. Less so these days, far less so. Rarely, in fact.

Those of us who encounter that deadly intersection of Clavey Road and Route 41 are especially leery of trucks.

We know its gruesome history of devastation, sudden death, frightful burns, and ruined lives.

OCCASIONALLY, an offending truck driver is maimed or killed. More often, he escapes, leaving a trail of carnage and agony.

Trucks are vital to the movement of goods, to sustaining the flow of commerce. A truck driver's job is gruelling and thankless.

You couldn't pay me enough to sit in the driver's seat for even a week, high above the roadway, surveying from that crow's nest the movement of hundreds of small, defenseless vehicles, each staking out a patch of asphalt in their comings and goings.

It's not merely well-maintained trucks and alert, trained, careful drivers we're dealing with.

It's booze and pills, failing brakes and bald tires, highway cowboys and hot-rodders, excruciating fatigue and impossible deadlines. Together they pose the constant threat of instant death for innocent victims.

I drove to Mississippi a while ago — all the way on super interstates. It should have been a breeze, only 689 miles from Lake Forest to Greenwood, yet I felt tense and paranoid most of the time, hounded every inch of the way by a thundering herd of motorized pachyderms, relentless and powerful and often seeming out of control.

AT 55, they rode my tailpipe, closing in on my back seat. At 70, they kept up and often passed me, losing ground only on a long uphill incline. If I had jammed on my brakes for any good reason, like a stray child or a dog, I would have been reduced in seconds to a charred statistic.

Driving the Pennsylvania Turnpike several years ago, I

remember vividly hurtling down the mountainside through the blackish night and pounding rain, my wife, two daughters, and I, virtually fleeing for our lives.

They were gaining on us, effortlessly closing the gap, those shadowy giants looming against the sky, great round eyes glowing, their incessant throaty rumble assaulting our ears.

WE STRAINED TO outpace them, but it was as if we were standing still. We could barely see the road ahead. A certain panic overcame us. As my youngest whimpered, my wife dug her nails into my arm. The roar of our pursuers was fearsome and unreal. We felt almost doomed.

Suddenly, from out of the inky nowhere, a savior appeared. In a deft, daring maneuver, he cut between us and our pursuers. They stampeded past us and disappeared into the darkness.

We were saved. We sat limp but overjoyed. Wearing a wide-brimmed hat, our intrepid rescuer emerged from his vehicle with its flashing red lights.

I was shaken by his first crisp words: "May I see your driver's license?"

HIS RADAR SAID I was going 77, which I did not dispute. After all, I was fleeing to save my family from those relentless pursuers, who must have been doing no less than 85 miles per hour.

My speeding ticket, he droned, would cost me $79. The ritual over, I had the last word:

"Officer, do you fellows ever stop one of those damn fool truck drivers, or only us potential victims?"

Silence. He snapped shut his ticket book. Our car shuddered as another great hulk thundered past us down the hill.

Think about it. How often do you see a 40-foot trailer/truck immobilized on an Illinois highway with blue lights flashing nearby and a state trooper dutifully writing out a ticket?

What is our defense, yours and mine?

Country boys in the Big Apple

I admit to membership in that legion of country boys (and girls) attracted by the gaudy glitter of New York, New York.

You're exactly right, I wouldn't want to live there, but I always feel a tingle of excitement when I have reason to go there. It helps that two of my daughters live and work and are utterly enamored by the Big Apple.

With a friend, I went there last week on a very brief business mission. We had time to take in a genuine off-off-off-off Broadway play in which the star was daughter Phoebe's incumbent boy friend. He wowed a standing-room audience of 27, including six in our group, and I must say the fare was better than some I've encountered under the guise of professionalism.

THE LADIES HAD other commitments, so my cohort and I went to dinner alone. We finally decided to "shoot the five hundred" and go to Manhattan's celebrated "21."

Gathering our aplomb, we entered through the wrought iron gates, paid proper homage to the string of maitre d's, and were ceremoniously ushered to a table beneath the famous mass of corporate and sports memorabilia which hangs from the ceiling.

John Henry, my associate, was munching a piece of melba toast, sipping a tall drink, and skimming the menu when he coughed slightly and then erupted in a series of much more vigorous coughs. I immediately had visions of being called on to execute the Heimlich Maneuver to keep him from choking to death.

Let's see, now, do I grab him around the chest from behind, pound his stomach, or just what?

Still unable to talk, he pointed to a line in the menu. I looked and then understood. I felt relieved. There was no medical emergency, except that I, too, suddenly felt a little sick.

HERE A BIT OF explanation is required. All of you who have ever been in military service, whether in war or peace, will remember a famous "dish" which has been a culinary stand-by throughout most, if not all, of the Twentieth Century.

It was mixed in huge vats and then ladled onto what was known grimly as "shingles." To describe the main dish, sailors and GIs down through the decades have used a word which is not considered proper for a family newspaper like *News/Voice*. I have always assumed this particular combination was served so widely and frequently by mess sergeants because it was easier and cheaper to make than mud pies.

That leads me back to 21's menu and John Henry's choking spell.

WHAT HE HAD spotted was an entree called "Chipped Beef a la creme." Get the connection? The price was $21.75. Right. $21.75. Understand the coughing fit?

John Henry quickly regained his composure, and we tried to decide what to eat. We both quickly ruled out the Chipped Beef on a shingle . . . er . . . ah . . . a la creme.

We were relieved to find something at least a little more in line with our budgets. First was a specialty of the house, Chicken Hash "21" for only $18.75. We guessed chickens must be something of a rarity in midtown Manhattan.

A STILL BETTER buy was the "21" Burger for a mere $18.00. We could only assume there were precious few beef cattle or McDonald's within miles of "21."

John Henry and I finally settled on red snapper and swordfish, respectively, both quite strangely priced in the same bracket as that exotic chipped beef. I soon had an explanation. My swordfish was quite tasty, but half as thick at a price 50 percent higher than some excellent swordfish I had a week later at a North Shore restaurant.

Finally, to cap our experience, we were advised in writing that 15 percent for the waiter, 5 percent for the captain, and 7 percent for the wine "sommelier" (waived since we had no wine) were being added to the bill.

As I said earlier, New York is perfectly okay for an occasional visit, but I'm always glad to get back home.

My wife, Martha, her nose slightly out of joint, said only, "Well, what do you expect if you insist on going to 21?"

July 28, 1983

Lament for a noble breed

There is something about Highwood Festival Days (starting today through Sunday), Lake Forest Day (next Wednesday) — and other suburban celebrations on the North Shore — that bring out the hometown flavor of those communities, and at the same time bridge the gap between the great urban metropolis, Chicago, and the myriad cities and towns and rural hamlets all across the vast expanse of downstate Illinois.

AS SOME MAY RECALL, about a hundred years ago — or so it seems — I ran for the United States Senate and thus came to know quite intimately "the rest of Illinois."

Campaigning downstate can be a rare, quite heady, and illuminating experience. Which it surely was for me.

All the cares and turmoil of the political rat-race melted away whenever my black Chevy station wagon was rolling south or west toward Stronghurst or Freeport, Ottawa or Kewanee, Princeton or Marion, Dwight or Watseka, Mattoon or Danville, Vienna or Paris, Melvin or Henry, or any of a thousand other "hometowns" beyond the long shadow of the colossus Chicago.

CAMPAIGNING DOWN THERE, out there, was fun. It was exhilarating. It was rewarding. It was enlightening.

It was a grind, too . . . 40,000 miles in a hundred days over soggy cowpaths and treacherous multi-lane highways, through fleecy clouds and dull gray fog, snow and sleet, always late, always frantic, always at least a little disorganized.

Four or five fitful hours of sleep a night, counting crowds and voters rather than sheep, and agonizing over the next day's speeches.

Handshake after handshake after handshake . . . big and firm, small and flabby, rough, soft . . . until mine were raw and calloused.

Voters, voters everywhere . . . chase them and corner them . . . climb over fences, into haylofts, out of snowdrifts . . . waving, grinning, laughing, clapping, talking, shouting . . . for days a red throat and bullfrog voice, and finally a raucous whisper . . . just enough left to make my case and tell my side of it to people of every size and shape, age and color, disposition, creed and nationality, on street corners and trains, in union halls, schools, churches, stores, courthouses, at teaparties, rallies, plant gates, town meetings, stock auctions.

It was a wearying grind, but it was fun and worth even the dull ache of defeat.

WHEN THEY THINK OF DOWNSTATE, many Chicagoans think vaguely of Peoria or maybe Bloomington and Champaign. Caterpillar's in Peoria, Adlai came from Bloomington, Champaign's a college town.

There are myriad provincial city folk who still conjure up visions of downstate as the land of hayseeds, the Saturday night bath, and twinkly-eyed old men swapping stories in the general store.

There *is* a bit of that nostalgia, for which no one need hang his head. But it may confound some of the more citified types to know that Downstaters, by and large, at least as I see them, tend to be more aware, better informed, just as worldly, and at the same time less harried, less frantic, more serene, more

32

content than the typical well-educated city sophisticates. Downstaters are bright, inquisitive, well-read, well-travelled, and considerably less full of themselves than many of their urban brethren.

Downstaters are generally more knowledgeable about politics. They are somehow closer to their government, more determined to take part in making it work. The Downstater more often knows his congressman on a first-name basis, phones his state legislator to comment on a sticky bill, possibly helps his precinct committeeman knock on doors. And he will never understand the Chicagoan's blasé tolerance of endless vote fraud, payroll padding, and corruption.

Campaigning in Chicago can be a pretty disheartening business. Approach a lady and thrust out your hand, and she's apt to scream and clamp a death-grip on her purse — or belt you with it.

You rarely get to see the full face of an apartment-dweller. All you glimpse is the one-eyed strip of face that squints suspiciously through the narrow opening when the door-chain is stretched taut. This sort of reception turns the legs to lead and the minutes to hours.

ON THE OTHER HAND, a campaign visit to a small town downstate is truly an event. Sort of like your own birthday party. You're a guest of honor and something of a celebrity. People want to see you and hear you out. You get a warm welcome on the street. The hearty handshake is returned just as heartily. A perfect stranger will practically drag you over to meet his wife. You may get treated to coffee in somebody's kitchen.

If you live in the great glass-and-concrete metropolis, it is easy to forget that this kind of life and this kind of people still exist.

In a certain sense, people like these are being hurried out of existence by computerized bigness — big business, big cities, big industry, big money, big ideas, big everything.

They are resented because they refuse to be caught up in

33

the riptide of modernity, because they are not shredded and buffeted by the agonies of the urban jungle.

PEOPLE LIKE THESE, who fashioned with their bare hands the American dream, are being disregarded, disenfranchised, and treated with sweeping disdain. Who needs them? They represent no tightly-knit, easily controlled voting bloc.

They are generally proud and self-sufficient, able to decide for themselves, fairly content with their lot — in other words, not easily bought off by the lure of more and more from bigger and bigger government, or the siren song of the questing politician.

They are a vanishing breed. Nothing much can save them. America owes its existence and much of its greatness to people like these, people who live and marry and work and die where their fathers lived and died. Sadly, the little towns and villages and their people — many of them — are destined to go the way of the bison and the whooping crane.

This is merely a lament for their noble kind.

Wednesday, March 26, 1986

Blame us, the media, but also Democrat leaders and voter ignorance, for the LaRouche debacle

Obviously, a man's judgment cannot be better than the information on which he has based it. Give him the truth and he may still go wrong when he has the chance to be right, but give him no news or present him only with distorted and incomplete data, with ignorant, sloppy or biased reporting, . . . and you destroy his whole reasoning processes, and make him something less than a man.

— Arthur Hays Sulzberger, 1948
Late publisher, *The New York Times*

Blame us.

Blame us, the sagacious, all-knowing media, from the smallest weekly, to the downtown press lords, to the glassy, staring eye of television.

Blame it on the *Chicago Tribune* and *Sun-Times, Bloomington Pantagraph* and *Kankakee Journal, Belleville News-Democrat, Aurora Beacon-Journal,* and the rest.

Blame it on the TV network outlets here, Channels 2 (CBS), 5 (NBC), 7 (ABC), on Channel 9, the Tribune-owned independent, and on their downstate brethren.

BLAME IT ON *News/Voice* and Pioneer Press and hundreds of other community weeklies throughout Illinois.

Blame it on Walter Jacobson, Steve Neal, Basil Talbott, Mike Flannery, John Madigan, Jim Ruddle, Bill Kurtis, Dick Ciccone, Hugh Hill, Dick Kay, Joel Weisman, Peter Nolan, yes, Bill Rentschler, and other presumed pundits who tell Illinoisans what's happening and why on the political landscape.

It may pain us to admit our monstrous flub, fellow journalists all, editors, reporters, columnists, commentators — as it rightly should — but we blew it, and badly.

The grotesque victories of two Lyndon LaRouche disciples on the Democratic statewide ballot must be blamed largely and directly on the news media. Not solely, of course, but we have earned the lion's share.

IF ONLY ONE recognized reporter or columnist in the entire state — from the *Tribune* or *Sun Times,* from a major TV station, from the wire services, even from the *St. Louis Post-Dispatch,* which covers the southern third of Illinois — had "smoked out" Mark Fairchild and/or Janice Hart in a probing, revealing interview or even a "backgrounder," that might have been enough to trigger the chain of "exposure" needed to change the disturbing outcome of this election.

But nobody, to my knowledge, not a single journalist, did it.

So immersed were the vaunted media "experts" in the conventional wisdom — that "minor," non-endorsed candidates have no chance — that they failed utterly in their basic duty to inform voters adequately and thus enable the people to choose wisely.

The essence of the First Amendment is that undiluted freedom which allows the press at its best to report and analyze and interpret fully and fairly, "without fear or favor." The Illinois press failed that test in this primary election.

Sun-Times publisher Bob Page said recently it is not the obligation of the press to be "fair," but rather to be "accurate." In this instance, the media failed the test of accuracy, for no one can claim "accuracy" when hugs gobs of vital information are omitted, for whatever reason, from accounts of major events.

IN A MARCH 12 story headlined "Aurelia (Pucinski) tags Edgar 'big spender.' " the *Sun-Times* reported blandly and incorrectly, "Both are unopposed in their party primaries."

And the day after the primaries, before the results were known, this line appeared in a *Sun-Times* election wrapup story:

". . . Nominated as their (Stevenson and Thompson) lieutenant governor running mates were Sen. George E. Sangmeister (D., Mokena), and Lt. Gov. George H. Ryan, a former House Speaker from Kankakee."

And ". . . Sanitary District Commissioner Aurelia Pucinski will take on Edgar for Secretary of State . . ." Wrong, wrong, wrong.

I can't claim *News/Voice* turned the hot light on the LaRouchers, but at least we acknowledged their presence in our statewide pre-primary summary. Elaine Fandell, our managing editor, wrote:

"In other statewide races, endorsed candidates have only token opposition. Illinois Senator Alan Dixon is opposed by Sheila Jones; Adlai Stevenson has two gubernatorial opponents, Larry Burgess and Peter Bowen; Stevenson's *probable* running mate for lieutenant governor, George Sangmeister, is opposed by Mark J. Fairchild; and Aurelia Pucinski, *running* for secretary of state, faces Janice A. Hart."

AT LEAST FANDELL was not so overcome by the "conventional wisdom" that she ceded automatic victory to the favorites.

Face it, the media let down the electorate and left Illinois with a dismal, dangerous mess on its hands.

In a few days since the fateful March 18 primary election, we have learned vastly more about the eccentric Lyndon LaRouche and his two hitherto obscure candidates, Mark Fairchild and Janice Hart, soon to become household words, than in all the days leading up to that day.

The shallow, slapdash job the media often do in covering elections, especially primaries, finally caught up on March 18 and dealt the public this sickening result.

Voters knew virtually nothing — how could they? — about the two LaRouche candidates. Many were left groping, virtually blindfolded, in polling booths throughout the state, assuming the names on their ballots were legitimate Democrats, having heard nothing authoritative to the contrary via the media, normally their prime source of information, or, for that matter, from their party leaders.

COOK COUNTY chairman, Eddie Vrdolyak, Mayor Harold Washington, and some downstate party chiefs left the statewide races off their sample ballots, presumably because of their intense focus on local contests. Adlai Stevenson apparently did little to boost his chosen running mate.

The LaRouche candidates bore straightforward, Anglo/-WASP names — Fairchild and Hart — which some said, "sounded American." Slated Democrats were Sangmeister, an able state senator unknown by the public outside his Will County bailiwick, whose German name had a Jewish ring to some ears, and Pucinski, whose Polish name smacked of Cook County politics to downstaters and reminded Chicago blacks of her father, Alderman Roman Pucinski, anathema to that key voting bloc. Such ignorance and prejudice, nasty even if largely unconscious, are both ominous and depressing.

Now Illinois faces the threat that the media will turn the LaRouche aberration into the dominant theme of an important election and thus trivialize and distort the outcome. The wildly inaccurate, media-promoted polls skewed the outcome and tipped the 1982 gubernatorial election to Thompson.

With the votes barely counted, the Chicago media in particular are dispensing — once again — the "conventional wisdom" that the primary success of Fairchild and Hart makes Gov. Thompson a "shoo-in" for a fourth term as chief executive, which has the flavor of wishful, less-than-objective reporting, and which is far from certain in today's fickle, unstable political climate.

The people of Illinois are entitled to a tough, issue-oriented, head-to-head clash of wills and ideas — Thompson versus Stevenson — free from the media's obsession to turn a vital election into a superficial sideshow.

IT WOULD HELP immensely if press and TV alike would submerge their fixation on the trivial, bizarre, and embarrassing, and concentrate instead on relevant, substantive, serious issues which affect the lives and livelihood of our state and its people.

Already it is the lot of the public — voters/readers/viewers — to be force-fed far more about the LaRouche contingent than they ever wanted or needed to know. If only a small part of the wretched post-primary excess had been served up *before* the disastrous primary! If only . . .

This overkill may serve to forewarn the public against the dangerous nostrums peddled by the LaRouche movement. Or, with the Rambo mentality prevailing even in the White House, such excessive coverage may give credibility to the LaRouche candidates and generate publicity they couldn't possibly buy.

Why such intensive coverage after the fact? Subconsciously, the media may be laboring under the delusion they are making up for their glaring pre-primary oversight, which, of course, simply is not so. Perhaps the major media are assuaging a certain buried guilt, if indeed the media suffer guilt, instead of freely ascribing guilt only to others.

FINALLY, SHAME ON YOU citizens out there who voted blindly or allowed your ethnic prejudices to guide your choices. Both candidates, for example, carried Lake County.

Writing last Saturday in the *News-Sun*, published in Waukegan, columnist Ralph Zahorik criticized the "folly of urging everyone to vote, vote, vote . . . As a result, hordes of well-meaning, shamed citizens are psychologically lashed into the voting booths to vote for people they know little or nothing about.

"It makes no sense to bludgeon people into casting votes in ignorance. In Tuesday's Democratic primary election, an uninformed vote was actually worse than no vote at all."

Amen. Who can quarrel with that logic?

Let's vow, fellow journalists, to do better by our "constituents" next time.

Don't blame it on the Japanese –

March 29, 1984

What's wrong with American business?

With all the grace of elephants mating in the African bush, America's corporate pachyderms have been grappling in grotesque ritual which portends no benefits whatever for a nation not fully recovered from a period of grievous economic ills.

Such were the Byzantine machinations of Bendix, Allied, Martin Marietta, United Technologies in 1982, and, earlier, of Dupont, U.S. Steel, Mobil Oil, and others among the nation's largest companies.

THIS TIME, it is the lumbering behemoths of Big Oil, with Standard of California proposing to swallow Gulf, Texaco devouring Getty, and Mobil taking over Superior Oil. To accomplish their conquests, these corporate predators will suck out nearly $30 billion from the finite national pool of credit, thus depriving myriad starving smaller companies of critical working capital, even survival dollars.

It is insanity. It is unacceptable. It should — but won't be — stopped dead in its tracks by Congress or the Justice Department.

No new jobs will be created, no new taxes paid. There has been no talk of greater efficiency or other obvious benefits of some logical mergers. Quite the contrary, jobs likely will be snuffed out and taxes reduced by the staggering, obscene costs of the mergers themselves and the complex consolidations which result.

A strong case can be made that acquisitions which add so dramatically to economic power and concentration are contrary to the public good. It is virtually impossible to identify one clear advantage for the mass of America's people or even for the employees of the companies involved.

THERE ARE, of course, as nature dictates, those who gain:

• Big banks and money merchants who make billion-dollar loans to often wretchedly-managed big companies, but routinely reject credit pleas from small business and the very entrepreneurs who created this nation's now-eroding industrial might.

• Investment bankers who advise and arrange and hustle for astronomical fees.

• Sometimes the shareholders and usually the surviving upper-echelon executives, who cut deals for themselves often out of proportion to merit.

We are treated to a blizzard of inane lawsuits, to accusations and epithets hurled back and forth by egotistical chief executives and their toadying hired guns.

WE WERE WITNESS to the sorry spectacle of Mobil's battery of lawyers rushing from judge to judge trying desperately to find an opinion favorable to their aborted takeover of Marathon Oil.

We watched as Mobil's chief antagonist, U.S. Steel, which ultimately took over Marathon, plunked down several billions of largely borrowed dollars to take home its prize after long years of unrelieved poormouthing about the sad state of its own beleagured industry and the unfairness of foreign competition, all the while sadly neglecting its outmoded steel-making facilities.

Chrysler Chairman Lee A. Iococca, who engineered his firm's near-miraculous comeback, rails at "this corporate cannibalism which doesn't create one more stinking job and helps make the credit crunch."

All the while, the Reagan administration sits benignly, approving as a maiden aunt, while one oil giant swallows another in what, at other times, would have been unacceptable economic combinations. Congress also has copped out after loosing meaningless thunderbolts of indignation.

A gutsier figure, Theodore Roosevelt, would have none of it.

"There is absolutely nothing to be said for government by a plutocracy," he wrote Sir Edward Gray in 1913, "for government by men very powerful in certain lines and gifted with 'the money touch,' but with ideals which in their essence are merely those of so many glorified pawnbrokers."

At the same time, in a classic example of contrary wrong-headedness, Reagan's Justice Department initially opposed the "survival" merger of Republic and Jones & Laughlin, two important components of a steel industry beseiged by foreign onslaughts and bleeding from every pore. On sober reflection, the opposition appears to have evaporated.

IN THE DEPTHS of the recent, prolonged recession, it was the powerful corporate behemoths — what Teddy Roosevelt called "the malefactors of great wealth" — which lopped off employees, closed plants, "redeployed" assets.

"Redeploying assets," in many cases, is a genteel euphemism for burying past mistakes.

There is a truism that big companies bury their mistakes, while mistakes — often only one — bury small companies. Giants like General Dynamics, W. T. Grant, International Harvester, and Lockheed, because of their size, resources, reputation, and momentum, were able for years to "bury" glaring errors of judgment, mismanagement, and inefficiency before they finally caught up. U.S. Steel's grab for Marathon, like so many other takeovers by big companies, was in many respects a cover for smug, marginal, myopic management.

George Shinn, former chairman of First Boston Corporation, investment bankers for the Fortune 500, noted:

"Big institutions always have to get bigger. It's because they have a huge overhead. It's always necessary to figure ways to avoid mediocrity and improve profitability. To do that, the institution usually gets bigger."

Not necessarily better. Just bigger.

YET PROLONGED recession and high interest rates — on the way up again and artificially high in any event — buried hundreds of sound, well-established, but thinly-financed smaller companies in the past several years.

It is these smaller companies — not generally the business giants — which constitute the spine and sinew and forward thrust of the U.S. economy. At an Economic Club of Chicago meeting in 1981, Treasury Secretary Donald Regan stunned Chicago's corporate elite by stating that 80 percent of all new jobs in the 1969–79 decade were created by companies with fewer than 100 employees.

And a new Roper poll shows 43 percent of the public has a "highly favorable view" of small business, but only 17 percent have such a feeling for most big business.

Startling? Not really. Not when one considers that the business pages overflow daily with evidence of past miscalculation, overconfidence, and arrogance by some of America's biggest, best-known companies, and in many cases a seeming disdain for the interests of their own employees, their customers, the general public and the larger community.

It is time to pay more attention to the plaintive, common-sense cries of Main Street than to the greedy, guttural urgings of Wall Street.

The four-way scramble launched by Bendix was nothing more or less than a handful of big egos playing high-stakes, real-life "Monopoly" in a game where only they — and a pack of lawyers and investment bankers —stood to gain, and gain handsomely, at the expense of practically everybody else and the nation at large. It is the same with the carnivorous scrapping over Gulf and Getty.

IT IS THE SOUND, small companies which must get attention, legislative relief, and especially financing support if we are to spur a resurgence of America's traditional commercial/industrial superiority. For it is these energetic, emergent, innovative firms forged in the entrepreneurial spirit, rather than the big, bureaucratic dinosaurs, which are positioned and motivated to lead such a renaissance.

June 30, 1983

What a deal to run a utility!

It dawned on me one day that the guys who run the electric company, gas company and phone company probably have the best and cushiest deals going in the wide, wide world of business.

After all, they don't have the same problem as other businessmen — selling their "products" and "services" at a profit against tough, dog-eat-dog competition.

I'M QUITE AWARE the utilities executives will scream as if stabbed at any such claim, the power/gas bigwigs claiming they go head to head with each other, even though I'm not aware of many homes lit by gas, and the phone fellows arguing that they're suddenly being deluged with countless competitors.

The fact is, however, that whenever the big utilities "need" more dollars to dress up their balance sheets, jack up the return for their shareholders, build new facilities or even cover up their own sins of mismanagement, they merely go before a state commission, where they maintain cozy ties, and get themselves a rate increase. Naturally, they always ask for more than they expect to get, so the state commission can give the illusion of driving a hard bargain, and the utility company can get about what it really wants.

Wouldn't you small business owners love that sort of arrangement? Take a local hardware dealer in Northbrook, Deerfield, Wilmette, or Glenview. First of all, you'd start out as the only hardware store in your area with an absolute monopoly on all that business. Not bad for starters.

THEN, FOR WHATEVER reason, you find yourself choking on a huge inventory of seasonal stuff your customers simply didn't choose to buy.

Your profits plummet, which means your shareholders (probably yourself, your wife and the kids) aren't getting a decent return (maybe none at all) on investment. So you can't afford to put those new lighting fixtures in the tool department, or take that long-planned trip to Hawaii.

No problem.

You simply amble over to the Illinois State Hardware Commission, taking along a lawyer with a little "clout" and some smarts in dealing with such august bodies, which, in light of your documented "hardship," allows you to raise all your prices by 25 percent. Suicidal under normal business conditions, but a bonanza when you have a lock on all the hardware business in your part of the North Shore.

THE LOCAL GAS, phone and power companies do exactly that on a more grandiose scale. In an actual case, Commonwealth Edison of Chicago last year ambled over to the Illinois Commerce Commission, accompanied by a real-live former Governor of Illinois, and all opposition to their extravagant demands — presto, chango — simply disappeared. Even the Illinois Attorney General, then running hard but unsuccessfully, as it turned out, to hold his seat — once a ferocious tiger in defending the interests of the beleaguered consumer/voter — was so dazzled by the Governor's presence that he turned pussycat and withdrew his table-thumping opposition.

Now, Robert B. Wilcox of Winnetka, chairman of the Chicago Energy Commission, a utilities watchdog group, predicts this area's electric and gas bills may double by 1986. At the same time, according to the *Chicago Sun-Times*, the Illinois Commerce Commission has accused Commonwealth Edison of "mismanaging its $1 billion-a-year fossil fuel bill, . . . repeatedly overestimating its fuel needs and hiding the problems."

Who pays the munificent legal fees of the former Governor? Who pays for the bungling and "mismanagement" by the utilities? Who else? The very same folks who keep receiving bigger gas and electronic bills reflecting those endless rate increases. You, you and you. All us consumers.

LET'S SAY you reach the point where you damn well aren't going to take another increase, and you organize a group of angry citizens to protest. The heat on the gas or electric company intensifies. Then what?

Easy. They fight back, of course, sending out their armada of lawyers, lobbyists and public relations staff to placate the politicians and editorial writers, running TV spots and full-page newspaper ads, making it seem almost sinful to object to the higher cost of heating or lighting your home. Who pays? Who else? Once again, we do, all us users of their precious power.

Nice work if you can get it, running a utility company.

47

Don't blame the usual 'whipping boys' —
Blame it on the 'non-producers'

- Don't blame it on the Japanese.
- Don't blame it on the labor unions.
- Don't blame it on the declining work ethic.
- Don't blame it on the politicians.
- Don't blame all our ills as a nation on all the usual whipping boys, each of which surely deserves a measure of blame.

BLAME OUR BIG troubles instead on what I term the "non-producers," a pot pourri of opportunists who are sucking this society dry, extracting ungodly sums from a finite pie without producing anything tangible, plucking the fruit of the land to an unconscionable degree, shifting the finite supply of money to fewer and fewer deep pockets, while picking the pockets of nearly everybody else.

- Blame the non-producers for America's decline as a competitive exporter of its goods to the world.
- Blame the non-producers for our inability to beat back the surge of imports to our shores.
- Blame the non-producers for the extreme uphill battle faced by small-business proprietors.
- Blame the non-producers for the growing struggle by more families — even solidly middle-class families — to make ends meet, to come out even at the end of the month.
- Blame the non-producers for the growing disparity between rich and poor.

Nobody, of course, should be expected to shoulder all the blame, but the non-producers deserve to bear a heavy share.

THE TERM "non-producers" is imprecise and in some respects unfair.

What I label non-producers are a fast-multiplying breed

48

who provide "services" for fees, commissions, and stipends without dispensing tangible goods in return.

One of John Naisbitt's "Megatrends" is the proliferation of "services" at the expense of products.

A consistent contribution made by the non-producers is to raise the prices — often dramatically — of all the goods we buy. Frequently the non-producers gang up, so to speak, and render U.S. companies, especially the huge number of small and mid-size firms, which produce 80 percent of all new jobs and represent the unheralded spine and sinew of the U.S. economy, unable to compete in the world marketplace.

THIS HAS TURNED the U.S. into the world's largest exporter of jobs at great cost to every last American.

Who are the non-producers?

Foremost among them is government, the vast and ever-growing bureaucracy at all levels, but especially the federal colossus, despite President Reagan's pledge to shrink government.

Following close behind is the massive, ever-expanding swarm of lawyers, accountants, consultants, commercial and investment bankers, stockbrokers, and other movers of money — the non-producers, who extract from rather than add to the pool of tangible goods.

Some of this is vital, of course, but we have passed the danger point. This nation, for example, has more lawyers than all the rest of the world combined. They snap and snarl, posture and fall all over each other, raising dramatically the level of litigation in a cantankerous and litigious nation, stringing out matters they ought to settle, costing each of us more dollars for whatever we buy.

AMERICA'S GREATNESS was fashioned as a skilled producer of goods and foods. America won World War II, and thus achieved global preeminence, largely because of its productive might, its ability to forge the weapons of war and the goods of daily living, as well as more than enough food to sustain our population and others as well.

49

As recently as 30 years ago, this nation's hard, lean efficiency in producing goods outstripped that of any other world power, whether friend or foe. It has turned to flab.

Now we are steadily, suicidally diluting, even giving up, that decisive edge, ceding industrial superiority to Japan, Germany, the Far East, the Third World. This is eroding American's stature and influence, relegating us to the status of "also ran," to a posture of reliance on others rather than on ourselves.

Little by little this is eroding our greatness as a nation.

It is the easy course, and it rationalizes the failure of our leadership over this past generation, those who have been instrumental in our drift toward mediocrity and subordinate status.

AMERICA IS STILL the world's best place to get rich.

But today, the riches of many are based on "betting right" in the money markets, making the quick buck, the huge fees, the easy return on risk-free loans. There is less stress on the painstaking building of a business which creates jobs and benefits the community. There is less of the character of perseverance, of hanging tough, if you will, often for years.

It is *character* we need most today to take on the hard tasks of remaking an America which we have been unmaking for three decades. It is a resurgence of the original American character.

Small business woes a-coming

I saw it coming last summer, and I didn't like the smell of it. Now I like it even less.

WHAT, PRAY TELL, does the acquisition of a giant California savings and loan by a New York-based international banking colossus have to do with an auto dealer in Winnetka, a home builder in Deerfield, a small manufacturer in Vernon Hills, an independent food store in Glenview?

Plenty.

First, the facts. Last August, the Federal Home Loan Bank cleared the way, despite intense opposition from California financial institutions, for sprawling, voracious Citicorp to take over Fidelity Savings & Loan Association of San Francisco.

Final approval of the deal by the Federal Reserve Board, which made Citicorp the biggest U.S. bank holding company, clearly heralded the early stages of unrestricted interstate banking.

THIS MEANS GIANT banking "systems" in seven league boots, led by expansionist Citicorp, will crisscross the nation in a relentless quest for deposits, loans, and other lucrative financial deals.

Closer to home, and less than a year later, Citicorp (and others), as I write this, is hot on the trail of First Federal Savings of Chicago, which got into financial difficulty along with countless other firms as a result of scandalous, all-time record interest rates during 1979–81, and which since has been disemboweled and put on the block by bloodless federal regulators.

Citicorp is hardly starting from scratch. Their loan and service offices, which by law can't accept deposits, and which legally circumvent restrictions on interstate banking, are strung out across the U.S. In their Atlanta operations alone, Citicorp already employs more than 300 persons. They are said to have an advance cadre of some 400 in Chicago.

In the high-stakes scramble for big bucks, many smaller, independent banks, rooted in and dedicated to their home-towns, will be bought up, crowded out, beaten down by the foraging giants of international banking.

WHEN THAT HOME BUILDER in Deerfield needs work-ing capital at the height of the construction season, he may be shocked to find the rules changed to his detriment.

Instead of sitting across a desk from the banker he's known since they played high school football together, he may find himself dealing with an unfamiliar, uptight, pin-striped, 29-year old Harvard MBA from Rye, New York, who's learning the ropes out in the boondocks before being "promoted" back to corporate headquarters.

The local businessman may suddenly be confronted with a scary scenario that includes a remote bureaucracy, distant credit committees, bland disinterest, possibly even an unjusti-fied loan turndown, and his own towering frustration as he attempts to keep his business afloat and growing.

Walter B. Wriston, Citicorp's driving, demanding chairman, who seems to cotton primarily to lords at his own level, views himself, as do his financial peers, as near undisputed king of the financial hill. His aim is bigness, dominance, a carving up of the pie among a handful of big financial institutions pri-marily for the benefit of a thousand or so big public com-panies, a sprinkling of foreign potentates, and themselves, especially, of course, Citicorp.

WRISTON'S PHILOSOPHY is enough to make a small businessman lapse into chronic insomnia and ulcerated colitis. Listen to what he said four years ago at a conclave of business and financial tycoons in Hot Springs, Virginia:

"The drastic tightening of credit doesn't mean the end of the world. It means the less creditworthy won't get it."

What Wriston meant is that smaller companies with little or no clout, the less important customers of the big banks, won't get it. Many, denied adequate credit during the grim recession of the past two years, already are dead and buried. Others this day are clinging by their fingernails and may never recover.

Walter Wriston, banking buccaneer, would rather take over a faltering $2.9 billion savings and loan in California — followed by another prize trophy in Chicago — to spread Citicorp's dominance than ration those same funds among hundreds of deserving, creditworthy, but "starving" smaller companies.

Citicorp, of course, may not finally bag its Chicago prey. The competition is impressive: Sears Roebuck and First Chicago, among others. If not First Federal, however, someone else; the trend is unmistakable, and, with the acquiescence of the Reagan administration, inevitable.

IF SMALL BUSINESS PEOPLE understand what's coming, they'll certainly try mightily, somehow, to head it off. Independent businessmen from sea to shining sea ought to be jawboning, even threatening, their congressmen and U.S. Senators this very minute.

Interstate banking, now a looming reality, may be the most critical threat ever to the survival of smaller, privately-owned companies, the spine and sinew of the American economy, and the national cornucopia of new jobs, new ideas, and new products.

Steel import curbs will be costly to all

The conventional wisdom, as dispersed by Big Steel and the United Steelworkers of America, is that this nation would be severely damaged and many jobs lost if import curbs aren't imposed on foreign steel.

The fact is the damage would be far greater if Big Steel gets its way. What the public doesn't understand is that the *users* of steel — thousands of small companies nationwide as well as huge Illinois employers like Peoria's Caterpillar Tractor — provide *20 times* as many jobs as *all* of the Big Steel producers put together.

The matter of steel import policy clearly is an issue of great significance to the nation.

MY INSIGHTS ARE based directly on my role as chief executive officer of several small steel fabricating companies with several hundred employees which depend on our ability to buy first-quality steel at prices which enable us to compete in a dog-eat-dog, worldwide marketplace.

With its highly effective lobbying apparatus, Big Steel has made its case to Congress and the public. In certain respects, it is highly distorted and certainly one-sided. What damage imports may do to the steel industry is more than offset by the benefits to hundreds of fabricators of steel, like ourselves: thousands of their employees, and millions of consumers, who buy countless products made from steel.

Let me cite a specific example. Our company, Jackson Forge Corporation, makes custom forgings for such major companies as Chrysler, Mack Truck, Clark Equipment, Cummins Engine, Dana, Warner Gear, and others.

During the recent deep and prolonged recession, our sales declined by 50 percent. We took aggressive steps to beef up our marketing in preparation for the inevitable economic upturn. But when it came, we found ourselves frozen out in the early stages, largely because of domestic steel prices which were too high to allow us to be competitive. We were high on quote after quote to our customers and prospects because of these relatively high steel prices, which were critical to us as a maker of material-intensive forgings.

WE WERE COMPLETELY unsuccessful in getting the major domestic mills to give us prices which would enable us to compete with imported forgings and with competitors buying foreign steel.

This forced a hard decision on us. We, too, would buy some foreign steel. With the arrival of our first shipment from abroad, our domestic suppliers came flocking to our door, suddenly "discovering" they could make certain price concessions. Our decision to buy some steel abroad — even though it represented only 30 percent of our total requirements — literally saved our life.

Since then, with a competitive price mix on steel, our sales are up 81 percent over the past nine months and we have returned to modest profitability. There is not the slightest doubt in my mind that our imported steel gave us the bargaining clout we needed to buy at reasonably competitive prices from the big domestic producers.

The most pressing problems of *most* steel companies do not stem primarily from foreign competition. While some companies, like Inland Steel, for example, have been run with vision and competence, some of the largest firms in the industry are now victims of their own long-term arrogance, complacency and shortsightedness over two decades or more. While some visionary companies like General Electric were resisting excessive union demands some years ago, Big Steel (and the auto companies as well) were giving away the store, taking the easy way out, and creating impossible future conditions. Some steel producers have been out buying oil companies and savings and loans while ignoring their steel-making facilities. Now they want a government bailout that would benefit them but surely hurt their customers and the American public.

SMALL AND MEDIUM-SIZED companies, their employees, and the American consumer should not be penalized and perhaps driven out of business and out of work to atone for the past sins of Big Steel. It seems inevitable to me that the major steel companies will immediately raise their prices the minute foreign competition is curtailed, inflicting severe, even lethal, damage on defenseless smaller companies with limited alternatives.

The ultimate decision on this matter, according to U.S. Trade Representative William E. Brock, will be made by President Reagan before the election, and presumably will consider the impact of import relief "on U.S. consumers and the economy as a whole," as well as "the concerns" of companies like ours.

It would be unfortunate if the President decides this critical issue on the basis of political considerations. Pressure for import curbs from the key industrial states will be intense in the next 60 days or so, yet the tradeoffs would be severely damaging to the public, to the users of steel and their employees, and to our relations with our world allies.

This column was adapted from Bill Rentschler's testimony before the U. S. Senate Foreign Relations Committee on July 6, 1984.

An agenda for U.S. 'greatness'

The battle for the bones and fossil riches of Phillips Petroleum is yet another chapter in the systematic dismantling of America's greatness.

The corporate raiders — Icahn, Jacobs, Posner, Boone, Pickens, and their ilk — crouch in the underbrush, stalking their prey, those companies whose assets are "undervalued," whose cash reserves and other liquid assets have been accumulated prudently, whose stock is fairly widely dispersed — and, when the moment seems ripe, lunge for the kill, that is, of course, the takeover.

They bill themselves as benefactors of the forgotten shareholder, but the biggest owners of stock generally are the huge institutions and money managers rather than the "little guy" they profess to champion.

THE GIANT CORPORATE takeovers assuredly do not benefit most Americans, but only the relative few. These enormous, multi-billion dollar conquests should be understood for what they are: monuments to greed and the "fast buck," for that is what accrues to the raiders, even if they are unsuccessful in their quest. The company under assault may succumb to "greenmail" and buy back its stock from the raiders at extortion prices, usually to save top management's power and pelf.

By a mile or two, Art Buchwald probably is the most perceptive humorist, perhaps even philosopher, of our time. He writes with pungent brilliance about "the beauty of takeovers.

"You don't have to produce anything, or employ people, or worry about Japan. . . ."

Thus are sown the seeds of our decline.

WE ARE INDEED in the process of dismantling — and not replacing — the machinery of production which won

World War II and made us the envy of our planet. Today, some seem content to accept second or fourth place behind the Third World.

Today, we deride our smokestack industries, squeeze out small farmers, deny the capital needs of little and mid-sized businesses — and in the process erode the strength and critical underpinnings of our economy.

At the same time, possibly beyond recall, we are spawning a parasitic, fast-multiplying, increasingly virulent and opulent stratum of non-producers, the vaunted service and professional elite which demands an ever-larger bite of a shrinking, finite pie.

WHO ARE THESE so-called non-producers?

- They are the lawyers, who for big bucks hire themselves out to unravel the complexities they create, all the while creating still more and greater complexity.

- They are the investment bankers, who create the Machiavellian strategies of takeover for ungodly fees.

- They are the accountants and consultants, commodities brokers, stockbrokers, and pawnbrokers, the whole conglomeration of fee and commission merchants.

- They are the big bankers, pressing, straining to erase the bars against interstate banking, and trample or absorb smaller community banks. The financial revolution is underway at full throttle, and it, too, threatens the fragile fabric of American greatness. The big banks mostly treat John and Jane Consumer and small business people as barely tolerable nuisances in their unbridled quest for big deals. They have loaned massive sums to shaky foreign governments, and they provide billions for massive mergers and takeovers, while they starve small business and charge consumers 10 or so points more than their prime corporate borrowers.

PRESIDENT REAGAN, who steadfastly wraps himself in the American flag and seizes as his own the rhetorical turf of small-town, God-fearing, family-oriented, ethically-pure America, hastens the accelerating trends toward bigness, centralization of economic power, and deregulation, which more and more seems to mean letting the corporate giants do whatever they damn please. Secretary of Commerce Malcolm Baldrige this week, for example, calls for the further easing of anti-trust regulations which already have been loosened to allow the most outrageous economic combinations.

The greatness of America was fashioned by its entrepreneurs, not by the ponderous, bureaucratic, greedy mentality of economic dominance, which holds the reins of power today.

We are weakened further by an easy, tolerant morality, a winking at wrongdoing in high places, even as the President speaks of a moral crusade. It is both corrosive and pervasive, and it eats away at the genuine idealism which motivated our founding fathers. It is manifest in the mediocrity and casual ethics of an Edwin Meese; in the continuing Presidential support of an indicted Labor Secretary whose time is consumed by his fight for vindication, and in the defense of too many not worthy of such support.

You and I, we must fight back. Here are some suggested planks for an incomplete Citizens' Agenda we must press on our elected representatives at both state and national levels:

1) Resist the pressure for interstate and statewide banking, which within a decade would wipe out or envelop most community banks, cut the borrowing life-blood of small to mid-sized businesses, impose higher prices on consumers for financial services, and end the era of personal relationships with neighborhood financial institutions.

2) Stem the tide of unrestricted, multi-billion dollar mergers, which sap the finite pool of available credit, and invariably hurt most those who are not an integral part of this massive, real-life Monopoly game.

3) Demand a serious, even ferocious attack on the Great Deficit Dragon, which President Reagan used to consider Public Enemy No. 1 *before* he became President, and which, if left unchecked, will ultimately wreck our prosperity and impose a terrible burden on our children and grandchildren. The cuts must be fair and deep, and must include sharp reductions in military waste and out-of-control defense spending, as well as hard scrutiny of Social Security and non-contributory federal pensions.

4) Nurture, aid, and encourage small business, which has created about 80 percent of all new jobs over the past 15 years and can do so over the next decade. Instead of offering the moon to General Motors for its Saturn plant, which reaps an abundant harvest of publicity for governors and mayors, we might recall that it is the Fortune 500 companies which abandon plants and lay off workers in cavalier fashion. Most such big companies have *reduced* employment in the past several years. If Governor Thompson had spent more time in Illinois during his eight years in office rather than traversing the globe on so-called economic missions, and had helped 125 small companies get established in Illinois each of those years, the 1,000 new companies might well have created 50,000 to 100,000 or more stable new jobs and reversed the tragic job outflow under Thompson.

5) Be cautious in responding to the siren song of "high tech," which clearly is not the panacea for all our economic ills. High tech is deeply rooted elsewhere, gobbles up voraciously huge amounts of speculative money, and does not produce for the most part great numbers of jobs. The battlefield is littered with high tech casualties.

6) For Illinois, with its "broad shoulders and stackers of wheat," stress innovative small manufacturing companies, many of which at first blush appear bland and unexciting, but may quickly grow with aggressive management to 100 or 200 or 500 employees. For the most part, Illinois, and especially

the Chicago metropolis, are saturated and overburdened with service industries, what I have described earlier as the "non-producers." We need companies which turn out products, which fill needs, which create jobs. We must forego glamour and promise for substance and immediacy.

7) Finally, we cannot tolerate in America, in Illinois, in Chicago, two societies — one rich or at least comfortable, and getting more so, the other poor and getting desperate. Under our umbrella of affluence, there must be room for those who are poor, ill, infirm, retarded, jobless, unable to cope — or we surely must expect unrest, mayhem, violence, and rising crime.

If this be so, our claim to greatness will be diminished, and, in truth, unjustified.

Let us rise to the challenge and assume as citizens the responsibilities of greatness.

'Didn't you used to be Barry Goldwater?'... and encounters with other notables

Thursday, August 23, 1984

**An intimate look at Barry Goldwater...
as the 1964 GOP presidential nominee returns
to address the 1984 convention delegates**

Twenty years ago, at its National Convention in San Francisco, the Republican Party nominated U. S. Sen. Barry Goldwater of Arizona to be its Presidential nominee. *News/Voice* Editor Bill Rentschler was an elected delegate from Lake County to that convention. Based on his association and periodic visits with Goldwater over that span of time, Rentschler has written this exclusive, wide-ranging interview and assessment of the Arizona senator, who, Rentschler says, "preached the canons, paved the way, took the blows for the ascent of Ronald Reagan."

Last night, Goldwater addressed the GOP delegates assembled at Dallas in a nostalgic return to the convention podium.

63

BARRY GOLDWATER AND I sat in a barren waiting room in the Rockford (Illinois) airport, awaiting the arrival of reporters for one more press conference.

It was the presidential campaign of 1968, Nixon versus Humphrey, and Goldwater, typically, was tending to party chores.

Sprawled wearily in a plastic chair, the 1964 Republican Presidential nominee, who was buried by Lyndon Johnson in the wake of John F. Kennedy's assassination, took a moment for reminiscing.

EYES DANCING, he told me of the old lady who approached him hesitantly on the street a few years ago after his annihilation in that campaign.

"Excuse me, sir," she asked softly, "didn't you used to be Barry Goldwater?"

The Senator from Arizona smiled. Barry Goldwater, somebody ought to tell that lady, will always be Barry Goldwater.

Fifteen years later, in March of 1983, I sit across the big desk in his private domain in the Russell Senate Office Building, a wall of airplane photos, mostly military, to my left, a thousand or so memories all around us.

I FOCUS ON the powerful tanned hands folded in front of him. He has a way, one on one, of creating calm. The voice is even and measured, the gaze steady, unflinching. The rugged cowboy face seems chiseled from a block of oak. He is 75 now.

The face is familiar, harshly weathered, eroded by two decades of hard decisions and full living since he stood at the lectern on July 15, 1964, in San Francisco's Cow Palace before a fervent, wildly-applauding Republican throng that had thrust on him its nomination to be President of the United States.

"It's good to see you again. How do you feel?" I ask, knowing he has recovered in the past couple of years from triple bypass surgery and endured two operations to install plastic hips.

"Never better," he responds, jaw thrust forward almost belligerently to make sure I understand.

WE CHAT FOR a moment or two about nothing much, and then I ask what is the most striking change in America between then, when he was a Presidential candidate, and now, the Spring of 1983. He does not hesitate.

"Damn few people put the country first anymore. All they give a happy damn about is themselves. Politicians, businessmen, everybody, you name 'em. That's the big change. For the worse.

"When I came to the Senate (in 1953), people were far more dedicated, committed to this country. Today, whether it's the Senate or the boardroom, they're concerned mainly with their own employment, hanging onto their jobs, taking care of old Number One.

"That's true across the board. We have such lousy management in most big corporations. No guts, no brains, cover their asses. That's about it."

BARRY GOLDWATER is warming up.

"Some of us (in Congress) work our tails off down here. We Westerners can't get home every weekend like some of those Eastern fellows who put in a Tuesday-Wednesday-Thursday week and then duck out.

"We don't spend enough time anymore defending the United States. We've still got a great country here, but you'd never know it to listen to some people. The rank-and-file press is pretty decent, but TV stinks, just plain stinks."

Goldwater was philosophical about his Presidential trouncing when we talked about it that day long ago in Rockford. He continues so.

"Bill, I knew the minute I heard the news Jack Kennedy was shot that I had no chance to be President. Jack and I were a good matchup, a real contest. He was Hah-vahd, I was the new West. He was the darling of the Eastern establishment, the liberals and intellectuals, I was the hard-nosed frontier conservative. It would have been a damn good race. But then it was all over . . ."

HIS VOICE TRAILED off and he looked beyond me.

"I had no chance against Lyndon. There was the sympathy factor. There was no record to run against. We were both from out West. He was President, and the press was all over me."

Were you ahead of your time? I asked him.

"Not really. It was the distortions I couldn't overcome. The media put horns on me, made me into a zealot. That's not Barry Goldwater."

TRUE ENOUGH.

Goldwater never was the knee-jerk reactionary some made him out to be. He still resents those who grind their special axes, in his view, by wrongly invoking conservative nostrums.

He proved that once again when he defended, in salty words-of-one-syllable vernacular, President Reagan's choice of Sandra Day O'Connor for the Supreme Court by snapping, "Every good Christian ought to kick (Rev. Jerry) Falwell right in the ass."

Vintage Goldwater.

THE MORAL MAJORITY'S Falwell, an outspoken anti-abortionist, condemned the O'Connor choice. Goldwater, labeled an "extremist" of the far right in 1964, took after the Falwell forces with six-guns blazing:

"I'm getting a little tired of people in this country raising hell because they don't happen to subscribe to the position a person has. A President could offer the Lord's name for some position and you would find some of these outfits opposed. I am probably one of the most conservative members of the Congress and I don't like to get kicked around by people who call themselves conservative on a non-conservative matter . . .

66

"If it is going to be a fight in the Senate, you are going to find Old Goldy fighting like hell."

THAT TIRADE tells a lot about the craggy, cantankerous Arizonan.

As the patron saint of modern-day conservatism, Barry Goldwater preached the canons, paved the way, took the blows for the ascent of Ronald Reagan.

In that campaign of 1964, Reagan got national exposure by articulating the conservative credo on national television for Goldwater. The polished orator then as now, Reagan made an impact that upstaged Goldwater and left the former actor as heir apparent.

While Goldwater has avidly supported the philosophy and ascent to the Presidency of his protégé, he is by no means a blind adherent.

HE ERUPTED IN RAGE when it came to light last April that the Central Intelligence Agency, with the covert approval of the White House, had mined the harbors of Marxist Nicaragua.

In a stinging letter to CIA Chief William J. Casey, Goldwater wrote:

"The President has asked us to back his foreign policy. Bill, how can we back his foreign policy when we don't know what the hell he is doing? Lebanon, yes, we all knew that he sent troops over there. But mine the harbors of Nicaragua? This is an act violating international law. It is an act of war. For the life of me, I don't see how we are going to explain it."

Goldwater's outrage triggered a sharp, bipartisan Congressional rebuke of the CIA action and clearly embarrassed the Reagan administration. Even the President's closest Senate confidant, Paul Laxalt, voted for an anti-mining resolution.

THIS, TOO, WAS in the Goldwater mold: Say what you believe and let the chips fall. Follow your conscience ahead of old partisan loyalties.

In their heyday, Goldwater and Nelson Rockefeller, four-term governor of New York and Gerald Ford's vice president, were viewed by public and media alike as bitter philosophical adversaries, the Arizona senator a passionate advocate of right wing dogma, the New Yorker a flaming eastern liberal.

"Not at all," Goldwater once told me. "Our differences were probably not much more than an accident of birth, of environment, where we grew up and lived."

He compared his pioneering, populist, entrepreneurial forebears, who headed west and founded a department store empire in then-virgin Arizona, with those of Rockefeller, born into a family of unlimited wealth and power and social prestige.

"GUYS LIKE THAT often turn liberal to ease their guilt over all that money," Goldwater chuckled.

"If Nelson had my Arizona upbringing, and I'd been raised by nannies on Park Avenue or one of those fancy estates," he mused, "things might have been a whole lot different."

Then, as an afterthought, "Did you know my mother was the first Registered Nurse in the State of Arizona, and she died at 97 from too much Bourbon?"

A secretary pokes her head into the office; the Senator has warned me his day is crammed with commitments. I rise to leave.

USING HIS POWERFUL arms, he hoists himself up from his chair and takes a painful step, leaning heavily on a cane with a terrier's head carved into its handle.

"The left hip isn't working so well," he grimaces.

I move around the desk to shake his hand and ask him in parting about his passion for flying.

"I've got 55 years in as a pilot. I can still fly, but only solo in helicopters these days or with another pilot. I won't run the risk of taking somebody down with me."

MANY OF THIS TIME and place don't understand Barry Goldwater. Perhaps because his agenda, his notion of public service, are as guileless and unbending as those of a lonesome range rider from another era.

From my encounters with him through the years, I am persuaded Barry Goldwater's measure of each big issue is simply what he perceives to be best for his country. Nothing more, nothing less.

There aren't many of that sort left in America when we need them most. Pity.

June 7, 1984

___

Notre Dame's Hesburgh defies nuclear 'insanity'

Father Theodore Hesburgh is not by any rational standard a peacenik, nuclear freak, Soviet dupe, or starry-eyed liberal who treats lightly the security of this nation.

Father Ted — his nickname around South Bend — has been the peripatetic president of Notre Dame for a record 32 years, during which time he has become one of a handful of America's most respected, outspoken, and caring national leaders.

Last month, I heard him deliver a blunt, sobering warning at the annual meeting of Business & Professional People for the Public Interest, a private Chicago agency devoted to environmental, legal, and civil rights reform.

"Where we are headed is nothing less than insane," he says. "We are drifting toward what Einstein in 1945 described as unparalleled disaster. We seem bent on reducing this planet to the lifeless, pitted surface of the moon."

FATHER HESBURGH warms to his subject. He speaks calmly, evenly, but his words are laden with emotion. He conveys a sense of disbelief that President Reagan and others in power aren't doing more to stave off ultimate disaster.

He speaks grimly of "no more children, no more smiling faces," and of "terrible burns, cancer, genetic damage for those who survive.

"We and the Russians this very moment have in our nuclear arsenals a million times the power that was unleashed at Hiroshima and Nagasaki, between us enough power to destroy the world 14 times over."

HE PAUSES, seemingly taken aback by the appalling enormity of his own words.

"We are proposing to add 30,000 more warheads over the next decade. It is impossible for me to believe we would do this knowingly and willingly. Can you believe we are spending one million dollars a minute on armaments, weapons of destruction?" he asks his rapt listeners.

At 67, Hesburgh is a resolute figure at the lectern, with square chiseled features, dark, penetrating eyes, wavy, gray-black hair swept back from his forehead and temples. His face is set; he seems committed and unswerving in his message. Around the room, heads nod in agreement and there are other signs of assent.

Then, firmly, "We have hoaxed ourselves into thinking there is an answer in sheer military superiority. We use the Orwellian word 'deterence,' which really means indiscriminate and colossal murder of humanity. There is idiocy in that reasoning.

"No matter what your religion, even if you have none, there is no possible way to think it is moral to kill 100,000,000 human beings on that first day."

THEN, A RAY of hope.

"There is an answer. We must start talking. It's long overdue."

What Hesburgh calls "my conversion" came two-and-a-half

years ago. Since then, he has worked tirelessly to unite the leadership of science and religion in a worldwide crusade against nuclear confrontation.

He is relentless in this endeavor which he considers his ultimate mission in life.

"It is incredible to me that *our* leader and *their* leader have not sat down to talk since Jimmy Carter signed Salt II. This is a political problem, plain and simple. Let's solve it. We *must* solve it."

BY NOW, Hesburgh's mouth is a straight line, his jaw taut.

"We play a chess game. But what is our most quintessential common interest, theirs and ours? Peace. Survival.

"We must launch a moral revival. We must touch off a groundswell for peace. There is no other course, for humanity is threatened with extinction. There are no subtleties. It is a monster, and we must get rid of the monster."

He returns to the children, "so full of hope and yearning."

"Why should we leave them a legacy of darkness?"

And then he sits down to resounding applause.

July 14, 1983

Dutch Smith: true 'Renaissance man'

Often these North Shore communities where we live are celebrated for affluence and even power.

That is the superficial side.

WHAT MAKES THEM stand apart is the genuinely remarkable, eclectic mix of people who treasure these places as their hometowns.

Dutch Smith was one of these.

Dutch Smith — formally Hermon Dunlap Smith — comes

as close to being a true Renaissance man as anyone I've known or known about.

In this age of hype and hyperbole, the term "Renaissance man (or woman)" is bandied about freely and bestowed on too many undeserving by the breathless media.

Dutch Smith truly was that rare being.

He was indeed a builder, "the complete citizen, a doer of deeds," as one colleague described him, and his life was "an incredible litany of leadership and accomplishment," as another said.

BUT HE WAS MUCH MORE, and, by my measure, much more than accomplishment is required of the true Renaissance man.

What made him different from most of the rest, and made him stand taller and more fully rounded, was his marvelous sense of humanity and compassion.

These qualities shone through and bathed the church at his funeral services in May.

James H. Douglas, Dutch's friend for 77 years, said simply, "Two weeks ago, on his birthday, I was with him when he welcomed the blooming of trillium and mertencia in the woods close to his house. . . ."

While he "has earned distinction in many fields," Mr. Douglas continued, "I feel he would like us to think of him particularly in his devotion to education . . . and to his hopes for progress towards tolerance and understanding, a more peaceful world."

LIBBY HAIGHT FOLLOWED with a small story which she said showed her grandfather's rare capacity for expressing love in a quiet but tremendously meaningful manner.

When she was five, Libby recounted fondly, she "committed the heinous crime of pushing my two-year-old cousin, Temple, off the end of the Thornecamp dock" at Desbarats (Canada), where the Smiths spent their summers.

"My mother, Debby, was suitably outraged and informed

72

me that I could not go swimming. Being quite literal minded, like many five year olds, I thought she meant I could never swim again for the rest of my life. I fled to my cabin where I sobbed loudly for what seemed like hours but what was probably about 15 minutes.

"The screen door squeaked open," Libby continued. "Pop (which is what his grandchildren called Dutch Smith) walked in, asked me what was wrong."

"I told him, 'Mommy said I can never go swimming again'."

"I don't think she really meant that," Pop said. When Libby insisted, her grandfather suggested quietly, "Well, let's go talk to her about it."

"With that," she said, "he raised me up, and I rode into the main lodge on Pop's shoulders. I felt as if I was returning to the palace with the king. I had been redeemed. Pop still loved me."

SCARCELY AN EYE was dry in the overflowing church.

She went on: "All the members of our small army have their own memories of Pop. . . . Long live his example to us all as a human being of wisdom, commitment, integrity, and love. Love not only for his family, but the entire family of man."

Finally, the minister read a prayer found by his children among their father's papers:

> Slow me down, Lord. Ease the pounding of my heart by the quieting of my mind. Steady my hurried pace with the vision of the eternal reach of time. Give me, amidst the confusion of the day, the calmness of the everlasting hills. Break the tension of my nerves, and muscles with the soothing music of the singing streams that lie in my memory.
>
> Help me to know the magical, restoring power of sleep. Teach me the art of taking Minute Vacations — of slowing down to look at a flower, to chat with a friend, to pat a dog, to read a few lines from a good book.

Remind me each day of the fable of the hare and the tortoise that I may know that the race is not always to the swift: that there is more to life than increasing its speed.

Let me look upward into the branches of the towering oak and know that it grew great and strong because it grew slowly and well. Slow me down, Lord, and inspire me to send my roots deep into the soil of life's enduring values that I may grow toward the stars of my greater destiny.

—Amen.

THAT PRAYER might have been written for Dutch Smith, whose deep sense of humanity added the dimension that made him truly a Renaissance man.

Thursday, August 16, 1984

On the trail with the Vice President

He looks much the same as the graceful, slender first baseman who captained a good Yale team four decades ago. His hair has receded a bit at the temples, but it is still mainly brown. These days, his waist is a little thicker, and he wears metal-rimmed glasses with owlish lenses.

When he speaks, it is an easy mix of Connecticut, where he was raised in understated patrician opulence, and Texas, where he made a middling fortune in offshore oil and ascended the political ladder. He also throws in "gonna" and "lemme," which links him to our Midwest and the South. For emphasis, he chops the air and occasionally bangs the lectern with a good southpaw stroke.

This time, in late May, it is Greenville, Mississippi — "my fourth visit in 18 months to the great state of Mississippi," he tells his rapt partisan audience, wanting to make sure his devotion isn't lost on even one of the 600 or so guests, who paid up to $500 apiece to hear him.

IT IS ENTIRELY possible there never has been a more dutiful Republican foot-soldier than George Bush, who has risen through the ranks to become Vice President of the United States.

Ronald Reagan's circumspect running-mate patiently waits his turn in the President's shadow, doing his oft-thankless, ill-defined jobs with style and a certain becoming reticence, staying almost defiantly clear of the presidential spotlight, carrying the President's message to all points of the compass.

Bush is in Mississippi again to boost freshman Republican Congressman Webb Franklin in his tough catfight with Robert Clark, the same black foe he edged by 3,000 votes in 1982. But Bush also is there — no mistake about it — to sell Ronald Reagan and George Bush in the Old South.

At the lectern bearing the portable Vice Presidential seal, Bush stands dwarfed beneath a mammoth American flag in a huge, normally barren arena festooned this night with masses of colorful spring flowers. He looks the earnest preppy, a little somber in gray suit and maroon tie, but trim and bouncy at 60. There is about him a still-boyish enthusiasm.

HE WASTES LITTLE time.

"I'm here," Bush begins, "because I want to help continue what we started in 1980 . . . to see that every man, woman and child will be afforded an opportunity to share in the American dream . . . and to assure peace, which we can never have unless we are strong."

Early on, he takes a sharp swipe at that old hobgoblin, Thomas P. (Tip) O'Neill, Jr., Democratic leader in the House, who is, "the most partisan guy ever to hold such an office" and whose "major failing is that he believes all this stuff he says.

75

"The Democrats want you to forget how bad things were four years ago. It's taken a full two years to get the economy on the mend . . . The country is better off, far better off than when we took over, and Americans have refound their old optimism," Bush tells his listeners, who are peacock-proud they've attracted such an illustrious figure to their comfortable river town of 40,613.

IN A SUDDENLY confidential manner, Bush leans forward, clutching the podium:

"I office two doors down from the President. I know how he works and how he thinks. He makes all his decisions based on a few principles, and, by golly, he's willing to stick with them when the going is rough.

"You've gotta like his firmness, his decisiveness. Whether the Russians like or not, they *must* respect President Reagan. It's critical that we stay strong . . . There's a new mood of assuredness because America is safer today.

"Lemme tell you, I get sick and tired of carping, melancholy critics . . . We will not negotiate from weakness, but we *will* negotiate," Bush says emphatically.

ON GRENADA, the Vice President praises his boss for "acting before a crisis became a humiliation," reminding his listeners that there were "more than a thousand potential hostages there."

Then he switches to a theme which is likely to be the keystone of a grinding Fall campaign:

"Family, faith, neighborhood, and work. When have you heard an American leader stand up for these values? That's the essence of what this President is all about, what he believes in. Why should people be denied the right to pray in public schools?

"There's new confidence in this country today, more hope for the future. That's our 'good news' message."

76

AS HE RETREATS, waving and grinning broadly, the Mississippians give him a standing ovation.

Bush, the team player, is doing his job all across America, reciting faithfully the litany of Republican "accomplishments," selling the Reagan "record."

This, of course, is the same George Bush who served dutifully as GOP National Chairman during the trauma of Watergate, as our first envoy to mainland China, as director of the Central Intelligence Agency, the same George Bush who, as a Presidential candidate four years ago, derided Reagan's "voodoo economics." Now he must defend the President's economic nostrums, the massive deficit, interest rates that are too high measured against sharply lower inflation. More recently, in his simple honesty, he is less emphatic than the President in denying plans for some sort of tax increase in 1985, and the press pounces like a tiger on a gazelle, eager to exploit even the slightest inconsistency.

The selection of Geraldine Ferraro as his opposite number inevitably elevates his profile sharply this Fall and may cause him anxious, awkward moments.

After November, win or lose, things will change dramatically for Bush. If the Reagan-Bush ticket wins, the President will be an instant lame duck and the Vice President will begin discreetly carving out an identity of his own as he looks ahead to 1988. If they lose, Bush will move briskly to mobilize a campaign apparatus geared to win him his party's nomination four years hence. To do this, he will have to best the likes of Baker and Dole, Kemp and DuPont, and sundry others.

Either way, it will surely be an ordeal and a test for this essentially decent and able public servant. For all this, he may some day be President.

Whether nine or 99, you 'know' Mickey!

"What's wrong with this country," one of America's best-known elder statesman told me a few weeks ago, "is too many 'fat bellies.' Their money belts cut off their circulation."

Mickey Rooney talking, a show-business legend for six decades of this Twentieth Century, a monument almost as familiar as the Statue of Liberty, and, remarkably, the same irrepressible imp at 63 who played Andy Hardy, the kid next door, in another era.

Fat bellies. Mickey was referring disdainfully to the chieftains of some of America's biggest companies, "who never have an idea themselves and won't accept anybody else's because it wasn't theirs."

Mickey Rooney has ideas — thoughtful, often controversial, ones — on *everything*.

Mickey gives off sparks. He literally radiates ideas.

His conversations are marvelous vignettes in pantomime. Why just talk when you can act? He sings, he shouts, he jiggles, he bounces, he mimics, he orates. He is pure creative genius. He moves with the quickness and agility of a 15-year-old.

I flew to California with some associates and a load of Charmglow grills to do a day's worth of photos and commercials with Rooney at Rancho Bernardo Inn outside San Diego, where he was winding up a run of his phenomenally-successful musical, "Sugar Babies."

I've known Mickey for six years or so — it seems like 50 — and he is, by all odds, the "most unforgettable character I've ever met."

HE IS WARM and loving, mischievous and outrageous, brassy, cocky, wildly creative, incredibly articulate. Some

78

actors — including at least one of global prominence today — need cue cards and teleprompters. Mickey himself runs rings around any script writer. He is a master of the impromptu, utterly spontaneous, beguiling, hilarious when he lets go.

At the same time, he is a completely disciplined trooper. He slaved over a series of gas grills in broiling southern California sun for three solid hours and outlasted the sagging photographer, limp ad agency troops, and all the rest of us. When he started to glisten, they mopped him off and powdered him down, and he simply kept up his antics as the ultimate backyard barbecue chef, outdoing himself time after time.

Mickey agreed a while ago to become the "spokesman" and "personality," a worldly, witty ambassador, for a widely-known line of consumer products. Off the top of his head, he dubbed their portable table-top gas grill "The Mic-nic" and promptly coined a catchy slogan: "Take the Mic-nic on your next picnic." And all of a sudden he wants to open a string of restaurants where everything — steaks and ribs, fish and chicken, baked potatoes and sweet corn, shish kebab and gas-grilled hamburgers — would be cooked only on these distinctive brand-name grills. Talk about creative . . . and irrepressible.

At 63, he's the lead in a major TV film — "It Came Upon a Midnight Clear" — on NBC this Christmas season. When "Sugar Babies" ends its long run, he's looking forward to "DuBarry Was a Lady," with co-star Ann Miller, which he will dedicate to the late Ethel Merman. And a couple of years down the pike, it will be a musical based on the old comic strip, "Maggie and Jiggs," with Martha Raye.

BUT HIS ULTIMATE dream is Mickey Rooney's Talent-town USA, a nationwide network of studios "where children grow," where they are "lovingly" taught the performing arts by carefully-selected teachers.

Some 800 aspiring kids from 6 to 16 right now are learning the rudiments of tap, ballet, drama, piano, voice, and other "disciplines" at the very first Talentown USA studio in Azusa, California. The walls are lined with old photos of Mickey, Judy Garland, Jackie Cooper, Shirley Temple and other child stars of that memorable cinematic era.

"Our kids have so little opportunity to grow, to achieve their full potential. I can't think of anything more satisfying than to help them, to give them incentive, to show them what they're capable of," Mickey says. "They won't all make it to the big time, but they'll be better for it, and their lives will be more meaningful. That's what I want to do more than anything else with the rest of my life."

At 16 months, when he was still Joe Yule, Jr. — not yet Mickey Rooney — he broke his upper leg in a fall at the long-gone New Jackson Hotel at the corner of Halsted and Jackson in Chicago. With the insurance money, his parents, vaudeville barnstormers, took him to California. The rest, as they say, is history.

MICKEY HAS "played" the White House for every president since Franklin D. Roosevelt.

"Reagan can't lose," he says. "It's unfair to pit Mondale against him. It's like Spectacular Bid against some nag."

He was the hottest of all box-office attractions for several years in the "Golden Age of Hollywood." He hit bottom, too. Now he's back on top, soaring, feisty, ebullient, qualities that never waned even in the worst of times.

This is quite a guy, this pint-sized atomic wonder. Who among us, whether nine or 99, doesn't "know" Mickey Rooney as Andy Hardy, the beloved prankster of the '30s and '40s, or as the poignantly-retarded Bill in the recent award-winning TV-movie? He is truly one of a kind, an original, an American entertainment legend.

Chuck Percy: Can he win again in '84?

An astute Republican "insider" told me he expects Charles H. Percy to lose his Senate seat in 1984, "possibly" in the primary next March 20, but "almost certainly" in the November election.

IT COULD HAPPEN.
There are quite a few Illinois Republicans of a certain stolid, unbending school who would love to see somebody, in fact anybody, Republican, Democrat, or Holy Roller, oust Percy from the United States Senate.

They attribute to him in various combinations and varying degrees most of the virtues of Elmer Gantry, Little Lord Fauntleroy, Rasputin, and Joe Stalin.

Through his two decades in public life, Chuck Percy, by some strange blend of alchemy, has indeed drawn an uncommon amount of flak, mostly from his fellow Republicans. Even though he is one of the most prolific vote-getters in Illinois history, he is never entirely "safe" because of the undercurrent of uncertainty, yes mistrust, which seems to swirl endlessly about him.

I've known Percy since before he formally entered the political arena, when he was touted as a *wunderkind* of the business world. We've found ourselves intense adversaries a fair number of times on our assessment of issues, philosophy, and especially people, where our judgments most often have diverged.

I did not support Percy initially in his bid for Governor in 1964; twice, under pressure from two Illinois governors, he backed my opponents when I ran for the U. S. Senate.

YET I SAY without hesitation that Chuck Percy ranks high among the handful of public figures I've known reasonably

81

well whose integrity and motivation I respect most. Nothing counts more.

Others who come instantly to mind are Senators Barry Goldwater of Arizona and Mark Hatfield of Oregon, and two former congressmen, our North Shore stalwart Bob McClory and Walter Judd of Minnesota.

Across the aisle, there are the likes of Wisconsin Senator Bill Proxmire (another who raises hackles) and U. S. Rep. Paul Simon of Carbondale, ironically a likely Percy foe next year. In state government, I respected Governor Otto Kerner and thought he generally stood above the rest.

If there is another quality in Chuck Percy that stands out, it is a combination of basic decency and deep-felt compassion, the latter an element sadly lacking these days in the high councils of the Republican Party.

ON THE FOURTH OF JULY, I spent a leisurely hour and a half interviewing, probing, questioning, digging, listening, visiting wth Percy.

"How have you changed?" I asked him toward the end.

"I still believe the same things," he told me. "I could give the same speech today I gave when I first ran for the Senate in '66."

I took him at his word and dug out with the help of his staff Percy's speech to the Illinois GOP state conference in Springfield on January 29, 1966. Here is some of what he said:

> My friends, I am running for the Senate as a progressive Republican. As a party, we have sometimes avoided the word "progressive." There is no reason that we should. Certainly, the Republican Party is not opposed to forward motion, to *progress*. It was our own Everett Dirksen who led the fight for the most important progressive legislation of the 1960s — the Civil Rights Act of 1964.
>
> If we are to succeed as a party in 1966, or *ever,*

82

we must not merely tolerate progress — we must become its champion.

We must make it unmistakably clear that we will not betray the traditionally progressive position of our party on civil rights by subtly appealing to a backlash vote of white resistance.

We must work to uplift the lives of millions of poor Americans, 90 percent of whom have lived under Democratic rule in southern and urban America for the past several decades.

We must actively confront the crisis of our once great cities — cities whose decay is evident to all who will look — cities which have been ruled essentially by Democrats for years.

We must stop mouthing empty platitudes about government being bigger than it was 30 years ago, and start finding ways to make it *better*.

If we do these things, we will move America forward, which is what we all desire.

If Chuck Percy runs for a fourth term on the essence of those few words, and stays with that basic theme of moving America forward, I have no doubt he'll win again in November of 1984.

If . . .

Thursday, November 8, 1984

A fallen Senator, a call for wisdom

It is past midnight in one of those look-alike mirrored rooms somewhere in the Hyatt Regency downtown, and the Reagan landslide has been confirmed at last by the people, rather than just the polls and pundits scrambling to get there first.

83

Restrained and ladylike as always, Loraine Percy stands a little behind her husband on the stage, her face gray with fatigue and resignation.

CHUCK PERCY, still running, still pumping adrenalin, tells his anxious troops, "We're going to win this," and some few still hope he may be right.

With the keen intuition of a devoted wife, Loraine Percy seems to sense it is not to be this time around, but her face is a mask and she is not about to betray her inner feelings.

Eighteen years a senator, now at the pinnacle as chairman of the influential Foreign Relations Committee, and suddenly it is ashes for Chuck Percy, a good and decent man and public servant.

The gods, he must feel, are conspiring against him, when a wealthy Californian, whom he doesn't know from Adam, spends thousands of dollars in Illinois to buy billboards depicting Percy as a "lizard," Percy tells his backers, even though the precise symbol is a chameleon.

IT IS OVER NOW, and Illinois will not be plunged into darkness. The new senator will be Congressman Paul Simon. We said of him in an editorial last March: "We know of few in public life whose integrity approaches that of the idealistic, yet highly practical legislator from tiny downstate Makanda. We admire his compassion and concern for 'people' needs."

The landslide, about on a par with Richard Nixon's 49-state sweep against McGovern in 1972, was a personal tribute to Ronald Reagan, that and not much more. There was no mandate.

There were practically no coattails, as the Republicans lost a little ground in the Senate and gained less than expected in the House.

We have entered an era of personality, perception, and money in American politics. It all seems so superficial and calculated. There was practically no deep discussion of issues which bear on the very fate of mankind. Walter Mondale was widely ridiculed for suggesting a tax increase might be needed to trim the mountainous, dangerous deficit.

PEOPLE RESPONDED to what they perceive as a kindly patriot, a grandfatherly John Wayne.

They responded, too, to what they perceive as a renewed pride and spirit and self-esteem in America. That is good, if it does not trigger a spate of chest-beating and nationalistic pomposity.

As we move toward the new century, true leadership, wisdom, and sensitivity for all our people — rather than empty sloganeering and narrow ideology — are imperatives in the equation for American greatness and even survival.

Thursday, January 30, 1986

Bishop Tutu speaks of love, human values, freedom for all people

You are struck first by his size.

He is a tiny, wiry man standing perhaps five-four, weighing no more than 120 pounds.

Yet when Bishop Desmond Tutu begins to speak, he becomes a giant, one whose passion and love fill and overflow a cavernous ballroom.

Bishop Tutu came to Chicago last Friday, and I attended a civic celebration in his honor.

HIS HOST, Mayor Harold Washington, linked Tutu with two others — Martin Luther King, Jr., and Pope John Paul II — who, he said, "made a great moral imprint on Chicago" in their visits here.

Famed Illinois poet Gwendolyn Brooks read for the 1,500 guests from her moving "Johannesburg Boy," which tells of places in South Africa "where the hurt black of our skin is forbidden."

Let us "end state-sponsored terrorism" as it exists in South Africa," demanded the Rev. Jesse Jackson in his invocation.

There was resounding applause as the Mayor turned the microphone over to the diminutive Anglican bishop and recipient in 1984 of the Nobel Peace Prize. Then perfect silence as the audience expectantly awaited his first words.

"I am quite, quite overwhelmed by your love, quite bowled over," he said, his gratitude expressed in a kind of melodious, English-accented lilt, gentle yet gripping.

TO BE SO HONORED in "this greatest city, with the greatest mayor. . . . and the greatest football team . . . (Roars of laughter and loud cheers) . . . has left us quite speechless with wonder and awe, really."

Bishop Tutu told of reading, in 1947, a tattered copy of *Ebony,* then a struggling magazine published in Chicago by John H. Johnson, now proprietor of the largest black-owned business in the U. S., which claims *Ebony* as its cornerstone.

"As much as anything else," he recalled, "the message on its pages set me on the road campaigning against oppression and injustice."

Then to his message.

God looks down on all His children with "divine self-satisfaction," Tutu said.

TO HIM, we are all "beautiful people . . . neat . . . something else . . . not just good, but very good . . . tremendous . . ."

"The Lord does not consider the color of one's skin as an index of one's value or worth, any more than a human being with a big nose should be favored over a person with a small nose."

"Each of us," Bishop Tutu barely whispered, "is an incredible work, a finite being made for the infinite."

"You and I," he told his spellbound audience, "are made for fellowship, togetherness, friendship. But we are not born

86

perfect human beings. We must learn how to be humans, to be considerate and compassionate.

"Apartheid is evil because it causes untold suffering. Families are uprooted, torn apart. We are seeking a new South Africa where all of us will be free.

"There can be no true freedom if one of us is not free. For then none of us is free."

THE GENTLE whisper is hard now and strong as his voice rises.

"I can see the day when (Prime Minister Pieter) Botha and (jailed opposition leader Nelson) Mandela will be together. This is not an unrealizable dream. God will tell them: Stretch out your hands and touch one another. He will open the glorious vistas of our great country when all will be free together."

Freedom for his country's 23,000,000 blacks, he vows, is "inevitable. . . . There is a witness to be borne, and God will not fail those of us who bear it fearlessly.

"I believe that nonviolence requires a certain minimum moral standard of those who would be appalled when they saw what police bullwhips could do to those protesting peacefully. It was to such a constituency that Dr. King could appeal. Sadly, I think that we (in South Africa) do not have a constituency which has this minimum moral standard.

"I speak of a moral issue. Are you for goodness or evil? Are you for justice or injustice?"

You sense the deep conviction in this man. You sense that history will prove him right, even though blood likely will flow before freedom comes to South Africa.

Outrageous Ed Koch, NY's mayor, 'tells it like it is' in Chicago

Audacious, outrageous Ed Koch, once and future King of New Yawk, New Yawk, and one of America's favorite stand-up comics, unloaded a barrage of opinions and anecdotes Monday that had a small group of Chicago's business elite alternately laughing, fuming, and agreeing.

He started tactfully at a luncheon of the Chicago Committee, sponsored by the Chicago Council on Foreign Relations, reminding guests that Chicago no longer is the nation's Second City, but has slipped to third behind his East Coast fiefdom and Los Angeles. A few pained chuckles.

Then he tore into Gramm-Rudman, the debt reduction bill which has been declared only semi-Constitutional by the U. S. Supreme Court, branding it "an abomination."

TREASURY SECRETARY James Baker, said Koch, keeps saying Gramm-Rudman requires *"only* a 5 percent reduction of the trillion-dollar budget.

"But that's not true," Koch insisted. "Only $300 billion is subject to reduction, and the rest simply isn't touchable. Gramm-Rudman rips the guts out of programs that serve people who live in cities."

The President's budget, Koch told the diners, will cost Chicago $436 million over the next two years, and "that money's got to come from somewhere."

New York will lose $1.4 billion over that same span, he said, but "we can stand it better than most."

Somebody wanted to know why so many Democrats go along with Reagan in the Congress.

"FEAR. PURE FEAR. The President is 'The Great Communicator,' everyone says. No question. You don't want to let him nail you as a big spender in an election year.

"You know, fiscal responsibility isn't a Republican idea. It's an idea your mother had. She wouldn't let her family spend more than they took in."

The balding, sharp-beaked Koch said of Reagan: "At least we won't have him to kick us around in 1988. We're lucky Reagan can't run again. Thank God he can't. Personally, I like him. His singlemindedness is what may make him the most effective President in U. S. history. I say that even though I disagree with him violently on lots of issues."

Speaking of differences between the two parties, Koch described the Democrats as "without question the majority party. What we stand for philosophically is what the majority wants, except when somebody like Reagan blurs the issues. We are more compassionate. The Republicans are . . . I don't like to use the word . . . predatory," he said, speaking to a predominantly GOP gathering in the Chicago Club.

KOCH WAS ASKED how he'd advise his Chicago counterpart, Harold Washington, to deal with the burgeoning scandal at City Hall.

The glib New Yorker, embroiled in a similar scandal in New York triggered by the same FBI informant, shrugged, "How do I know what your mayor should do?" This thought brought a round of guffaws. (Koch left our group at 1:30 to confer with Washington.)

Koch patted himself on the back for six consecutive balanced budgets, which he acknowledged is required by law in New York City.

Yet if Franklin D. Roosevelt had been required to balance the federal budget when he was elected in the aftermath of the Great Depression of 1929, "there would have been rioting in the streets, and we'd have had another Hitler in America," Koch said, adding that "FDR had no choice but to prime the pump to counter joblessness and other grave economic problems."

Why, he asked rhetorically, are things "so out of whack now?"

"Well, first of all, President Reagan's $750 billion tax reduction made a balanced budget absolutely impossible in his two terms.

"Second, he wants us to be armed, and so do I, because I don't think the Russians basically are any better than Hitler, but you can't balance the budget and increase military spending in a mindless way. You simply can't exempt any program from careful scrutiny if you're serious about balancing the budget. Reagan wants to shift the onus to us Democrats.

"I'm no expert on foreign policy, but I've got a few things to say anyway.

"The UN is a cesspool. This is hardly the first time I've said that, but they like me anyway over there. They understand me. Why should I give up my First Amendment rights just because I'm the mayor?"

ILLEGAL ALIENS, Koch said, "are killing us. Every business should be subject to stiff criminal penalties if they hire illegal aliens willfully and knowledgeably. But we should give amnesty to illegals who've been here for a year or more. No city should give aliens sanctuary if they come illegally."

"How do you size up the 1988 race for President?" he was asked.

"I hear talk about Bush and Kemp, but (U. S. Sen.) Bob Dole (Kansas) is by far the best the Republicans can put up," he said flatly.

"The most articulate speaker on the national scene today is our Governor (Mario) Cuomo. I believe he'll be running. There are other good Democrats, too, like (Sen. Bill) Bradley of New Jersey, (Rep. Richard A.) Gephardt of Missouri, and (former Sen. Gary) Hart. No, I'm not backing anybody yet. There'll be another six or seven in the race, and I want to look 'em all over before I decide."

Outrageous. Audacious. An authentic New York-type character. A curiosity in the heartland. Ed Koch. Only in America.

Rumsfeld eyes the White House as Searle sale nears

Timing, they say, is everything, and Donald Rumsfeld's timing through the years has been impeccable.

Once again, the magic seems to be working for Rumsfeld, a longtime Winnetkan and chairman of Skokie-based G. D. Searle & Co., the family-controlled pharmaceutical house whose earnings have surged along with sales of NutraSweet, their high-flying, branded artificial sweetener.

It happens that the Searle family's desire to diversify their vast holdings coincides almost perfectly with Rumsfeld's hankering to get on with his quest for the highest office in the Free World.

ANY DAY NOW, you may expect to read of the sale of all or part of the Searle company, whose parts are likely to fetch more total dollars than the whole. When Don Rumsfeld leaves the enterprise he turned around, he will bid adieu with a tidy fortune in stock option cash and a sense of considerable satisfaction, since Searle was his first and only private sector job of substance.

Before 1985 ends, my guess is that Don Rumsfeld's name will be added frequently and insistently to those of George Bush, Jack Kemp, Howard Baker, Bob Dole, and Pete DuPont as credible contenders of the U. S. Presidency.

At 52, Don Rumsfeld ranks among the shrewdest, toughest U. S. political figures of the past two decades. He has displayed a remarkable knack of dodging disaster and being in the right place at the right time, not merely by happenstance. Some would attribute this to luck, but I hold to the notion you pretty much make your own fortune for better or worse. Rumsfeld has made his.

When I was running for the U. S. Senate in 1960 as a mere "boy" of 34, a bright, cheeky kid named Don Rumsfeld phoned my campaign headquarters one day and volunteered to help. We snatched eagerly at all volunteers, and that's how I first came to know Don, seven years my junior.

TWO YEARS LATER, he leapt into the race in a new, remapped North Shore District to succeed Marguerite Stitt Church, the *grand dame* of the Congress then and a North Shore idol to this day at 92 years. Not many gave him much chance of defeating a well-regarded state legislator, Marion Burks, then better known than Rumsfeld. Shortly before the primary balloting, however, the *Chicago Sun-Times* broke a front-page exposé linking Burks with a somewhat vague and unsubstantiated insurance "scandal." Burks was badly hurt, and Rumsfeld unexpectedly emerged with the GOP nomination in a safe Republican district.

Once the primary result was sealed, the insurance "scandal" evaporated like a puff of smoke, and Burks was left wondering why the sky had fallen on him. Thus was launched a quite remarkable political career in which the final chapters remain to be written.

Rumsfeld went on to serve three terms in Congress, but got itchy as its seniority system and sluggish ways stifled his progress.

In 1968, I was asked by Richard Nixon to head up his Presidential campaign in Illinois. Overcoming my early concern that Nixon was politically dead after his 1962 defeat for governor of California, I took on what I knew would be a tough challenge. I did so out of respect for Nixon's grasp of issues and his brilliance in the area of global strategy, which, incidentally, exceeded that of his successors, including the incumbent President.

THE POPULAR, RISING Rumsfeld struck me as a good choice for Cook County chairman as I began stitching together a campaign team. I felt his clean cut image would help Nixon even though it was obvious the Congressman would be more a figurehead than an activist leader.

It turned out Rumsfeld was a jump ahead of me. At the same time, he was dickering with Nixon and national campaign chief John N. Mitchell, later Attorney General and a prime Watergate figure, for a loftier, more visible post in the campaign structure. Shortly, he was announced as a Nixon "surrogate," who would represent the candidate on the stump nationally, and later, a floor leader at the GOP convention which nominated Nixon.

Those close ties with Nixon provided the escape hatch from Congress which Rumsfeld sought.

The newly elected President made good use of Rumsfeld's political savvy and talents in a succession of major posts, including poverty czar, chief inflation fighter, and eventually White House aide at the very epicenter of power. Thus Rumsfeld became a trusted and certified Presidential insider from the beginning of Nixon's first term.

ONE WHO SERVED WITH Rumsfeld and knows him well once described the square-jawed Navy and later Princeton wrestler as "a guy who could leap out of a window on the ninth floor of a burning building and hit the ground running."

He said it with grudging admiration for Rumsfeld's skill in emerging unsullied from the toughest political scrapes and even disasters.

It may be that Rumsfeld sensed the gathering storm that would be known as Watergate. With his keen instinct for timing, he escaped both Washington and the White House with a propitious appointment as U. S. Ambassador to NATO in Brussels scant weeks before the unfolding of the scandal that toppled the Nixon administration.

Despite his intimate association with the former President, who was pardoned by Gerald Ford and permitted to resign in disgrace, Rumsfeld, unlike other key Nixon confidants, among them John Ehrlichman, Bob Haldeman, John Mitchell, and Jeb Magruder, has largely escaped all taint. Such is his way.

QUICKLY, HE BECAME a fixture in Gerald Ford's White House, first as Chief of Staff, then Secretary of Defense. With Jimmy Carter's narrow victory in 1976, Rumsfeld exited to the private sector, postponing for awhile his 15-year career in the public arena. Under President Reagan, he took leave of his duties at Searle for a seemingly unproductive stint as Middle East envoy.

Don Rumsfeld — "Rummy" to his pals — has clear eyes fixed intently on the Presidency. There may be detours and denials, but that is his obsession.

Time will tell his ultimate fate, but a word of caution: Don't bet the family silver against Rumsfeld.

Thursday, July 11, 1985

The 'shining legacy' of Adlai Stevenson, 1900--1965

The elder Adlai Stevenson, a native son of Illinois, former Governor, twice Democratic candidate for the Presidency, ambassador to the United Nations, who lived in Libertyville and frequented the North Shore, died 20 years ago this month. This newspaper column I wrote on July 24, 1965, shortly after his death. I voted for Ike, but what I said then about Stevenson and what he stood for seems just as valid two decades later.

• • •

HONORS MOUNT FOR Adlai Stevenson of Illinois, fallen America statesman.

They come from all over the world, from countries in

94

Europe and Asia, and from new lands hacked out of the African bush. They come from small towns and teeming cities in every corner of his native America. They come from the great and the ordinary, from people of every color and faith and political persuasion.

Some would deride as insincere the often effusive tributes from Adlai Stevenson's political foes, but they miss a fundamental point: that it is possible to honor and respect an adversary even as you strive mightily to defeat him. You admire his good fight, the talents he possesses that you may lack, his courage in the face of withering attack.

The widespread homage paid Adlai Stevenson reminds us of other significant facts of life in these United States: that most Americans pursue in their own strange ways the same objectives — peace, justice, equality, happiness, material well-being. And that most deep cleavages stem from conflicting notions of how to achieve those common ends.

I frequently found myself in disagreement with Adlai Stevenson on the means to reach goals we shared. I disagreed with what I felt was his tendency, lately somewhat tempered, toward accommodation in foreign affairs, and with his undue reliance on federal solutions to most of our domestic ills.

BUT I RESPECTED him as a man who gave unstintingly of himself to public service, as one whose rare eloquence stirred his countrymen to high purpose, as a man of warmth and wit and compassion.

Who can forget his wry opening remark in a speech shortly after he had been buried by General Eisenhower beneath an avalanche of votes? "A funny thing happened to me on my way to the White House. . . ." — a winning, even endearing comment by a man with heavy heart but a rare sense of irony and perspective.

We need in our land more men whose support of their convictions is staunch, fervent, even passionate. Stevenson was one of these. With a public eloquence surpassed in our time only by Churchill, Adlai Stevenson made his case with graceful, memorable phrase. He presented his own, and often in the UN, America's point of view with notable skill and distinction.

There is all too often a tendency for those who disagree with a particular line of reasoning to seek to demolish the man rather than the validity of his argument. This course usually cloaks the weakness of their case. If these dissidents were to be scrupulously fair, they would not attack or demean or seek to derogate their foes, but rather would articulate more forcefully, more effectively, more compellingly their side of the controversy.

A THOUGHTFUL DIALOGUE between antagonists — who are quite likely to be seeking similar ends — pierces the murk, enlightens the audience, solidifies the objective, clarifies the purpose, and strengthens the resolve. This is good. It is even necessary, where freedom of speech prevails. Our nation is the beneficiary when there is searching give-and-take on the great issues of the day. Those who seek to stifle debate or force adherence to some "official" position do their country no service.

Surely it is better to light a candle than to curse the darkness. Adlai Stevenson sought always to throw shafts of light into dark corners. This was his great gift. He contributed notably to understanding on this shrunken planet of ours, and to enlightenment — of the American people, of all the peoples of the world.

This is Adlai Stevenson's shining legacy.

From Watergate's ashes, Richard Nixon bedazzles America's publishers

It was inevitable that Richard Nixon would rise one day from the ashes of Watergate.

Whatever his flaws, there is no denying his extraordinary grasp of global affairs, which easily surpasses that of his Presidential successors.

Nor can any reasonably fair-minded observer question his decisive imprint on the main issues of his time. It was Nixon, remember, in his first, momentous term as President, who ended the military draft, which was rending the nation, and opened the corridors of communication with Red China, the remote colossus of the Far East, a move that shifted the balance of world power toward the U. S.

By the time he had defied long odds, returned from the political dead, and ascended to the White House in 1969, the old gut-fighter, who was anathema to the media and the liberal colony, had become more the tough-minded pragmatist than right wing ideologue.

LAST MONTH in San Francisco, Richard Nixon came all the way back to confront his ancient enemies of the Fourth Estate. If ever there was proof of the adage that time heals, this was the classic case.

The fallen President spoke in the overcrowded ballroom of the elegant Fairmont to the nation's newspaper publishers, from the mightiest, like the *New York Times, Washington Post, Los Angeles Times,* and *Chicago Tribune,* to proud, aspiring upstarts like *News/Voice.*

They hung on every word of his 90-minute virtuoso performance, rendered without a scrap of paper before him, and at the end, most gave him, somewhat sheepishly, a rising ovation. Leading the cheers was Katherine Graham, publisher of the *Post,* which had most to do with hounding Nixon out of the White House.

It was obvious Nixon, playing a role of professorial showmanship, relished the chance to lecture his influential audience. Waiting to go on stage, the former President, whose "approval" rating by Gallup has climbed past 50 percent since his resignation under excruciating pressure following the Watergate scandal in 1974, toyed with his food and sipped a glass of milk, occasionally waving to somebody he spotted in the crowd.

NOW 73, HE appeared pinkish and healthy, his jowls still prominent, but with no semblance of the five o'clock shadow which once made him look villainous to his detractors. He wore a perfectly tailored navy suit with navy-and-white striped tie. He seemed relaxed and in command.

Nixon's main theme was the urgency of aid to the Contras in Nicaragua, and he made Ronald Reagan's case with the consummate skill of a first-rate trial lawyer.

"We don't like dictatorships," he told the publishers and their wives, but we must learn "to distinguish between different degrees of evil." The pragmatic Nixon.

The role we played in toppling the Marcos dictatorship in the Philippines was "universally applauded," he said, while 65 percent of Americans oppose aid to the Contras, which is "far more important to U. S. strategic interests than the Philippines."

Nicaragua, Nixon said, "meets the test" for U. S. aid. The country is ruled by "an oppressive communist regime that hurts the people there."

If the ruling Sandinistas prevail, they surely will threaten Central American stability, and especially Mexico, which he described as a country literally "waiting for a revolution."

"Make no mistake," he stressed, "if the Sandinistas are freed, they will create enormous problems for us."

THE CONTRAS *"could* succeed," he said, with "adequate support." Nixon pointed out the Soviets have pumped in more than $500 million to the ruling regime over the last five years, and Libya and Syria have contributed twice that much.

The $100 million so strongly urged on a reluctant Congress by Reagan is " not nearly enough."

The former President said our objective is not to "overthrow" the Sandinistas, but rather to "apply enough pressure" to force them to negotiate, reduce their militia, stop taking aid from the Soviets.

Nixon admitted the Contras are "not saints" and have been guilty of various atrocities, but "guerilla wars bring out the worst."

Faced with questions of another Vietnam developing out of our expanding role in Nicaragua, Nixon said emphatically the "best way to avoid our involvement is to provide aid now."

IF WE DO SO, and are successful, there will be positive ramifications far beyond Nicaragua, resulting in the first example in history of "stopping a communist-backed dictatorship regime."

Nixon reflected on the "enormous frustration of playing a leading role on the international stage."

"I understand that frustration," he told publishers, alluding to Winston Churchill's 1946 assessment of the "awe-inspiring accountability" of world leadership in his heralded "Iron Curtain" speech.

Speaking of the on-again, off-again support of U. S. global policy by our European allies, Nixon explained that at various times they "like, envy, and hate us, but in their hearts they know without the U. S. playing a major role, peace and freedom would not survive."

When he ended his long, penetrating discourse, his audience gave him a noisy ovation. Before it was over, 80 to 85 percent were standing in tribute to a masterly performance.

IN THE TOUGH questioning period that followed, Nixon continued in control and at ease.

• "I support the President on Libya." The U. S. did what it had to do "precisely and effectively," issuing a warning first, exhausting non-military options, and confirming Moammar Khadaffy's direct involvement in terrorist acts.

"Plans must be made now to determine what action we'll take next." Nixon said flatly that the bombing option is "past" and the next logical step probably is a "blockade that would cut off his export of oil."

• "I don't have a good answer (on the five remaining) hostages . . . As much as we feel in our hearts, the U. S. cannot be held hostage to hostages."

• What might he have done differently in his Presidency? "Just destroy all the tapes," he blurted out. That triggered a roar of laughter and applause from the crowd.

• He branded the Gramm-Rudman-Hollings deficit reduction bill "brilliant short-term politics, but disastrous long-term statesmanship."

CONGRESS AND the President, he said, "must face up to the budget and do something about it."

• His greatest single achievement? "The opening of China. . . . made a long-term difference. . . . lost me many of my longtime hawkish friends." In the domestic area, he cited his "cancer initiatives of 15 years ago. . . . we're making progress."

• If the economy stays good through 1988, Vice President George Bush will be "nominated and elected by the Republicans to continue the policies of Reagan." If there is a "slide" in prosperity, the GOP convention, he predicted, will be "wide open" and the Democrats will "have a chance."

With a broad brush, he ticked off the list of possibles for the Presidency in both parties.

Of the Republicans, his list went like this:

- Bush — "Best qualified."

- Rep. Jack Kemp — "Most charismatic."

- U. S. Sen. Bob Dole — "Smartest."

- Former Senate majority leader Howard Baker — "Shrewdest."

- Evangelist TV preacher Pat Robertson — "Best communicator."

NIXON DIDN'T mention such other potential contenders as his former Chief of Staff, Illinois' Donald Rumsfeld; Reagan's good friend, U. S. Sen. Paul Laxalt; former Delaware Gov. Pierre S. DuPont IV, or Illinois Gov. James R. Thompson.

On the Democratic side, he called "front-runner" Gary Hart, the Colorado senator, "impressive and thoughtful, (but) too cerebral to be a good Democratic candidate."

He described New York Gov. Mario Cuomo, who later addressed the publishers, as "a savvy politician" whose style is "more poetry than prose. . . . who speaks from the heart." He is "very formidable," Nixon said, but weak in foreign policy.

Chrysler's charismatic Lee Iacocca would be tough, but he can't "tolerate fools, which is a very dangerous thing in a politician."

It was vintage Nixon from the perspective of the now seemingly mellow elder statesman. Say what you will about the former president, about his warts and integrity, and many to this day harbor only venom and disdain, he nonetheless has the best brain and global reach of any President since Eisenhower. Give the devil, as it were, his due.

Portrait of an Earthy Plainsman

Of all the 535 men and women drawn from across this nation to serve in the 90th Congress, the one dominant figure, towering over the rest, clearly was Everett McKinley Dirksen, native son of Illinois and Minority leader of the U. S. Senate.

This is my profile of that earthy plainsman, surely the great legislative genius of our time. It seems appropriate on the eve of this primary election of 1986, exactly two decades after Dirksen "mesmerized" a Chicago audience gathered to honor him.

• • •

A TALL MAN, now bent with the weight of years, walks with measured gait along the flat, fruited plains of Illinois toward the yellowed pages of history.

You know somehow where he is going.

And you know he senses and relishes his fated role as mover and philosopher, as one around whom legends will grow, as one whose memory will linger.

This man is Everett McKinley Dirksen, steadfast helmsman for that little crew of Republicans in the United States Senate.

They honored him in Chicago one late April evening in 1966, when the biting wind belied the promise of spring, at one of those big, glossy, often deadly dull $100-a-plate dinners.

Without a note or scrap of paper before him, he "preached" for one solid hour and twenty-two minutes more, surely long enough to bore stiff most anyone except perhaps his forgiving family.

YET FROM THE moment Everett Dirksen set free from deep in his innards that first velvety syllable, those sated, af-

102

fluent diners — 1,800 in all — leaned forward toward him and strained to hear every word as if life itself depended on his next one.

Before Dirksen rose, the bony young minister from the little frame church in his native Pekin spoke reverently of the Senator as "one who stands among us, but towers above us."

That set the stage. Then Everett Dirksen shuffled to the lectern, blinking in seeming surprise at the glare of TV lights he contends with almost daily.

The celebrated silvery locks were tangled and awry. A huge carnation made a white splotch on his black suit. The massive head, the sagging face were thrust forward, and tired, watery eyes peered over horn-rimmed spectacles into the sea of admirers. He looked for all the world like the fabled cowardly lion from cinema's Land of Oz.

There was in the great ballroom the perfect silence of expectancy, for most of them had savored the Dirksenian thunder before.

Then the words began to come, resonant, rolling, soft and almost inaudible at first. He told a gnarled old story about a grateful cow, one of his oft-repeated favorites. Half the crowd had heard him tell it before, yet they wandered almost gleefully alongside him to the punch-line, and then roared with laughter, feeling he had permitted them to share with him an intimate moment.

WHAT HE SAID was not new. Some would brand it corny or trite, the same old clichés about God and motherhood and freedom and all that. The empty sophisticates might dismiss him as out of touch with these frenetic times.

But you know somehow this man is not shallow or calculating or emotionless. You can see an incandescent glow in those tired eyes when he talks of freedom.

A medical curiosity with an impressive catalogue of ailments, he suffers not from the limiting myopia which afflicts and restricts so many of his colleagues and contemporaries. His mind scans the ages with a certain graceful sweep. It searches the archives and draws easily on the great books and fine minds of human history.

There is an element of grandeur, a certain homely wisdom about this righteous, earthy plainsman. His is a dying breed, towering like the shaggy mammoths above the gray flannel prodigies who are guided by polls, surrounded by faceless aides, preoccupied with the cosmetics of image.

"No, you can't eat freedom," Dirksen purred, "or buy anything with it. You can't hock it downtown for the things you need. When a baby curls a chubby arm around your neck, you can't eat that feeling either, or buy anything with it. But what in this life means more to you than that feeling, or your freedom?"

HE HAD MUCH ELSE to say that night in Chicago. Here are a few random wisps of his "conversation" with 1,800 dinner companions:

• We must glue our eyes on the cause of freedom. It's the one thing that counts. The quiet, insidious erosion of freedom is taking place constantly . . . They're trying to remake us from stem to stern, trying to subvert our principles . . . It is time for those citizens who believe in the durable values to stand up and be counted. . . ."

• "There would have been no civil rights bill without us Republicans. That bill was written in my office. . . . The Negro should come back to the Party of Lincoln."

• "Americans today are a prosperous but unhappy people . . . there is frightful turbulence and discontent and bewilderment . . . Not the least confused are those in Washington as they caterwaul and wander aimlessly about. . . ."

• "That burglar they call inflation is eating into every paycheck . . . When it goes out of control, then controls go on, and you don't have freedom. . . . "

• "Some of these kids think it's smart and fashionable to burn draft cards. But they only do it when the TV cameras are there. I think it's smart-aleck nonsense. . . ."

• "George Meany (president of the AFL/CIO) asked for my support on the repeal of 14-B (a labor reform bill). 'You fairly wrench my heartstrings,' I told him, 'but you'll never get my vote'."

• "The reapportionment fight is just beginning. If you know you're right, you're not discouraged by one lost battle. We'll fight it out to let the people decide. . . ."

• "We have a monster government . . . unmanageable . . . the individual gets lost."

• "Many people don't care, but I will never let the freedom of these neutrals be impaired."

• "We Republicans must invite all sorts of people to come over and help us: the rank-and-file of labor, housewives, Negroes, young men, those who believe in constitutional government, those who want victory in Viet Nam."

• "There are only three issues this year: peace, freedom, the preservation of our free-enterprise system. . . ."

THESE ARE FRAGMENTS. He said a good bit more in those fleeting eighty-two minutes. Then they stood up and cheered this man, who likely in 1968 would be the Republican nominee for President by acclamation if he were ten or a dozen years younger.

There is much of the Shakespearean "ham" in Everett Dirksen, and he is quick to admit it. But here, too, is a legend who still lives and works his legislative sorcery, the only one of his kind and stature and character in the Senate.

Some chide him for his flexibility, his ambiguity, his easy

camaraderie with the White House. He baffles friend and foe alike, for there is in him none of the unbending rigidity of the man who opposes only for the sake of opposing. This rankles some fellow Republicans and confounds his opponents.

He chooses his fights, selects his battle sites with the care of a shrewd general. He has learned in four eventful decades of public service that the effective warrior must above all live to fight another day. So he rarely courts the bloody nose, seldom picks the fight he is bound to lose. But on all the big issues where peace or freedom are involved — civil rights, reapportionment, Viet Nam, Section 14-B, the nuclear test ban treaty — he is there at center stage, playing a lead role, making his stand.

They called him the Wizard of Ooze, and once they said it in derision, but now they recall it with affection and awe born of respect.

For Everett McKinley Dirksen will be around awhile, stalking the marble corridors with the ghosts of Clay and Webster, Taft and Borah, long after most of his colleagues — and we — are gone and forgotten.

Thursday, October 18, 1984

Night at Comiskey with Prince Michael

It would have been a perfect Saturday night, heavy with fog and drizzle, to curl up with a good book and go to bed early.

Instead, I found myself planted on a wet plastic folding chair in soggy, foggy Comiskey Park, about 300 feet from home plate in deep right center field.

I admit I asked for it. I got carried away at a Better Boys Foundation charity auction a few weeks back and found myself the proud and somewhat bewildered possessor of four tickets to a Michael Jackson concert. That's right, you know, *the* Michael Jackson.

So that's how I ended up last Saturday night with my wife, Martha, and two daughters, Marthie, 24, and Hope, 11, at a major league ballpark on a night when any sort of tolerably sane game would have been called off. At least it wasn't cold.

I MUST TELL YOU all about it. For me, it was a genuine happening. I did something like it once before. Exactly 20 years ago, I took my first born, Sarah, then 14, and a friend to the International Amphitheatre to hear the Beatles. Actually, the din and general chaos that night were so ear-splitting I couldn't hear much of anything, but I do remember it vividly. The former *Daily News*, later *Tribune* columnist and onetime mayor of Glenview, Jack Mabley, was the emcee that night, and I've never forgiven him.

Anyway, here we were last Saturday night at Comiskey Park with a chance to experience the fabled Michael Jackson and his entourage. Hope was vibrating with sheer excitement, while Marthie, excited, too, kept saying Michael Jackson just *wasn't* Bruce Springsteen, which is about all I knew for sure.

Walking out onto the field, which, after being churned into muck for three straight nights, can't possibly be ready for baseball next April, was in and of itself awe-inspiring for a kid from Hamilton, Ohio, whose taste in music runs to Cole Porter, Rogers & Hammerstein, and Lena Horne.

Out in left-center field was a massive stage whose superstructure stretched nearly 100 feet to the top of the upper deck, where majestic home runs occasionally land. Above the stage was a huge video screen. On each side of the stage was a gauzy, curtain-like panorama featuring two gnarled, spreading oaks set in rocky terrain. This prompted a certain amount of early ooh-ing and ah-ing, barely a pale sample of what was to come.

WE PROCEEDED ACROSS the sodden, gummy field to our folding chairs, each properly molded to hold a generous

107

puddle of water. We found ourselves little more than 100 feet from the stage, a bit off-center, with the giant exploding scoreboard before us.

Early on, Martha, my observant wife, spotted five blue "porta-potties" within easy striking distance. This instantly banished all claustrophobia and made her evening.

It was still light when we arrived. We had been warned that traffic would be horrendous, so we started very early, naturally encountered no delays or obstacles whatever, and arrived at 5:45 for a 7 p.m. kickoff, even though there was to be no batting practice. Like everybody else, we were "frisked" by metal detectors.

At this point, the old ballpark was fairly empty, and people were trickling in. Hucksters were selling ponchos made, I'd guess, from old Kleenex, and what they called "binoculars," for $6.00, take your choice. The glossy, oversized program, with Michael and his five brothers unaccountably clad in safari gear on the cover, went for a cool ten bucks. The regular ball park food fare, hot dogs, popcorn, cokes, and the like, were sold at standard White Sox prices. Wisely, there was no beer.

The evening started quietly. The early arrivals were docile and curious, milling around without purpose, wide-eyed as they viewed the monster stage and high scaffolding out front which held eight spotlights on swivels aimed at the stage.

BY 6:30, PEOPLE were pouring in, many on the young side, but not exclusively, a surprising number of families, a fairly even mix of black and white. My three ladies hunkered down under their green and purple raingear, watching and waiting, while I meandered about in the mud. Two banks of powerful baseball lights along the third base line pierced the fog and cast an eerie glow over the scene.

I was feeling a little glum. After all, I had expected earlier this very day to be watching the Cubs shellack the ultimate world champs from Detroit. Harrrumph, Michael Jackson.

108

At 7 sharp, with a fair smattering of seats unfilled, the lights went out and the crowd started screeching. This must be it, I surmised. Onto the darkish stage came a solitary figure. The audience cheered wildly as the spotlights revealed a quite ordinary, pale, youngish man in a shiny red-and-black costume.

To the beat of some unfamiliar (to me) music, he started juggling. You know, juggling, what a juggler does. That's right, a juggler. At a Michael Jackson event, mind you.

ANYWAY, HE WENT ON for 20 minutes or so, his juggling enhanced by psychedelic, ever-changing lights, his whole act seeming incongruous and quite mundane on this night of nights. Still, we were moving inexorably toward the big moment.

But not quite yet. We would first be treated to a new "torture" video presentation by CBS on the big screen above the stage. Somebody—presumably the Jacksons—began screaming, "Its torchaaa," as a surrealistic ritual unfolded, complete with clawlike fingernails, jungle beat, bejeweled masks, dancing skeletons, and lethal blades emerging in narrow passageways — amid much loud sound, gore, and colored smoke. Can you picture all that?

Lights on again . . . 7:30 now. The low-hanging cloud cover takes on a yellowish hue as the city lights reflect up against the canopy of mist . . . tension mounting, only a few empty seats, a little snapping and squabbling in the muddy aisles . . . one family of four evicted because their tickets were for *last* night. (Boy, did that lady chew out her husband!) One young thing with fluorescent green hair prances down the aisle . . . another with glitter sprinkled on bare shoulders . . . still another in black leather pants that must have been sprayed on . . . a boy of six or seven, eyes dancing, wearing a sparkling white Michael Jackson glove and saucer-sized button, in a wheelchair. Lots of restless milling and unease now. All in readiness, on with the show, clap, clap, clap . . . My-kel . . . My-kel . . . My-kel . . .

An hour has dragged by and now the stage is dark again until a shadowy figure appears with green lightstick to stir the crowd into a frenzy for the big moment. We are nearing *the* moment. Now it is here, and it defies description.

THE EARTH BEGINS to rumble. Thunder rolls ominously. Purple light colors thick smoke curling about the stage. Great, ugly, hairy creatures lumber into view to the beat of frenetic music. Lights play on a glittering sword imbedded in a giant stone. Who shall pull it out? (Three guesses, and only the last one counts.) Several pretenders fail. A terrible simulated storm ensues, with lightning flashing, laser beams in gaudy colors piercing the sky. Those great oaks painted on the curtain sink to earth. Many in the audience are screaming and stomping.

Calmly, a heroic, shrouded figure, face covered, appears to tug at the sword. Effortlessly, he removes it from the stone and plunges the blade into one of those giant beasts. Off comes the mask, and Michael — who else? — stands before 35,000 adoring fans and a handful of skeptics.

This by any standard is an extravaganza which succeeds only by continually outdoing itself. The sound is often raucous, the staging riveting, the tempo exhausting.

Now it is Michael and his five Jackson brothers rising on platforms above the stage, silhouetted against blinding white lights punctuated by colored lights, Michael in glittering field marshal jacket, tight black pants, spats, and, oddly, black loafers, exhibiting a form of turbulent kinetic energy, his features smooth and almost girlish, his soprano voice piercing. The other Jacksons are mere foils.

THE FOCUS ALWAYS IS on Prince Michael, dripping from the frenzy of his movements. With rare force, he belts out a song whose title sounds to me like "Human Nature." The uncompromising light bathes a face that is unmarked, childlike. Laser shafts of fuchsia, turquoise, gold, and aqua radiate out from the stage and dance across the Comiskey stands and light towers.

This is an irrepressible showman. The lights turn to deep blue. Michael exhibits all the supple moves, incisive kicks, head fakes, rubbery legs, his celebrated "moon-walk" — all part of an endless repertoire.

We are transported into a surrealistic otherworld. The beam solely on Michael, he shifts suddenly, unexpectedly to gentleness, at once emotional, plaintive, grieving, vibrating, eyes closed tight in an exquisite anguish.

"She's out of my life," he intones, writhing, tortured by his lost love. It is vintage stuff from this callow talent, a matchless showman standing alone in the burgundy mist, head bowed. The song ends.

Many in the audience, including everybody ahead of us, are rocking and bobbing, stomping and standing on their chairs, caught up in the excitement. It seemed mainly a natural exuberance. We saw no booze, smelled no pot, saw nothing "suspicious."

AFTER 35 MINUTES, Michael drifted offstage and brother Jermaine, a bigger, ruggeder Jackson in tight, form-fitting turquoise leotard, took over. His is an older face, a still harsher beat, a more conventional, less subtle style. But he clearly has his fans.

Soon, Michael lopes back, refreshed, reinvigorated, possibly showered as well. The audience, rapt, mesmerized, comes alive again, chanting, clapping, rocking.

One skeptic turns to me and mutters, "I'll give 'im three years, and nobody'll remember 'im."

A change of pace, as spider-like monsters with lighted tentacles and gleaming blue eyes descend from the sky on Michael. Trapped, he is enveloped and presumably dead. A satin sheet is placed over him, as the music turns mournful, but that is not to be. In a blinding flash of light, smoke, and noise, the sheet is whisked away, and our hero reappears, bedecked in red and gold lion-tamer jacket with epaulets. He

111

seems none the worse for wear, and the audience thinks it's all pretty exciting. It's certainly not easy to doze off at a Michael Jackson rendezvous.

One of his big numbers, I was told by my daughters, is called, "Beat It." I couldn't pick up the words and innocently asked Hope if he was singing "Peanut." She silenced me with a withering look.

THE JACKSONS RETURNED to their "first" number — "I'll be there" — sentimental, cool, more wrenching emotion, unrestrained exuberance, sadness — the gamut of human feelings packaged to sell. Michael, I thought, dancing, moving, showed the lithe, graceful, effortless coordination of a gifted athlete, a poet in motion, a master of ballet, a gazelle.

The stage is suffused with red smoke, and the Jacksons seem swallowed by flames.

The colored lasers reach across the crowd and touch the light towers, the beat gets more intense, and it is over.

Martha and I are limp. Hope is giddy and glassy-eyed. Marthie still thinks Springsteen is better. We've witnessed a glittery tableau, a fleeting page from a history of our times. I'm glad. It has added one more facet to our lives.

'You've got to be taught to hate...

September 15, 1983

You've got to be taught to hate ...

Think. Think carefully about these powerful words by Oscar Hammerstein from the famed musical, "South Pacific":

> You've got to be taught to be afraid
> Of people whose eyes are oddly made,
> And people whose skin is a different shade,
> You've got to be carefully taught.
>
> You've got to be taught before it's too late,
> Before you are six or seven or eight
> To hate all the people your relatives hate —
> You've got to be carefully taught.

I believe that. Kids don't start out hating. There are no born bigots. Put a child of two or three on the kitchen floor with a mixed bag of other kids — white, black, yellow, brown, misshapen, mentally slow, whatever. They'll play happily, brothers and sisters, unless an adult injects some signal of prejudice.

LIKE THE PARENT who says: "I've never really had anything against Jews. Or blacks or orientals." He's telling his

113

kids he deserves a medal for his broadminded acceptance of Jews — and prejudice is thus implanted. The Ku Klux Klan, Nazis and other hate groups spew their venom. We remember when teen-agers carried signs reading "Nigger — Beware" in Marquette Park.

Kids don't think up such obscenities. It is the parents who all too often goad and organize and sow those seeds. Many, I suspect, are proud as their red-blooded offspring throw bricks and scream filth.

MOST OF these same parents doubtless are dedicated churchgoers. Yet hate and prejudice clearly mock the teachings of all religions. We would do well all year long to remember the Bibical admonition that the Lord loves all His children, and loves us neither more nor less because of our differences.

March 15, 1984

A lasting gift money can't buy

The most valuable thing you can give your children — or grandchildren — is abundant love. Of course. But there is another priceless gift you can bestow on *your* small child. You can't buy it with money, only a little of your time.

You can *read* to your children. Ten, fifteen minutes a day is enough. It will create a gratifying closeness. Your child will be ready for serious reading and communicating — ahead of the other kids — when he starts school, often before. He'll develop a love of reading likely to remain all his life. You can read the same books over and over to a small child. You can buy decent, lively children's books for dimes rather than dollars — or borrow them from one of our splendid North Shore libraries.

BEFORE OUR DAUGHTER Hope, now 11, was a year old, I used to gather her in my arms with her bottle in a big wing chair, and read to her in a kind of drowsy sing-song from books I loved as a child. She didn't understand, but she responded even then to the familiar sounds, and those nightly sessions — a ritual for years after for her mother and me — have been a highlight of Hope's day — and ours.

You and I are called on each day to read and write and communicate. To establish the reading habit early and pleasurably give your child a decisive head start. And the times I've spent reading to my children will always be among my happiest memories.

'Bill, I'd never lie to you . . .'

Nothing sets me squirming more than the fellow who tells me in unctuous, supersincere tones:

"Bill, you know I'd never lie to you."

AT THAT POINT, my fingers start tightening around my wallet, and red lights flash furiously before my eyes.

Beware of the individual — salesman, repairman, lover, lawyer, butcher, politician — who persists in telling you how honest he is. That sort, I've found, almost invariably has ulterior motives and will lie or waffle whenever it serves his purpose. The honest man simply doesn't feel the need to tout his integrity.

In the wake of Watergate, there surfaced an expedient brand of politician who's made a career out of peddling his honesty. They may even believe what they and their image-polishers keep telling us. But it's just a matter of time until the skeletons start rattling in their closets.

You'll find that people and politicians noted for high standards and bedrock integrity don't make a fetish of telling everybody they encounter how honest they are.

EVERY ACCOMPLISHED con man since time began launches into his pitch by trying to sell you and other potential pigeons on his honesty. You always knew, didn't you, that some of our noblest politicians rank high among the most skilled of all con men? I won't mention any names. You can make your own list.

Early in the 17th century, Shakespeare in *Hamlet* warned us to look out when "the lady doth protest too much . . ."

Amen — and beware!

Thursday, January 2, 1986

A Creed for Everyman: Unity, not division

As we enter 1986, and the final 15 years of history's most turbulent and momentous century, America needs above all a creed that will encourage unity rather than division.

This richly-blest nation must not permit itself to be badgered and bent, steered and ruled, by those who cluster at either extreme of the spectrum of national opinion.

We are submerged in a glut of festering, deep-rooted intolerance, frenetic, synthetic gaiety and ostentation, callous unconcern for the woes of many who hurt, hunger, bleed, suffer.

Instead of shrill, shallow partisanship, we must fashion a sound, durable, and compelling philosophy to preserve at once the greatness of America and freedom in America, as it moves our country forward and answers the diverse cries of it people.

HERE IS A creed meant to bind together all Americans and all Illinoisans rather than rend apart our people, a Creed if you will, for Everyman:

• I believe our essential greatness was fashioned — not by latter-day pretenders or our own myopic contemporaries — but rather by the hardy few who carved America out of the wilderness, threw off the oppressor's shackles, gave us our laws and government and precious tradition of freedom.

• I believe that an even greater America lies before us, and that we can climb any mountain or meet any challenge by combining the tested wisdom and timeless principles of the past with new knowledge and new methods, with vision, imagination, unselfishness, and a flat refusal to accept defeat.

• I believe that every American in truth is an uncommon man, different from every other, possessed of hopes and fears and pride and feelings all his own. We respect his dignity. We honor him as a human being. We do not cynically lump him with others in a class or voting bloc or nationality group. We do not pander to his prejudices. We do not segregate him by the color of his skin, by the money in his pocket, by his race or religion. We seek the best *for* him and *from* him.

• I believe that lofty slogans are empty to the man who is hungry, to the man whose child is sick, to the man who finds himself out of a job, to the man who exists in the grimness of the ghetto. I believe that a nation which follows unflinchingly the path of freedom and free enterprise can be warm and understanding and compassionate, and, without resorting to socialist quackery under any other name, extend a hand to those who are unable to help themselves because of age, illness, poverty or calamity.

• I believe we must make our big cities livable again. We must cleanse the air and make the streets safe. We must untie transportation knots, clear old slums, build new homes, and stimulate cultural and recreational opportunities for all. We must demand prudent, honest government and wipe out corruption, boss rule, and waste. We must bring hope and self-respect, dignity and education to those who live and despair in the metropolis.

• I believe the years ahead will prove that the nations of the world can live together in peace, but this aspiration will require all the toughness and resolution, the courage and patience, not found in men of little faith or little hope.

• I believe we cannot guarantee our safety and security simply by amassing an ever-greater arsenal of the weapons of annihilation, if in the end they destroy our solvency and impede our quest for durable peace. I believe President Eisenhower's warning of the ascendancy of the "military/industrial complex" has become a frightening reality which even now precludes our ability to meet our most urgent domestic priorities.

• I believe we must take an unpopular position when we believe it is the right one, and to oppose what we know is wrong, even though we may be tarred by the brush of obstructionism.

• I believe we must be ever-vigilant of our freedoms, that we must resist even seeming small intrusions by the stormtroopers in our midst, that we must understand freedom is indivisible, and that encroachment on the freedom of any one citizen erodes the freedom of every other American.

• I believe we must end without procrastination the cruelty and sheer waste of discrimination. Even as we pursue this noble and essential goal, we must be cautious to respect and not trample the rights of others.

• I believe, too, in the rule by law; in firmness and reason in our conduct of foreign affairs; in enduring peace with justice and honor and concern for the God-given rights of all the world's peoples; in broader and better job opportunities for all; and in a common sense, disciplined treatment of our fiscal affairs.

• • •

The message is clear. We Americans must go forward together, trusting one another, believing in each other, seeking always areas of accord, or we shall neither grasp the soaring opportunities, solve the nagging problems, nor keep our bond with humanity in this perilous Nuclear Age.

Let us hope history will credit these generations with meeting head-on the exacting, perplexing, rugged challenges of our time. And let each of us in his own way play a decisive role.

October 13, 1983

Measure of 'success'

What is success? The answer has tormented great minds.

In what I found to be a thoughtful, in places poignant, editorial in *News/Voice* last week, our Executive Editor, Pat Shaw, pondered the question, noting especially the loss of "human value" when our focus on material "success" and "wealth" and "power" transcends the spiritual and decent and compassionate.

Pat's editorial set me thinking, remembering, and rummaging.

I CAME UP SOMEHOW with Ralph Waldo Emerson's definition of "success," which I had put aside years ago because it caught well some of the values which are important to me.

Success, wrote Emerson, is:

119

To laugh often and much; to win the respect of intelligent people and affection of children; to earn the appreciation of honest critics and endure the betrayal of false friends; to appreciate beauty; to find the best in others; to leave the world a bit better, whether by a healthy child, a garden patch or a redeemed social condition; to know even one life has breathed easier because you have lived. This is to have succeeded.

That may not cover everything, but it includes much of what success means to me. I would not mind being judged by Emerson's measure.

April 26, 1984

Life's 'ambiguity' takes 'maturity'

"Maturity is an ever-increasing capacity to deal with ambiguity."

THESE ARE THE words of Moorhead Kennedy, an Iranian hostage for 444 days, who was a recent guest preacher at Lake Forest's Church of the Holy Spirit.

His words constitute a thought worth pondering. You must zero in to appreciate what he is getting at and how it applies equally to the urgent and trivial matters which affect each of us.

"Ambiguity," he explained, means that very little in life is conveniently black or white. No point of view is irrefutably, absolutely right or wrong. The Russians are not all bad, and we are not all good.

It is "moral absolutism," Kennedy said, which precipitates

much woe, stalemate, and rancor, whether global, national, local, or personal. This is so whether the issue is abolition, as it was in Civil War days, abortion today, or countless other divisive issues which stir their adherents to fierce advocacy and often a blindness to any other point of view.

WHAT KENNEDY'S words meant to me — and I applaud him for them — is that a defiant, unyielding certainty and smug self-righteousness, whether by extremists of left or right, as well as some who consider themselves in-between, reflect a harmful immaturity which rends nations and families and renders virtually insoluble some of our most nagging concerns.

Our readers have discovered by now that *News/Voice* and its editor are hardly weak-kneed or wishy-washy. We nonetheless subscribe to the view that some of those seemingly most insoluble challenges would melt away if both sides came to the "bargaining table" in an open mood of mature compromise.

The world — our own communities and workplaces — surely would become better places if that spirit and good sense were to prevail.

Thursday, April 18, 1985

Message to our young readers: 'There's a place for you . . .'

NOTE: Some years ago, I was invited to deliver the sermon at the 1st Annual Youth Day Service of St. Paul Missionary Baptist Church, an all-black congregation on Chicago's South Side. My remarks were beamed to the church's young people, mainly between the ages of 10 and 19. I came across the text of that sermon recently, and because it seems to apply as much to North Shore young people now as South Side black youth then, I have chosen to repeat it as this week's column.

• • •

America is crying out today, almost desperately, for wise and enlightened and compassionate leaders.

A vast leadership void exists in our country. You young people can and must one day help fill it. You must start preparing yourself now. You must set your sights on roles of future leadership. The hunger for constructive leadership exists in every area of our society: education, business, science, religion, politics, law, diplomacy, medicine, social work, everywhere.

And the opportunity was never greater for you who prepare yourselves, who set goals, who are willing to make certain sacrifices.

Let me suggest now to each of you a set of beliefs, a way of life, a personal creed which may help you assume a measure of leadership and achieve what you want out of life:

1. Believe in yourself. Love thyself. Be proud of yourself. Stand tall. Of all the people on earth, there's not another person exactly like you. You are somebody, a very special person, a unique individual. Never forget that. It is most important if you are to achieve on earth what you want to achieve and what you are capable of achieving.

2. Reach for the stars. Set high standards and seek with all your energies to reach them. A famous Chicago advertising executive, Leo Burnett, once said something like, "Reach for the stars, and while you may never quite catch one, you will never come up with a handful of mud." And that's good advice for each of you. So keep your sights high and your standards high — and that will help you achieve more than you think possible in your lifetime.

3. Always do a little more than you're expected to do. Don't try to get away with a little less. When you're assigned a chore by your teacher, employer, mother or father, go the extra mile, even the extra foot. Do a little more. They will notice and be grateful, and such an attitude will bring you great satisfaction and big dividends.

4. Do something for somebody else. No matter how hard or bleak your own life may seem, there are plenty of others worse off. So find a way to help them, to help even one person. Your life will be richer for it.

5. Honor and respect your parents. They've worked and sweated and prayed for you. You may think they're old-fashioned and out of touch, not with it, not so cool. But they're your parents, and they deserve your love and respect. Whatever you become, they will deserve credit and thanks.

6. Be true to yourself. Be honest with yourself. This means being honest even when it hurts. This means doing the right thing even when nobody's watching. You may be able to kid most people, but you can't really kid yourself. If you set high standards for yourself, and if generally you stick to them, then you are being true to yourself. Few who betray themselves ever really succeed.

7. Get involved. Try to make the world a little better. It's a great, big world, overwhelming, awesome. What can *I* do, you ask yourself? Maybe you can't reform the world overnight, but you can make your street, your school, your church, your home a little better. If everybody did his bit, it would be a far better world for all the rest of us.

8. Keep the faith. You've heard it said often: Keep the faith, baby! You'll have reasons to lose faith in the course of your life. Some people will betray your trust, others will fail to keep promises. But these breaches are not reason to turn sour against the whole world. Don't let that happen. Believe in people. Trust in God. In other words, keep the faith, retain your faith.

9. Try your hardest. Never do less than what you're capable of doing. You won't always succeed, but you'll know in your heart you tried. Nothing is sadder than the terrible waste when a man fails to live up to his potential, when he falls short of achieving what everybody knows he could achieve. Try hard — it's a good feeling, and it's the only way to make the most of your God-given abilities.

10. Set goals for yourself. Try to decide where you want to go, where you want to be five years, ten years from now, and how you can get there. Change them whenever you need to along the way. You can't know now where you'll be half a lifetime from today, but you've got a far better chance if you plan and dream and work toward specific goals.

11. Look up to somebody. Identify with somebody. Don't be embarrassed to have a hero or two. Pattern your life — parts of your life — after somebody you admire. Ernie Banks, Dr. Martin Luther King, a fine young man like your own Youth Chairman Jerry Washington (now an Illinois State Representative), your father, mother, teacher, minister, a political or business leader. Don't be reluctant to believe in somebody and to learn from their trials and triumphs.

12. Be kind. Kindness costs nothing, and yet it can mean so much. A kind word, a kind gesture, any small act of kindness may be remembered forever — and you'll know inside you that it was the right thing to do.

13. Get an education. Do everything that's required — whatever you must do — to get an education. Go as far as you can go in school. Don't drop out, despite all the temptations. The benefits of that education will be with you all your life — and it will help you in so many ways to get where you want to go and achieve the goals you want to achieve.

14. Never give up. You'll encounter setbacks along the way, setbacks that seem ruinous and even final. They'll depress you, crush your spirit for the moment. But you must refuse to accept defeat. Make sure your setbacks are only temporary. Fight back. Learn to defy hard luck. Learn from adversity. Never stop trying, for there's always another way, another day, usually a better way. Take heart from the knowledge that many of the world's most renowned leaders throughout history overcame immense obstacles, rebounded from crushing defeat, and refused stubbornly to yield to seeming disaster.

There is one final bit of advice which I believe is vital to your mental and spiritual health and well-being. To be successful in the best and broadest sense of that word, to achieve a full and rich and satisfying life, you must **banish all hate.** Leave no room in your heart for hate. Hate is a cancer which eats away all that is good. There will be times when you think hate is justified, when hate is almost impossible to avoid. For there is meanness in the world, and prejudice and unkindness. Even so, you must turn away hate, and rise above hate, for hate will injure you most of all and in the end it may consume and destroy you.

But it is not enough only to banish hate. Above all, **you must learn to love.** Listen with me to these words of St. Paul to the Corinthians, words which will enrich your life and the life of every human being who hears them and responds to them. You will not really go far or achieve much or attain lasting peace of mind unless you learn truly to love your fellow men.

So hear and heed these words of St. Paul:

"Though I speak with the tongues of men and angels, and have not Love, I am become as sounding brass, or a tinkling

125

cymbal. And though I have the gift of prophecy, and understand all mysteries, and all knowledge; and though I have all faith, so that I could remove mountains, and have not Love, I am nothing."

Love suffereth long, and is kind;
Love envieth not;
Love vaunted not itself, is not puffed up,
Doth not behave itself unseemly,
Seeketh not its own,
Is not easily provoked,
Thinketh no evil;
Rejoiceth not in iniquity, but rejoiceth in the truth;
Beareth all things, believeth all things, hopeth
all things, endureth all things . . .
And now abideth faith, hope, love these three;
but the greatest of these is Love.

Finally, **believe in your God.** "Open up your heart, let Jesus come in" — in the words of the hymn we sang here today. Pray. Ask for God's help, and thank God for what you are and what you have, however little it may seem to you.

Remember . . . there's a place for you on this earth. You are somebody, somebody different than any other somebody. With God's help, you can make of your life whatever you are determined to make of it.

Once over lightly

October 6, 1983

This week's moral: Beware of experts

One of the things wrong with the country today is experts. Put another way, what this country needs is fewer experts.

Many experts, I've found, really aren't. They just claim to be. Which is smart, because it can be quite profitable to be regarded as an expert in almost any field.

Take stock analysts. The *Wall Street Journal, Crain's Chicago Business,* and various business writers frequently quote stock analysts, thus conferring upon them expert status. For example, a reporter rings up an analyst at Bare, Bones & Co., the big investment banking house, to get the inside scoop on what's happening at Goldpolo, Inc., until recently a highly-touted stock. In sonorous jargon, the analyst/expert gives the low-down on why Chairman I. M. McWasper fired the whole executive team, sparing only the executive chef and curator of art, and what as a result will happen to Goldpolo's stock.

I READ SUCH learned comment with gimlet eye. Most such analysts, my research shows, are a year or three out of some MBA program, haven't so much as run a lemonade stand, and, in fact, have never toiled in the real world of

127

marketing, manufacturing, and profit-making. Most analysts, I've always supposed, mouth weighty gossip they pick up from other analysts over lunch at McDonald's or riding the Northwestern in from Wilmette or Glencoe. Yet a lot of trusting souls equate the pronouncements of the analysts with the wisdom of the Delphic oracle because, after all, they're experts, aren't they?

Another breed of expert is the restaurant/food critic, who treats the substance of survival as something between an art form and purest ecstasy. Their gourmet patter has become a space-eating staple in the food sections of newspapers, including ours, and chic magazines. One assumes thousands of famished folk won't life a fork without the astute, play-by-play guidance of their favorite culinary expert. As for me, I usually feel stuffed before I get past the third paragraph. I suppose it's a great way to visit a string of exotic eateries as guest of honor. But I'll never understand why either you or I should savor minced mussels just because some finger-lickin' expert eater tells us they're yummy.

A somewhat pretentious counterpart of the food expert is the wine expert, who makes plain old smashed grapes sound like a blend of holy water, Listerine, and the elixir of eternal youth.

ECONOMISTS ARE WIDELY thought to be experts in economic matters. Don't you believe it. Put two economists in a room and you've got total disagreement. After all, the Federal Reserve Board's economists, led by economist/expert/chairman Paul Volcker, managed, in very few months, to butcher the U. S. economy, resulting in an all-time high prime rate, record bankruptcies, skyrocketing unemployment, disaster in the housing and construction industries, etc., etc., etc. That's expertise? Yes. That's what experts will do if you give them half a chance. As a reward for such expertise, President Reagan recently appointed Mr. Volcker to another term as Fed chairman.

Yet another of the genus expert is the sports expert. This is the time of year when the baseball expert hopes his readers have short memories. His fervent prayer is that his readers and perhaps his boss, the editor, have forgotten by October what he told them in good faith during spring training about who by now would be the reigning major league hot shots.

Most of these intrepid forecasters, experts in any and all games played between our two oceans, start the virgin baseball season with a clean slate, an unblemished record, and a cadre of naïve, trusting, and forgetful fans. It is generally an unshakable axiom among sports experts, as with political experts, to cling to the tried and true, year-in, year-out contenders, thus invariably missing by light years if a rebuilt also-ran emerges from the pack and surges to the fore. Sports experts rationalize this sort of unbecoming conduct by a brash ball club by ignoring it as long as possible and then brushing it off as an "upset" impossible to predict in advance. What it more often means is that the expert did a lousy job of evaluating the ascendant team's talent, leadership, and motivation, or perhaps the steady decline of the perennial favorites.

So much for sports experts.

WHEN YOU CHIP away several coats of bright paint, you ofttimes discover that the so-called experts, who are paid to be expert and celebrated for their expertise, are no more expert than you or I. Often less so.

Oh, well, one more childhood illusion shattered.

The moral: Beware of experts.

'Say it ain't so . . .'

THERE IS NO FORCE on earth which can end my life-long love affair with major league baseball.

Lately, however, I've seen some things which raise a few doubts.

As an aspiring Hall of Famer struggling on the weed-infested vacant lots and rock-hard ballfields of my native Hamilton, Ohio, the thing I remember most vividly is the painful sting of the bat in my hands when I hit the ball too far down on the handle, especially on a chill spring day.

And the even more excruciating bone bruises in the palm of my hand when I caught a line drive in the pocket of my flimsy first baseman's mitt with the padding largely gone.

I REGARDED THAT PAIN as a necessary rite of acceptance among the bigger guys and better ballplayers, and I endured it.

No more. Today's major leaguers, except possibly for somebody as old as Yaz or Pete Rose, or our own Fergie Jenkins, wouldn't have the vaguest idea what I'm talking about.

These days, a brawny, hairy-chested long ball hitter strolls up to the plate with a menacing look, pauses, and then adjusts his soft white leather batting gloves like a debutante about to enter the country club on her big night. Batting gloves. If I'd tried something like that when I was a kid, I'd have been hooted out of the lineup and chased all the way home. Still, I figure batting gloves might have added 70 or 80 points to my middling average, surely enough to get me a shot at the big leagues.

After topping one to the pitcher for the third out, our hairy-chested hero trots out to his place in right field with a piece of equipment guaranteed to make even his mother look like a slick fielder. This secret weapon is the modern-day mitt.

As any true fan knows, this engineering marvel is a little smaller than a toilet seat, snaps shut on a ball like an alligator's jaws, and extends the fielder's reach about the length of another arm. It has been established that a volley of shots from a .38 won't penetrate the pocket; the spent bullets fall harmlessly to the grass.

BY CONTRAST, I PLAYED a passable first base with a mitt about the size of a butterplate strung together with a rawhide lace. On a sunny day, if I held my mitt up to the sky, I could make out cloud formations by squinting through the pocket.

That's all over and done, and I certainly don't begrudge today's ballplayers their vastly superior equipment with which to pursue their craft. But I must admit I was shaken by one recent revelation.

I had occasion after a game to visit the dressing room of a major league team which, out of respect for the young and starry-eyed, I shall not identify. For a moment, I thought I had entered the inner sanctum of the Joffrey Ballet. For there, in front of a large theatre-type mirror, were three of my heroes in the intricate process of blow-drying their hair to tousled perfection. Alas, times change.

ALL I COULD THINK OF, before I slunk out, was the immortal plea by the disbelieving ragamuffin who confronted "Shoeless Joe" Jackson after he was accused of throwing a World Series game in the infamous "Black Sox" scandal of 1919.

"Say it ain't so," the stricken lad begged his tarnished hero.

131

He'll muddle along, hope for the best

I have a confession to make. I ladle too much sugar into my coffee and onto my cereal. I'm not wild about yogurt, cottage cheese, sunflower seeds, alfalfa sprouts and most of the other certified health foods my wife and daughters tell me are essential to my well being. What's more, I neither jog nor do those nautilus/aerobic/whatever exercises.

MY DAUGHTERS predict dire consequences as a result of such irreverence and say I am neither chic nor sensible.

They may well be right. Then again, I feel great doing things my way. I eat what has taken me this far in life. I learned from a teacher somewhere back in grade school that milk and eggs were well-nigh the perfect foods, and I still consume my share of both. By instinct and natural fondness, I do eat some things labelled as healthy these days, like apples and bananas, fish and fowl, and most vegetables.

And I've never smoked!

As for exercise, I'm for it — in moderation. I play a little tennis, swim a little, run up stairs, but I don't run myself into the ground. I don't have shin splints, arthritic knees, or fallen arches, as do some card-carrying jocks I know.

I LIKE BARRY GOLDWATER'S observation about exercise. The Senator, now nearing 75, says he's exercised all his life, played vigorously at every sport, and, in his words, "That's the reason I can't walk today." (Two implanted hips.)

No fads for me. I think I'll just keep doing and eating what's worked for me so far and hope for the best in the years ahead.

A zany/not-so-zany look to the future

Editors tend to settle back in big, overstuffed chairs during the Christmas holidays and put down for their loyal readers either sombre or saccharine visions of the future.

Much of what they write is presumptuous, pointless, silly, and ultimately wrong.

In that hallowed tradition, I offer the following:

• Defense contractors will be issued formal federal "Licenses to Steal," thus removing them from the confirmed crook category and legitimizing grand larceny.

• Similar licenses will be issued at the state level to gas and electric utilities, with license fees to be split between the State Treasury and the Governor's campaign reelection fund.

• Leading business schools will offer courses in the techniques of becoming a skilled federal informant, which often will pay more in cash and perks than top executive posts in Fortune 500 companies.

• All FBI agents will be required to obtain degrees in drama, especially the impersonation of legitimate businessmen, honest lawyers (Ha!), and upright judges. Immunized witnesses will be taught to mouth pre-taped testimony convincingly and with straight faces.

• Lie tests will be required of all federal and state employees, except known or admitted liars at the level of cabinet member or above, and appointees whose position requires legislative consent. U. S. Attorneys, FBI agents and immunized witnesses will be granted special exemptions.

133

- Attorney General Edwin Meese will move in federal court that the U. S. Constitution be suspended when it conflicts with initiatives of the Justice Department.

- By the end of the 1980s, all homes selling for less than $150,000 will consist of one medium-sized room. Available options at extra cost will include front and back door, sink, toilet, space heater, and light fixture. Four-bedroom, two-bath homes will start at $999,999.95, with 60 percent down and the balance over 48 months.

- For the convenience of the FBI, contractors will be required to install electronic bugs in all new homes, office buildings, and courthouses, and lie detectors in the confessionals of Catholic churches.

- Neiman-Marcus will offer the Sears Tower in its 1990 Christmas catalog.

- Most homes will be heated by a combination of warm beer, old furniture, and pet manure. Higher-priced homes will be heated by funnelling political speeches through hot air ducts.

- The standard household toilet will function as a combined garbage disposal unit, tropical fish tank, and hot tub.

- Root canals will replace heart bypass and hysterectomies as *People Magazine*'s "in" medical procedure.

- There will be more vegetation indoors than outdoors, with a major boom in green concrete lawns. As a result, stock analysts will tout companies which build all-weather tennis courts. The carpet industry will suffer as architects specify dirt floors in most new homes to create an outdoorsy ambiance.

• Most of our protein requirements will be supplied by worms and other insect flesh. Worm ranches will flourish on the few remaining vacant lots, driving lot prices out of sight. Wormburgers will be popular at fast food restaurants

• Vegetarians will subsist largely on flowers. Vegetables, as we know them, will be sold by florists and used mainly for decorative purposes. Zucchinis and artichokes will be in, and trendy brides will carry bouquets of carrots and bibb lettuce.

• Scientists and government agencies will determine that edibles packed in cans and boxes, and protected by foil or cellophane, cause cancer, and are therefore inedible. They will be banned.

• The prime interest rate will be set by a select committee of Mafia loan sharks and New York bankers chosen at large by the chairman of the Federal Reserve Board. This is known as price-fixing and is illegal for everyone except bankers. The chairman of Citicorp will chair the committee and be addressed as "Your Excellency."

• All professional sports seasons will be expanded to 12 months each year. Monday night football will be cancelled and replaced by Tuesday-Wednesday-Thursday-Friday-Saturday night football. Baseballs lost in snowbanks will be ground rule doubles. Wives convicted of murdering their sports-addict spouses will be given suspended sentences.

• It will be possible to obtain peanuts, candy bars, hot dogs, pop, beer, pizza, scorecards, T-shirts, and caps by inserting old Susan B. Anthony dollars and other loose change into your TV set. Air sickness bags will be available so no devoted TV fanatic ever has to leave his set.

• TV weathermen will appear first on all TV news shows, be assured by contract of on-screen exposure for at least 20 minutes during each half-hour, and receive double pay during blizzards, tornadoes, severe thunderstorm warnings, hailstorms (stones of one-half inch or greater diameter), and wind-chill records. Anchormen will be reimbursed for razor hair-styling and three piece designer ensembles.

• Insurance companies will not be required to pay claims. They will merely collect premiums, cancel coverage, and increase rates.

• One out of every two Americans will be a lawyer. No citizen will be permitted to appear in court unless he is represented by two or more lawyers. Ordinary non-lawyers will have to retain a lawyer and prove they have done so before entering a supermarket, boarding any form of public transportation, applying for college and/or job, and attending professional sports events.

• U. S. imports of Mercedes motorcars will be reserved exclusively for lawyers, doctors, professional athletes, and former Pentagon officials. Restricted suburbs will be developed and zoned only for lawyers, doctors and occasionally, certified public accountants. This may be unconstitutional, but there will be plenty of lawyers around to test the concept in court. Houses there will be equipped with walk-in vaults, barred windows, and hot-and-cold running white wine.

• Students will be recognized as a new occupational category and presented with gold watches at final graduation exercises. Ph.D. degrees will be awarded to college students who, after at least six years of higher education, can read five out of seven Interstate highway signs, memorize the instructions on a self-service gas pump, and write an essay, in 25 words or less, explaining what they got out of college.

• An additional advanced degree will be awarded every succeeding five years to students who satisfactorily complete

136

all the requirements. Such students will not be required to enroll, attend classes, take exams, or otherwise interrupt their self-monitored quest for personal growth and self-enrichment.

• A new militant organization — NOPE (National Organization for Pet Equality) — will become a potent political force. Pets will have access to all public restrooms and will be granted equal time on radio/TV talk shows. Rabies shots and annual de-worming procedures will be mandatory for all pet owners. Flea collars will be optional for pets and people. Pets no longer will be called by demeaning single names (e.g., Spot or Fluffy). Otherwise, they must adopt the last name of the family with whom they live (e.g., Spot Reagan or Fluffy Rostenkowski) and apply for Social Security numbers. Pets will not be denied credit because they are pets.

Well, there you have it.

Unpublished, 1975

A toast to the double bed in the White House

The most reassuring news to come out of Washington, D. C., in ages is word that President and Mrs. Ford will share a bed and bedroom in the White House.

What's more, it's their own bed, moved over from suburban Virginia, a link between Grand Rapids USA and the jaded capital city, not a historic hand-me-down from President Andrew Jackson or some other prior denizen of the White House.

Bully for Jerry and Betty! That revelation ought to give all the President's constituents renewed faith and a good feeling about the first couple.

There's something wholesome and comforting about the double bed. It says a lot about people. It's hardly the ideal arrangement for a confirmed loner. Double-bed fans generally are agreeable folk with fewer hangups, willing to put up

137

with a random elbow in the ribs, tolerant of buzz-saw snoring, probably on good terms with each other.

Those are good qualities in a President, probably as valid in gauging his potential as some of the impossible benchmarks set by the President-graders in the media and thought shops. The sort of give-and-take cultivated in a lasting double-bed union ought to help the President deal with such diverse groups as Congress, the Russians, the oil and milk lobbies, labor leaders, and others.

Admittedly, it's not big news when a married couple beds together, yet all our recent Presidents, going back at least four decades to Franklin D. Roosevelt's first term, slept in solitary splendor.

When married couples, even Presidential pairs, sleep in separate rooms, you have to wonder why. It may mean nothing much or plenty. Maybe (1) they just aren't too fond of each other, so they keep different schedules and lead different lives, or (2) one is suffering from a contagious disease or dreadful allergy, or (3) their house is too big (the White House has well over 100 rooms) and they feel guilty about all those empty rooms, or (4) at least one of them has such habits as eating catsup on cottage cheese in bed, flailing all night like a washing machine gone amuck, and playing tapes until the wee hours, or (5) any combination of the above.

Apparently, and happily for all of us, the Fords are untroubled by such torments. This allows the President — with tranquil, rested mind — to concentrate more fully on affairs of state.

And there's an added bonus. When the new President climbs into bed, aching, battered nerves frayed after one of those days all Presidents (the rest of us, too) endure, his devoted wife will be there beside him to administer the sort of relaxing back-rub that beats tranquilizers all hollow. President Ford is the sort of fellow who will return the favor. That ought to make all of us out here feel a little better, too.

So a toast to the double bed in the White House! May it symbolize a new era of good feeling in America.

Phone call from the sky:
'Keep my spaghetti warm!'

You probably won't believe what I'm about to tell you, but then again maybe you won't be as nonplussed as I was. After all, I'm more than a little amazed that my about-to-be 12-year old daughter is quite adept with a computer.

Anyway, a few weeks ago, en route home from Dallas, I phoned my wife 18 minutes out of O'Hare at 20,000 feet straight up to tell her I'd be a little late for dinner. Aren't you just a little dazzled?

Come on, now, that's a giant leap beyond those cordless phones you can use in your backyard or on the porch. Especially so for a kid who once made his own "telephone" by stretching wire taut between two tin cans.

ANYWAY, MY BUSINESS associate, a confirmed yuppie who's hooked on everything the fast-track set buys or covets, was carrying in his attaché case a Motorola cordless cellular phone.

Casually, as we neared Chicago, he pulled it out of his case, and, with the bravado of a riverboat gambler flashing a winning hand, dialed his home number, making sure he had the attention of a few nearby kibitzers. He talked on for several minutes, as more passengers leaned into the aisle and eyed his new-fangled toy in action.

By the time he handed it to me, he was the focus of admiring, wondering glances, several grave questions, and quite a few "wows."

Martha wasn't at all sure I was being serious when I told her from whence I was calling. She even suggested I may have dallied en route home and drained a glass or two. She also told me she'd keep a little left-over spaghetti warm.

IT WAS AFTER I hung up that the fun began. A skeptical

139

stewardess came meandering down the aisle, smiled a saccharine smile, and, in a voice heavy with sarcasm, gave us the treatment reserved for difficult passengers.

"Well, boys, shall I bring back the drink cart, ha-ha-ha?"

My ever-gentlemanly cohort, Gerald, asked if she'd like to make a call.

"Like to where? I can *walk* up to see the pilot."

"Give me a number," Gerald persisted, as all eyes turned to this little vignette-in-the-sky.

"Okay, okay," she humored him. "How about 214?" . . . and then she rattled off seven more numbers after the Dallas area code.

GERALD DUTIFULLY "touched" them into his amazing machine, listened for the ring, and handed it to the thoroughly unconvinced stewardess.

She held it to her ear, peering down from on high with a disdainful smirk.

Gerald handed her the phone.

Taking it gingerly, as if it might be alive, she held it to her ear.

A LOOK OF PURE amazement remade her face.

"Margie?" Her voice was small and tentative.

Then: "MARGIE," still questioning, followed by "M-AAA-R-G-I-EEEEEE," a near-shriek that resounded through the plane.

She talked self-consciously with Margie for a minute or two, then sheepishly handed the phone back.

"I would never have believed it," she told us, still wide-eyed, even though word is out that commercial planes are soon to be outfitted with phones for passenger use.

AS WE LEFT the plane a bit later, she was prepared for us. With a touch of ceremony, she presented two bottles of "first class" wine wrapped in blue American Airlines napkins, a token of appreciation for her experience.

140

The wondrous world of cordless telephones provides all sorts of tales. I bought one for my car about a year ago despite snide comments from my wife along the lines that "boys never outgrow their toys, do they?" Anyway, it has proved invaluable time after time as a business tool. Once recently, when a huge truck ran me off a country road in blinding Wisconsin snow, I was able to summon help from a snowbank.

On another occasion, less urgent, I was telling Hope I'd be home in about 10 minutes as I pulled into the drive-in lanes at the bank to cash a check.

"Love ya, darling," I said to end the conversation with Hope.

THE TIMING WAS exquisite.

Back came the perfect rejoinder.

"Love you, too. Say, you're just about the friendliest one we've had through here recently. What can we do for you?"

Startled, I looked up, and saw the three tellers roaring with laughter inside their glass booth.

Ah, the wonders of modern-age electronics.

Thursday, August 9, 1984

Take all health rules with a grain of salt

Okay, everybody, salt up!

Salt's back on the "in" list, after years as an evil substance responsible for narrowed arteries and other grievous human ills. That's the word based on a study of some 10,000 human guinea pigs over many years.

How many sufferers from high blood pressure, on their

doctor's advice, ate meal after meal that tasted uniformly like wet cardboard because salt was denied them?

There is one immutable principle in understanding each and every health and nutrition rule: Like Chicago's weather, if you wait around a while, it will change.

IN A SIXTH GRADE hygiene class, I was told the two "perfect" foods were milk and eggs. I took that lesson both seriously and literally. To this day, I drink milk and eat eggs, guiltily, of course, because now they are supposed to be prime sources of cholesterol, that lethal clogger of arteries. Still, I reason, there must be some good in those "perfect" foods, so I've merely cut down rather than cut out and hope for the best.

Everything you've ever enjoyed is suspected these days of causing cancer. The bony finger of the medical/nutritional spoilsports was pointed at coffee for awhile. I can't even remember if coffee is presently on or off the skull-and-crossbones list, but I continue to savor my several cups a day.

I load mine with plain old refined sugar — the real stuff — which is under severe and relentless assault as a health-sapper.

Well, maybe, but I prefer straight sugar to those little pink and blue envelopes containing artificial sweeteners. If sugar kills me, I'd rather succumb to the real stuff than to man-made substitutes. After all, the experts, given enough time, publicity, and research dollars, can foul almost anything and create life-threatening hazards undreamed of when life was simpler and less "scientific."

TAKE BACON. I do on occasion because I consider it a treat. Bacon is compared by cancer researchers to a cup of hemlock. What am I to tell you, except it tastes good and certainly embellishes my lethal poached eggs?

I wait confidently, knowing it's only a matter of time until some researcher, working feverishly in his dimly-lit garage, discovers something to change dramatically the present tarnished image of good old eggs and bacon.

Voila! Three slippery, uncooked slices laid across the forehead will become the sure cure for migraines. Or bacon bits sprinkled generously over shredded cigarettes will give serious runners that extra kick on the back stretch.

Wait a while. Whatever you know for sure in the wonderful world of health and nutrition is guaranteed to change by 180 degrees sometime before you expire from all the wrong advice the "experts" have laid on you.

Thursday, January 9, 1986

What's a Navistar?
You'll never guess and never remember

Let's hear it for Navistar!
How's that? Navistar?
Yes, Navistar.
What the devil is a Navistar? Or who?
A new Navy fighter plane?
Nope.
An aerobic exercise program?
Sorry.
A battery-operated toy submarine?
Wrong.
The successor to Halley's Comet?
Wrong again.
The latest Pentagon ripoff?
A belly-dancer's navel bauble?
A miracle laxative?

None of the above. Please don't get funny.
Well, what is it then?

Navistar is the exciting, modern, avant garde name of a famous old company, International Harvester, a venerable Chicago institution. You know, the McCormick reaper and all that.
You're kidding.
No. They announced it earlier this week to 15,000 employees worldwide on some kind of satellite hookup. They said Navistar is "our" new name.
How did they explain it?
Well, they put a lot of junk into a computer about the new 21st century International Harvester, and out came Navistar.
You *are* kidding.
No, this is the new image of the old Harvester. Nobody knows what it means, but maybe it's got something to do with hitching their old wagon to a new star. Get it? Or something.

WHO MADE UP the new name?
Some outside consulting firm that deals in corporate images. They fed all this stuff in, and out popped Navistar. Pretty slick.
Did the Board of Directors approve the new name?
They must have.
Did they pay the consulting firm?
Thousands of dollars.
You can't be serious.
I am. Why do you think a lot of nice old companies with friendly, familiar, reassuring names have their names changed to names nobody understands or remembers or likes?
Darned if I know.
Easy. These corporate image firms have a right to make a living, too, just as much as lawyers and accountants and politicians.
Will the new name help International Harvester, I mean Navistar, make a little money?
That's asking quite a lot.

144

Pssst, here's how to speak Southern

I spend a good bit of time in the South, especially Mississippi, where I have business interests. Some of my friends down there have been coaching me in talkin' Southern so I don't stick out like a sore thumb and embarrass them with my abrasive Yankee speech.

This random sampler of definitions and usage is a reader service to help you-all talk and listen right, and not embarrass yourself, when you're down South.

Myan: Human male. "That myan over yonder just winked at me."

Airs: Mistakes. "Ah already seen three airs in that newspaper article, and I ain't even halfway through it yet."

Idinit: Term used by genteel southerners who wish to avoid saying ain't. "Might hot today, idinit?"

Gitcher: Go fetch. "Annie, gitcher gun."

Raffle: Long gun. "Nobody gonna bother me when ah got ma raffle with me."

Nan moll: One mile less than ten miles. "Ah reckon the store's about nan moll over thataway."

Frahdy: End of work week. "Thank God it's Frahdy."

Kamoan: Invitation to return. "Kamoan home, Bubba, yore forgiven."

Yawl: Southern catch-all phrase. Singular or plural. "Yawl hurry back now."

Momenem: Mother and family. "Be sure to give my best to your momenem."

Hep: To aid or benefit. "Ah cain't hep lovin' ya, Lucy Belle."

145

Hey: Greeting used instead of hello or hi. "Hey, Bobby, how ya doin' there, myan?"

Lahf: The state of living. "What ya ever gonna do with yore lahf, boy?"

Let on: To indicate knowledge of. "She don't let on she knows her husband's been runnin' 'round with that blond waitress."

Libel: Likely to. "If he keeps it up, she's libel to shoot him daid."

Madge: State of wedlock. "Their madge was annulled after only two days."

Pare: Strength, authority. "Ain't no pare like the pare of the President."

Phrasin: Very cold. "Put another log on the fahr. It's phrasin in here."

Prolly: Likely to. "Ah think ah'll prolly go to Memphis for the weekend."

Quare: Strange. "Grampa's been actin' quare ever since he fell off that merry-go-round."

Ratcheer: On this spot. "Put the bag down ratcheer."

Ahmana: Assertion. "Ahmana go to the store presently. Anything you want?"

Sprang: One of four seasons. "Sprang will be a little late this year."

Sawt: Common condiment. "Ahmana put some mo' sawt on this popcorn."

Shurf: County law enforcement officer. "The shurf's raidin' them topless joints agin. Must be an election year."

Tarred: Fatigued. "Ah'm plumb wore out, jes' too tarred to go tonight."

Thang: An object. "She's jes' the cutest lil thang."

Thow: To hurl. "That fella thows a real mean spitball."

Yale: Loud outburst. "When that kid got his finger caught in the car door, ya shoulda heard him yale."

● ● ●

I hope my Southern friends aren't offended. Why should they be? They keep tellin' me I sure do talk funny.

(With special thanks to Steve Mitchell, a pioneer in "How to Speak Southern," and Deane Tankersley, a Southerner who gave me the idea.)

Thursday, September 12, 1985

California can't touch the warmth and roots of our 'prosaic heartland'

We Midwesterners take a lot of guff. We suffer untold indignities.

We've kept the country afloat and well-fed for . . . lo, these many years . . . and now they're calling us "The Rust Belt" and consigning us to history's dustbin, blowing us off and burying us deep.

East coast types tend to look down their noses at us heartlanders as rubes, hicks, hayseeds, bumpkins. We're supposed to be uncouth, uncultured, unlettered, unwashed, and all those other rude words they call us.

Californians also ridicule us mid-Americans. They sniff that we're neither hip, chic, cool, avant garde, nor "with it," whatever "it" may be.

ARIZONA SEN. BARRY GOLDWATER, a crusty, plain-spoken sort, once put the Eastern elitists in their place by suggesting that the entire Eastern seaboard, but especially the New York-to-Washington corridor, ought to be sawed off from the rest of the U. S. and shoved, not so gently, into the Atlantic.

I volunteer singlehandedly to take on California.

There are those, my devoted wife among them, who consider California the quintessential paradise, the ultimate Nirvana.

Sorry, darling, but you know how I feel.

If you gave me — repeat, *gave* me — a palatial mansion overlooking the broad Pacific, a middle-six-, even low-seven-figure income, staff of 10, free hair-styling, in-house big band, and a lifetime supply of gourmet groceries, you couldn't induce me to leave Illinois for California.

Not for more than five days, anyway.

Who needs mud slides, forest fires, earthquakes, tidal waves, 18-foot sharks, falling Sequoias, the San Andreas Fault, Marvin Mitchelson, Beverly Hills, golden beach bums, and all that surface glitz?

YES I KNOW ABOUT the "unsurpassed" ambiance of San Francisco, where romantics "leave their hearts." After all, I've watched "Hotel" on TV a few times and even stayed there a few more.

There is a rootlessness to California, a magnetic, irresistible attraction for the restless, nomadic, groping, wanting, unfulfilled.

It is the perfect spawning ground for wild schemes, high fliers, persuasive phonies, weird and flaky lifestyles. It seems fitting somehow that Silicon Valley, the boom-and-bust locale of America's latter-day, high tech "Gold Rush," would germinate and play in California. Where else, pray tell?

148

For me, California's sprawl and vastness and impersonality will never match the cohesiveness and warmth, the tradition and roots, of mid-America's hometowns.

Maybe my perception of California is warped and askew. Maybe.

Go west, if you will, my friends, but let me live and die right here in the more prosaic heartland, the spine and sinew and soul of America.

If we care about justice...

This series of columns and editorials on the abuse of justice by federal prosecutors and other criminal justice officials was nominated twice for a 1985 Pulitzer Prize for Distinguished Commentary.

In his letter of nomination, *Chicago Lawyer* Editor Rob Warden wrote:

". . . William H. Rentschler truly has been a voice in the wilderness. He alone in the popular press in the Chicago area has championed the serious issues presented by the unscrupulous actions of public prosecutors. . . . The Pulitzer judges have an opportunity, in selecting William Rentschler for this important and deserved award, to encourage other media, locally and nationally, to support with renewed vigor the notion that is more fundamental to our democracy and more sacred to our way of life than any other — the notion of liberty and justice for all."

Author and communications executive Sid Cato told the Pulitzer jurors:

"What the courageous Mr. Rentschler has done is cry out against what he writes eloquently is 'erosion

151

*of our civil liberties' by the FBI, by the prosecution-
prone U. S. Attorney's office, by the courts. . . .*

*Think for a moment on this point: In fearlessly pit-
ting his columns and editorials against in-office law-
enforcement officials, and on the side of what he
deems right, Rentschler at a minimum has risked
ruin of his chain of newspapers. At worst, he has
subjected himself to investigation, harassment, indictment or imprisonment. . . ."*

• • •

May 3, 1984

'Rotten apples' defile justice

It is more than enough to make one throw up.
It is only ghastly alternatives we are offered.

ON THE ONE HAND, there is the posturing, preening
John DeLorean, accused of seeking to rescue his failing auto
company and flamboyant lifestyle through a massive cocaine
"deal" captured on video tape.

On the other, there are conniving FBI agents and manipul-
ative federal prosecutors, supposedly on the side of the angels,
but in truth amoral avengers guilty of buying witnesses, im-
personating bankers, staging events, reconstructing testimony,
and literally creating criminal conduct.

It is a travesty on justice, a depressing commentary on the
state of our highly-touted criminal justice system, a mockery
of last Tuesday's Law Day celebration, which is a national
testament each year to our badly warped, if idealistic, concept
of justice under law.

The bizarre DeLorean drama is not isolated. It has been

played out in various courtrooms with increasing frequency over the past 14 years, since U. S. Attorney General John N. Mitchell, Richard Nixon's close confidant and partner in law, guided through Congress the Omnibus Crime Bill in 1970, which for the first time authorized testimony by immunized witnesses *without corroboration.*

This meant any weasel could testify to anything so long as it fit the prosecutor's requirements. This measure gave hungry, self-promoting, marginally scrupulous-or-worse prosecutors the right to "buy" testimony by granting convicted or would-be criminals freedom from prosecution and often jail if only they would testify against government targets. Some U. S. Attorneys leap at the easy granting of immunity to nail visible public figures and parlay the publicity into political careers, lucrative private law partnerships, or prestigious judgeships. The abuses often are scandalous, the government's witnesses nothing more or less than confirmed crooks and creeps, yet federal judges routinely look the other way and thus become party to the scandal.

Chicago Lawyer, probably the foremost investigative journal in Chicago, has exposed serious, very possibly indictable offenses by the federal law enforcement apparatus which are studiously ignored by big downtown newspapers and TV stations.

WHY? SIMPLY, the mass media have become virtual "co-conspirators" in undermining justice by forging cozy relationships with Justice Department officials, including U. S. Attorneys and FBI agents. A handful of print and TV reporters have made careers and won countless awards by milking such ties for leaks, scoops, and damning, unattributed accusations and innuendo which compromise the right to fair trial no matter how vehement the denials.

In turn, these favored reporters puff the exploits and enhance the careers of their sources. Such is the stuff of tainted "justice" and irresponsible journalism.

The DeLorean case is one of a long list involving celebrities, officeholders, and visible public figures. Their stories have an eerily similar ring.

In the 1970s, Edward J. Gurney was a highly regarded Republican U. S. Senator from Florida. An ambitious U. S. Attorney chose him as a target and threw the proverbial book at him. Gurney was prosecuted twice and emerged totally innocent from the ordeal. But he never recovered, giving up his Senate seat and his solvency, ending $600,000 in debt from the monstrous legal fees which invariably accompany criminal charges.

ALL THEY WANTED, he said ruefully of his accusers, "was to hang a big hide on the wall."

There is the story of the late Otto Kerner, former Illinois governor, federal judge, general, and U. S. Attorney, whose reputation for integrity was unblemished through three decades of public service. His conviction was engineered by then-U. S. Attorney (now Governor) James R. Thompson, who granted total immunity from prosecution for the carefully-contrived testimony of two wealthy race-track owners, Marjorie Lindheimer Everett and William Miller.

Until his death after serving part of a three-year prison term, Kerner stated repeatedly that the witnesses against him were "bribed" by the immunity deal and "induced to lie" by Thompson. Thompson and his first assistant, Samuel K. Skinner, arranged a multi-million dollar federal tax forgiveness for Miller and later interceded with California authorities to help key witness Marje Everett, an obvious corrupter if Kerner was in fact guilty, obtain a racing license in California. She has been a recent guest at a White House social function.

One recent series of articles by editor Rob Warden and several reporters in *Chicago Lawyer* is a documented account of what seems a shocking "conspiracy" to obstruct justice among current U. S. Attorney Dan K. Webb, his crony and former associate Charles Kocoras, now a U. S. District judge, and criminal lawyer David Schippers. Shortly before the epi-

154

sode, Webb and Kocoras had vacationed together, and all three served in the U. S. Attorney's office under Thompson and his successor, Sam Skinner, now a high-priced defense lawyer with Sidley & Austin, Chicago's largest law firm.

STILL ANOTHER SHABBY episode involves Federal Judge Harry E. Claiborne of Nevada, long a thorn in the FBI's paw in its endless war against organized crime, who was indicted last Dec. 8 on charges of bribery, wire fraud, tax evasion, obstruction of justice, and filing false financial disclosures.

"His chief accuser," wrote *San Francisco Examiner* reporter James A. Finefrock, "is notorious brothel owner Joe Conforte. . . . Defense attorneys contended that the judge is the victim of a long-standing vendetta by federal investigators. . . .

"Conforte," said Finefrock, "returned to the U. S. in early December after three years on the lam in Rio de Janeiro, Brazil, which he called 'a paradise on Earth.' He fled there in 1981 to escape a five-year tax evasion sentence. In exchange for his cooperation, that term was reduced to 15 months, fugitive charges against him were dropped, and he was made a protected witness and kept in a secret location.

". . . Conforte's tax liability is estimated to be as high as $20 million," Finefrock continued in his article last Jan. 15. "Federal prosecutors deny reports that a deal has been cut to reduce what he owes to $3.5 million. Five years ago, another federal judge called Conforte 'a pimp sitting on the banks of the Truckee River thumbing his nose at the government.' Now he's the government's star witness." Shades of Otto Kerner!

So what else is new? The pattern is sickeningly familiar to all who watch the inner workings of our federal criminal justice system and are willing to speak candidly and openly of its manifold abuses.

This is our government conducting itself in the manner of the sleaziest slice of society, covering itself with slime, and defiling its sacred trust.

155

THESE EVER-BOLDER, unchecked intrusions threaten our liberties. "It's too much of a prosecutor's game and it is, in my view, scandalous," says Monroe H. Freedman, professor of law at Hofstra University, described by *Chicago Lawyer* as "a noted authority on lawyers' ethics."

Consider:

• The courts have largely abrogated responsibility for disciplining the prosecutors.

• Congress typically has failed to address a hard issue and set clear guidelines.

• The American Bar Association, by its near total silence, has given prosecutors a license to proceed without hindrance.

• U. S. Attorney Generals, mainly short-term figureheads, have been unable, disinclined, or unwilling to take control. The 94 U. S. Attorneys have the power to run amuck and trample the Constitution in their private fiefdoms, and the director of the FBI, former Federal Judge William H. Webster, seems almost to revel in the Abscams, the Greylords, the high-profile cases involving videotapes, wiretaps, and FBI agents variously playing bankers and Arab shieks.

In all too many cases, the only legitimate question which emerges finally is:
"Who, pray tell, deserves to be found guilty and given a stiff sentence, the defendant or his accusers?"
"There's a small choice in rotten apples," quoth Shakespeare in *The Taming of the Shrew*.

ISN'T THAT a sorry state? How long will we citizens tolerate such a bald distortion of our system's intent, and how long can the fiction of justice be maintained?

156

A real life script to scare, offend, and perhaps enrage

The script I am about to share with you is so bizarre and improbable it was rejected by every major movie studio and book publisher in the United States. Yet it includes all the elements of a sensational best-seller or blockbuster film.

The story involves a big-city judge charged with corruption, which is said to permeate the entire court system, and an ambitious, publicity-hungry prosecutor who is a darling of the media.

IT IS A SCANDAL of epic proportions. It has all the makings of a real Ellery Queen courtroom barn-burner. The judge is indicted in a blaze of publicity, and the whole town focuses on the outcome of the trial, which could be a landmark case in U. S. legal history.

But there is a completely implausible twist in the script. The federal judge assigned to the case, the preening prosecutor, and the tough defense attorney all turn out to be long-time cronies and associates who have proceeded arm-in-arm together through their careers thus far. Each cut his eye-teeth and learned the legal trade as assistants in the office of the same U. S. Attorney who has since gone on to high public office. The trial judge and the prosecutor, we learn, not only worked together, but vacation together in the North Woods and are intimate, back-slapping buddies. What's more, the prosecutor, bent on convicting, and the defense attorney, presumably equally committed to finding his client innocent, turn out to be former partners in the very same small law firm.

Well, you get the point. None of this rings true. Quite obviously, this scenario is too far-fetched to sell. Nobody's going to buy such an irrational, outlandish, unreal plot.

Nobody, that is, except the vaunted Chicago media, superstars of hard-hitting investigative journalism.

They bought the whole ludicrous script and fed it unabridged to their readers and viewers.

YOU SEE, gentle readers, the "script" is not fiction but truth, a real-life melodrama which casts gravest doubts on the integrity of our judicial system. You won't read this interpretation, this *non*-fiction account, anywhere else, certainly not in Chicago's daily newspapers.

What I'm talking about is last week's conviction of Cook County Judge John M. Murphy in the incredible Greylord soap opera which has been playing in the Everett McKinley Dirksen Federal Building for many weeks. Judge Murphy, whom I've never met nor laid eyes on, may very well be crooked as a dog's hind leg and guilty as sin.

But the whole sordid process of convicting him is a colossal affront to rule by law and the basic tenets of the legal system we tout as the best and fairest in all the world. The tragedy is that the judiciary, bar association leaders, prominent lawyers, and editorial writers, who ought to be outraged, are silent as stones, perhaps intimidated by the federal juggernaut which in its way has "controlled" the Northern District of Illinois since 1971, when James R. Thompson was appointed by President Richard Nixon to be U. S. Attorney in Chicago.

Let's start by understanding the cast of characters in this grotesque courtroom ritual.

THE PRESIDING federal judge is Charles P. Kocoras, a former Assistant U. S. Attorney who served under U. S. Attorney Thompson, who used that powferful job as a springboard to the Governorship of Illinois.

The prosecutor is present U. S. Attorney Dan K. Webb, a former Assistant U. S. Attorney under Thompson.

The defense attorney is Matthias K. Lydon, a former Assistant U. S. Attorney who served under, you guessed it, Thompson.

Our legal system is based on the adversary principle. The prosecution and defense have the obligation to spare nothing to arrive at the truth (apparently at times an outmoded concept), the former to convict, the latter to seek acquittal by every honorable means. The trial judge has the obligation to stand above the battle, to be impeccably fair and balanced and dispassionate.

How can that possibly be when three virtual "fraternity brothers" are the principal players in this particular trial? The appearance of impropriety at a minimum is overwhelming, practically begging for protest. At the very minimum, in a trial of this sensitivity and magnitude, it would seem Judge Kocoras might have withdrawn from the case. Perhaps Defense Attorney Lydon might have thought better of accepting Murphy as his client.

Rob Warden, editor of *Chicago Lawyer,* which is published by the Chicago Council of Lawyers, told me he considered the proceedings "outrageous."

One question occurs: Why would Judge Murphy entrust his fate to a lawyer with such ties? I can't imagine, unless somehow he was convinced in his shellshocked state that Lydon's relationship with Judge Kocoras and U. S. Attorney Webb somehow would redound to his ultimate benefit. We shall never know what Murphy's attorney said or implied. If Murphy were convicted — and clearly the deck was stacked against him — would Lydon talk to his cronies about a lesser sentence? This is no accusation, but surely it is the sort of possibility which might cross the mind of any disinterested observer.

THE PRESS NORMALLY is quick to condemn the "appearance of impropriety" where public officials are concerned. Surely the appearance of impropriety is a predominant element in this case, yet there has been no murmur of protest from the media.

So Judge Murphy is convicted, but there is much more. Lydon said he will appeal. He knows that is an empty, virtually hopeless gesture. Ask former Illinois Attorney General Bill Scott, former Cook County Commissioner Floyd Fulle, the family of the late Governor Otto Kerner, and all the other political victims of the past dozen years.

The Seventh Circuit Court of Appeals includes two former prosecutors, Judge William J. Bauer and Joel Flaum, both Thompson intimates of long-standing, and the court overall has a justly deserved reputation for sustaining the prosecution and not rocking the boat. If my research is complete, the Seventh Circuit has not overturned or ordered a new trial in a single high-visibility political-type case since Jim Thompson became U. S. Attorney. The U. S. Supreme Court merely declines to hear such appeals, no matter what the circumstances or conduct of the prosecutors.

But there is more to Greylord, enough to make a sensitive legal purist either weep or grind his teeth.

First, there was the planting of "bugs" in judicial chambers by the FBI. Standard stuff these days, but U. S. Supreme Court Justice Oliver Wendell Holmes described wire-tapping as "dirty business" in 1928, and a bit earlier Justice Louis D. Brandeis called it an "instrument of tyranny."

There was the FBI's technique of using agents and informants to give false testimony under oath in courtrooms.

There was the granting of immunity to sleazy courtroom "hangers-on," who were the key witnesses in the massive campaign to convict Judge Murphy, and who will testify again and again as the litany of indictments expands.

AT THE END, there was the showy prosecutor Webb hailing his courtroom triumph as "a resounding victory in favor of every witness," as if to say, "By golly, we got the jury to believe these creeps and convicted crooks and purchased informers."

The main witness, retired Chicago cop James LeFevour, was induced to testify — call it "bribed" — by being allowed to plead guilty to a misdemeanor for his long history of con-

160

fessed bribes and ticket-fixing, thus staying out of jail and retaining his police pension.

The deal the government gave him, crowed LeFevour, was "a lifetime opportunity."

We should beware. More than 2,000 years ago, Aristotle warned: "Of the tyrant, spies and informers are the principal instrument."

"God help that country," pleaded Archibald MacLeish several decades ago, "where informers thrive, where slander flourishes and lies contrive . . ."

There's still more.

Most Americans cling to the notion that a man is innocent until proved guilty. That has been considered a sacred precept of the U. S. judicial system. But not to U. S. Attorney Webb and his ilk, who have crushed it underfoot.

IN OPEN COURT during the Murphy trial, with no indictment or even prior accusation, the self-righteous, arrogant Webb charged Cook County Judge Richard F. LeFevour with fixing cases and taking bribes. The charges were based on claims by James LeFevour, Judge LeFevour's cousin, the admitted crook whose freedom and future depend on federal favor.

"One man's word is no man's word," wrote the German philosopher-poet Goethe nearly two centuries ago. "We should quietly hear both sides."

Judge LeFevour bitterly denounced both Webb and his cousin in a stinging statement:

"I am innocent. I bitterly decry and denounce the unprecedented way the accusations against me were brought forth and aired. I have been tried without a forum, I have been tried without confrontation by my accusers, and I have been tried without a right of cross-examination. In sum, I have been thoroughly tried, but I have had no trial as we know it in America. We certainly have taken a long step backwards to the ancient and long-repudiated practice of trying people by torture and ordeal. . . . No man should be forced to fight for his liberty, his position and his reputation as I am being forced to do. Any fair judicial trial in the context of the media uproar that the government has generated against me is going to be difficult if not impossible. But I will not falter, and I will ultimately prevail."

IT IS IRONIC that FBI director J. Edgar Hoover was quoted in 1952 in an FBI Law Enforcement Bulletin as follows:

"When any person is intentionally deprived of his constitutional rights, those responsible have committed no ordinary offense. A crime of this nature, if subtly encouraged by failure to condemn and punish, certainly leads down the road to totalitarianism."

"The press," said Justice William O. Douglas, speaking in 1953 to the American Law Institute, "will commonly reflect (or even create) the view that the end justifies the means. Those of us dedicated to the law must stand before those gales."

The Chicago media for the years since 1971 have consistently ignored "the means," however outrageous, feasted on the goodies and extolled the menu served up by a succession of self-aggrandizing Republican U. S. Attorneys, starting with Thompson and proceeding to Samuel K. Skinner (a partner of the big, prestigious law firm of Sidley & Austin and Thompson appointee as chairman of the sensitive Illinois Capital Development Board, which controls tens of millions in capital outlays), and now Webb. All were nominated by U. S. Sen. Charles H. Percy, the latter two under strong pressure from Thompson, who has prevailed consistently on Illinois' senior senator to take good care of his cronies.

One starstruck downtown reporter, in a highly adulatory paean, speculated last week that Webb, like Thompson, might become a candidate for governor "if his former boss and mentor (Thompson) is named to a federal position." Webb, of course, denied the speculation; they all do.

"Justice," said former President James Madison, a delegate to the Constitutional Convention, "is the end of government. It is the end of civil society. It ever has been and ever will be pursued until it is obtained, or until liberty be lost in the pursuit."

It is a sad day for justice in America when any person — judge or petty thief — be convicted in such a manner as this. Liberty may seem secure, especially to those of us who have known it always, but in truth, it is fragile and precious and always in danger of subtle assault. Let each of us assume our proper role in defending and preserving our liberties. For, as the patriot Tom Paine told us in 1795, "Those who expect to reap the blessings of freedom must . . . undergo the fatigue of supporting it."

Thursday, August 9, 1984

A turn toward justice?

Not guilty.

In a stunning reversal of a long, virtually unbroken string of guilty verdicts in high-visibility federal political prosecutions in Chicago, a lay jury Monday acquitted Cook County associate Judge John G. Laurie, a so-called Greylord defendant.

For those who understand and treasure fairness, balance, justice, and rule by law, this may prove to be a watershed decision, a turning point in a long, sordid process of one-sided "justice" in the Northern District of Illinois.

The jury decision discredits a sickening parade of sleazy federal witnesses and surely casts doubt on the FBI's ever-more-intrusive means of obtaining evidence.

OUR GOVERNMENT — yours and mine — threw everything in its awesome arsenal at Judge Laurie. The FBI, increasingly abusive of our Constitution and basic civil liberties, bugged judicial chambers throughout the Cook County system and, in Laurie's case, came away with barely audible tapes which his lawyer, Patrick A. Tuite, insists were "doctored" in Washington — by the FBI.

The posturing, publicity-drugged U. S. Attorney, Dan K. Webb, based his case against the highly-regarded, previously unsullied judge on three immunized witnesses of most dubious credibility.

Said Tuite after the trial:

"To make deals with scumbugs like (them) is an outrage. . . . The U. S. Attorney's office likes to believe what they want to believe, and it has happened so often in this building in the last few years. They pick a defendant, *then* try to find the evidence . . ."

HERE LURKS DANGER to our liberties and to the proper, honorable functioning of our criminal justice system.

Webb did not invent the methods used in this and other trials during his tenure as chief federal prosecutor in Chicago.

The technique of political assassination was perfected by his mentor, then-U. S. Attorney (now Governor) James R. Thompson, who launched his political career with the indictment in 1971 of the late, respected Otto Kerner, former Governor and federal judge, using as his star witnesses a series of rich corrupters.

Thompson passed on his know-how and technique virtually unabridged to his successor and sidekick, Samuel K. Skinner, and his former associate, Webb. These three intimates have controlled the powerful U. S. Attorney's office for most

164

of the past 13 years, a fact which itself has destroyed any semblance of independence and objectivity.

"The federal prosecutor has more control over life, liberty, and reputation than any other person in America," warned the late Robert H. Jackson, former U. S. Attorney General and Supreme Court Justice.

This prosecutorial troika has tended to strike fear into the hearts of many in Illinois. Few lawyers speak publicly to decry their abuses. The federal judiciary here, not including the few who have retained their balance, reflects a prosecutorial slant. Some defense attorneys, unlike Mr. Tuite, seem to have been intimidated or at least muffled The major media have functioned more as cheerleaders than as critics and watchdogs over our liberties.

THERE IS AN ARROGANCE that smacks of the police state. *Don't cross us, or you'll be next,* is the implied message.

That's why Judge Laurie's acquittal, by interrupting an unbroken pattern of "success," may be the best thing that's happened in a long time around the Dirksen Federal Building downtown.

It is ironic that *News/Voice* — purely by happenstance — is carrying this week a powerful Guest Column by philanthropist/activist J. Roderick MacArthur of Northbrook, which might have been written to encourage a turning of the tide. A few of his words are worth repeating here:

"Standing up for the civil liberties of other people is simply part of our loyalty to the human race. . . . They are automatically *owed* in their entirety to every citizen."

IT IS IRONIC, TOO, that the Greylord prosecutors suffered their rare setback as the American Bar Association was convening this week in Chicago, attracting such big names as U. S. Attorney General William French Smith, Chief Justice Warren Burger, and FBI Director William H. Webster.

The state of justice properly might have been their foremost concern, but Smith was railing against communism, Burger

165

(like some of the rest of us) was fretting about "too many lawyers," and Webster was proudly rationalizing the FBI's sneaky investigative techniques. All three seem largely oblivious to the erosions of our liberties inflicted by prosecutorial and investigative excesses, and, if anything, are supportive of such initiatives.

So, finally, it all comes down to us citizens. Those of us who love freedom must defend it diligently, speak up when it is threatened, and pay its price.

Let us show loyalty "to our human race."

Thursday, August 16, 1984

(An editorial)

'Tough on crime' rhetoric must apply to FBI, U. S. Attorneys, all others who break law

They're *all* "tough on crime."

Time after time in this campaign, Ronald Reagan will tell you he's "tough on crime." So will Walter Mondale, George Bush, and Geraldine Ferraro.

The same goes for Gov. Jim Thompson, U. S. Sen. Charles H. Percy and his opponent, Rep. Paul Simon, Sen. Alan Dixon, your Congressman, and your state legislators.

U. S. Attorney General William French Smith, FBI Director William H. Webster, Illinois Attorney General Neil Hartigan, and State's Attorneys Fred Foreman of Lake County and Richard M. Daley of Cook County will tell you they, too, are "tough on crime."

YOU WON'T FIND a public servant anywhere who will deny he's "tough on crime."

Gr-r-r-r . . . tough . . . TOUGH . . . T-O-U-G-H ! ! !

166

But are they telling the truth? Do they really mean it?

Are they truly for equal justice, or are they tough *only* on *some* crimes and *some* criminals?

How tough are they, for example, when the crime is committed by a U. S. Attorney or FBI agent or IRS official who is sworn to uphold the law and who is supposed to symbolize rule by law?

CONSIDER:

• Tapes obtained surreptitiously are altered to the detriment of the defendant.

• Witnesses are induced to lie by a prosecutor who thus suborns perjury.

• Crucial evidence is withheld from the defense by the prosecution.

• Persons not formally charged or indicted are besmirched and their rights to a fair trial compromised.

These examples have been charged or reported in the media.

THEY ARE overt acts, potential crimes, committed in recent, highly-publicized federal trials by U. S. Attorneys and FBI agents. Defense attorneys usually scream bloody murder, and in some cases, such abuses are scathingly denounced by presiding judges.

Usually, it stops right there, with nothing more than a mild slap on the wrist at worst, but more likely only a knowing wink.

Are those at high levels who profess so piously to be "tough on crime" prepared to demand prosecution and punishment for "agents of justice" who violate their oaths and commit

167

crimes in their overzealous pursuit of presumed wrongdoers?

It may be that the offenses of the lawmen, which rend the very fabric of justice, are in the end the most appalling crimes of all. But when was the last time you heard that a federal prosecutor or FBI/IRS agent was prosecuted for lying under oath, suborning perjury, altering tapes, withholding evidence, making public charges before indictment, badgering witnesses, abusing immunity — crimes that deny and undermine our sacred tenets of equal justice and rule by law?

WHEN? If ever.

It is time for our public officials to start pursuing this depressingly commonplace brand of *official corruption* with the same zeal some self-righteous, publicity-seeking investigators and prosecutors have expended in their noisy, media-rooted probes of Greylord, Abscam, Watergate, Federal Judges Otto Kerner and Henry Claiborne, even John DeLorean, and many others of stature, prominence, and visibility in our society.

News/Voice calls on our leaders from White House to courthouse to affirm — and prove by their actions — that they are as tough on crimes committed by the errant FBI and IRS agent, U. S. Attorney, State's Attorney, and state investigator *as on any other lawbreaker.*

Only the scrupulous equality of treatment for *all* lawbreakers will return this nation's criminal justice system to its ideal of *equal* justice for all.

We shall report to *News/Voice* readers any responses we get from our elected and appointed public officials.

Up to now, the silence has been deafening.

(An Editorial)

Clear message from a 'grass roots' jury

Nothing is more "grass roots" America than a jury.

Jurors, like most American citizens, want to trust and believe in their government.

But that trust was shattered last week for the jurors who acquitted John DeLorean.

Clearly, the DeLorean jurors and those who earlier found Cook County Judge John Laurie not guilty sent a blunt, unequivocal message to their government to curtail the shabby, underhanded tactics by which federal prosecutors and FBI agents sought to "hang" the two defendants, one a showy entrepreneur, the other a youthful judge.

SAID ONE JUROR after DeLorean's acquittal in Los Angeles: ". . . The way the government agents operated in this case was not appropriate, and I look forward to the future favorable impact of this case on the country."

Let us hope and pray that is the case, but don't bet on it. Both U. S. Attorney General William French Smith, a good, gray corporate lawyer with no credentials for the top job in Justice, and FBI Director William H. Webster, a former federal judge who shows precious little respect for civil liberties, were quick to say with cavalier disdain that the DeLorean decision would have no impact in the future on the very investigative and trial techniques which the jurors resoundingly rejected.

We call on Congress to act promptly to curb the abuses by our "agents of justice" which those citizen jurors in Los Angeles and Chicago see clearly as a threat to our concept of rule by law and our precious liberties.

Once again, the people are ahead of their leaders.

(An Editorial)

Time to fire or discipline errant prosecutors and judges if we truly care about justice

The 67-year-old judge is sentenced August 8 to ten years in prison following his conviction on bribery charges in one of the Greylord cases.

Less than two weeks later, the federal judge who presided and the federal prosecutor who accused are vacationing together in Georgia with their families.

These are facts, irrefutable facts.

It is a scandal which should rock the ramparts of criminal justice in America. It is a scandal which shrinks the importance of the penny-ante Greylord indictments and soils the image of the U. S. Attorney in Chicago.

It was a trial previously besmirched by the FBI's unprecedented bugging of judicial chambers, by the immunizing of sleazy, untrustworthy witnesses, by publicity so excessive it made a fair trial nearly impossible, and by the blatant posturing of the prosecutor, who made accusations in open court against yet another judge who has not to this day been indicted, even though five of his sons have been subpoenaed to appear before a grand jury.

IF THE FEDERAL powers-that-be, and all those concerned for the credibility and integrity of an already-tarnished legal system, genuinely care about fairness, equity, and true justice — all the platitudes they mouth with regularity — if indeed this were the case, U. S. Attorney Dan K. Webb would be fired forthwith and U. S. District Judge Charles D. Kocoras at a minimum would be severely censured by the Executive Committee of the federal judiciary in Chicago

It was Judge John M. Murphy of Cook County Circuit Court who was convicted in this farce-that-passed-for-a-trial.

There is every indication that the intimate Kocoras-Webb liaison virtually assured his downfall.

By contrast, in a case involving similar evidence and some of the very same witnesses, Judge John G. Laurie was acquitted. Laurie clearly benefited from what Edmund Burke in 1794 described as "the cold neutrality of an impartial judge," in this case the highly circumspect, impeccably fair Judge Prentice Marshall, who ran a scrupulously fair trial and denied the prosecutors such liberties as Kocoras routinely allowed his longtime crony Webb.

When "caught" vacationing together with their families at Callaway Gardens, a Georgia resort, by NBC/TV commentator Peter Nolan, Webb told Nolan he and his family were far removed from the Kocoras family in widely-separated cabins and that the two had seen each other only once in passing on the spacious grounds. Nolan flew unannounced to the resort, 70 miles south of Atlanta, on Thursday, August 23, and confirmed the two were ensconced in adjacent cabins, #829 and #830, no more than a dozen yards apart. Within two hours, Webb had fled, presumably returning to Chicago to fabricate the most plausible story when — and if — confronted by the normally adoring media.

"Webb lied to me — period," Nolan told me. "He knew he was lying. He was plenty nervous when I got him on the phone."

ARE THERE ANY courageous lawyers out there, some who truly give a damn? Are none willing to stand up publicly and denounce such conduct? Has fear descended over the legal community? Is it only apathy? Or a kind of jaded, what-the-hell acceptance?

The American Bar Association is headquartered here. Two of its past presidents live on the North Shore. There are the Chicago Bar Association, Chicago Council of Lawyers, and, in Springfield, the Illinois State Bar Association. The Illinois Supreme Court has established an Attorney Registration & Disciplinary Commission, which by its relative passivity shows that the legal profession cannot be counted on to "police" itself.

They are presumed to be the keepers of the canons of their profession. Yet they stand silent on a matter as critical as this, perhaps muttering and shaking their heads in the corridors, but not speaking out to condemn practices which clearly are wrong and which tarnish the notion of justice.

Notwithstanding such facts as these, Judge Murphy's prospects are gloomy. His appeal will be heard by the relentlessly pro-government Seventh Circuit Court of Appeals, which includes some of the great minds of the 15th century and two more former federal prosecutors, Judges William J. Bauer and Joel Flaum, both, like Webb and Kocoras, longtime intimates of Governor James R. Thompson, a Nixon-appointed U. S. Attorney who used that post to vault from obscurity to the Governor's mansion. Despite the outrageous conduct of the federal prosecutors in some of the major political trials staged by Thompson and his cronies, not a single conviction has been reversed by the Seventh Circuit.

IT MAY BE that some good will come of this sordid episode, the latest in a long series, most of which have escaped widespread public attention because of the cosy links between the publicity-hungry federal prosecutor's office and the Chicago media, especially the downtown dailies. The *quid pro quo* has been invariably favorable and frequent "news" puffery in exchange for an endless flow of leaks and occasional scoops.

Whither the press, protector of our freedoms and staunch defender of the First Amendment? Peter Nolan broke the story on Channel 5 of the two trial principals vacationing together.

The *Chicago Tribune* noted Nolan's news break with an article the next day, oddly bearing no byline, but including several damning quotes from Judge Murphy, whom a *Tribune* reporter phoned for his comments. That was all. I saw nothing whatever in the *Sun-Times,* and the *Tribune* didn't follow up

172

by asking Webb for an explanation or comment on his hurried return from Georgia. No editorial comment by either paper, and a major story died right there. Strange, it may seem, but typical of the unwholesome alliance that has existed for some years between the press and the prosecutors in Chicago.

Yet this episode may — and I say it with little conviction — this *may* mark the beginning of the unraveling of the "Thompson Cabal" (Oxford American Dictionary: ca•bal — 1. a secret plot. 2. the people engaged in it.), whose tentacles of influence have spread octopus-like through the federal prosecutorial apparatus in Chicago, the federal bench, and some of Chicago's biggest law firms. With Machiavellian cunning, Thompson and his cronies have applied unremitting pressure over the past 13 years to place unquestioned "loyalists" in high places.

The largely unwitting, but nonetheless willing, prime conspirator in the building of the Thompson cabal has been a well-meaning, if at times naïve, non-lawyer, Republican senior U. S. Senator Charles H. Percy, who has largely controlled key federal appointments since the death of Senator Everett McKinley Dirksen in 1969, except for the years when Democrat Jimmy Carter occupied the White House.

Percy's prosecutorial and judicial nominees during this period have been dominated by Thompson cronies. The latest of these, James F. Holderman of La Grange, whose nomination to the federal bench was announced last week, is yet another former Assistant U. S. Attorney from the Thompson stable, and, Percy says, a backer of his in Du Page County. Percy's choices in recent years have destroyed all semblance of independence and objectivity in the all-powerful U. S. Attorney's office and have eroded the balance in the federal court structure here. At the same time, in bowing to Thompson's pressure to nominate Thompson intimates Samuel K. Skinner and Webb to succeed him as U. S. Attorney, Percy has helped Thompson erect a wall around himself that precludes any investigation of Thompson's widespread improprieties as Governor.

If Percy has a potentially fatal Achilles heel in his tough race for reelection against U. S. Rep. Paul Simon of downstate Makanda, it is his seeming obeisance to Thompson, a governor barely reelected in 1982 by fighting off a recount with the help of U. S. Attorney Webb and a majority of the Illinois Supreme Court, including one Democratic justice who seemingly "owed" Thompson a favor.

IF THERE IS even a shade of doubt that Judge Murphy is innocent — our system, after all, is supposed to be based on a presumption of innocence and "reasonable doubt" — then the Webb-Kocoras *ménage à deux* is a scandal of major proportions. Even if he is guilty as sin, the prosecutor and judge have joined in an unwholesome assault on the canons of justice.

Listen to these stern words from the late Justice Oliver Wendell Holmes, Jr., of the U. S. Supreme Court in a 1928 opinion:

> For my part I think it a less evil that some criminals should escape than that the government should play an ignoble part. . . . If the existing code does not permit district attorneys to have a hand in such dirty business, it does not permit the judge to allow such iniquities to succeed.

It is almost as if Justice Holmes were speaking directly to U. S. Attorney Webb and Judge Kocoras.

Others through the years have sounded the same message, which is a virtual cornerstone of our legal system.

"It is better to risk saving a guilty person," wrote Voltaire in the mid-18th century, "than to condemn an innocent one."

At about the same time, Sir William Blackstone said, "It is better that ten guilty persons escape than one innocent suffer."

More recently, in 1961, Justice Learned Hand made a similar point: "I had rather take my chance that some traitors will escape detection than spread abroad a spirit of general suspicion and distrust. . . ."

In their zeal to accuse and convict, some of this day's prosecutors, especially in the Northern District of Illinois, have buried any such high-minded notions.

The subpoenas Webb served on five sons of Judge Richard LeFevour — who was publicly accused by Webb and since has been forced to step down from the bench — is a brazen attempt at the sort of intimidation we associate with Hitler's Gestapo or the Soviet KGB. Imagine the terror such a tactic would strike in your heart if it involved your children or those of a close friend or business associate! This is still thought to be the land of the free, where we are spared such intrusion and intimidation.

Yet the pattern is familiar.

"That U. S. Attorney's office over in the federal building . . . those young prosecutors have a Nazi youth cult mentality," former Gov. Otto Kerner, himself a former U. S. Attorney and federal appellate judge, told me ruefully after his media-fueled political conviction. At the time, a decade ago, the proud, patrician former governor was an inmate at the federal prison in Lexington, Kentucky.

"That group," Kerner said wryly, "can make a baptism sound like a drowning."

BUT WHERE THEY themselves are involved, the members of this tight, ambitious, and arrogant clique, everything's fair and above board. At whatever risk to myself — and I know first-hand how vindictive they can be — I intend to keep the white hot light of truth focused on the excesses of the "Thompson cabal." These *News/Voice* newspapers are modest in their dimensions, dwarfed by the downtown giants, but we are free to say what they dare not, so proscribed are they by their hidden agendas and their determination to maintain cosy ties with Illinois' power elite.

175

Freedom in Illinois — and possibly beyond, as Thompson maneuvers toward the Presidency — may repose in the hands and hearts of the 180,000 or so who read these newspapers, a fragment of the Chicagoland populace, but a body of citizens that is uniquely influential, involved, concerned, hardy of mind and spirit, sensitive both to subtle and brutal assaults on our freedoms and on the tenets of our free society.

You readers may well be our best hope, for, as Edmund Burke is so often quoted, "The only thing necessary for the triumph of evil is for good men to do nothing."

Thursday, May 2, 1985

No Pulitzer yet, but we'll keep making waves on the North Shore

"Sorry, Pop, you didn't win the Pulitzer this time, but we love you anyway."

That was daughter Phoebe calling from New York in the early dawn last Thursday. That's how I found out the Pulitzer jurors hadn't seen fit to anoint me, but that I'd won anyway.

I'd be less than truthful if I didn't admit to a twinge of disappointment.

I had no illusions about winning, and certainly didn't expect to . . . but after all, hope does spring eternal, lightning sometimes strikes, and anybody who holds a lottery ticket has an outside chance.

ALL SORTS OF PEOPLE—family, friends, perfect strangers, readers of these newspapers — made me feel very much a winner even to be nominated. They wrote, stopped me on the street, came up at parties and in the stores, congratulated my wife, and really seemed to care. I felt at times as if I'd hit the home run that beat the hated Yankees.

176

I guess I knew all along Pulitzer prizes for journalism are primarily the private preserve of the big metropolitan dailies.

Most newspaper people would kill for a Pulitzer. Their prestige comes from the fact that there are so few to go around.

Occasionally, somebody from a precocious community journal like *News/Voice* intrudes to take the prize — without knowing for sure, I suppose legendary William Allen White of the *Emporia Gazette* and the famed anti-segregationist, Mississippi editor Hodding Carter the Elder, won Pulitzers — but it's a distinct rarity when the ultimate award eludes the grasp of the top 50 or so big-city dailies, which dominate the Pulitzer board.

MOST PULITZER NOMINATIONS, I'm told, are made by the top brass of newspapers to recognize the superior output of their own staffs. Many are made by reporters, writers, and columnists in their own behalf, which they are encouraged to do under the Pulitzer rules.

Some presentations are elaborate. When I was a reporter years ago for the *Minneapolis Tribune,* which won countless awards, the joke around the newsroom was that we had "the best scrapbook department" in all of U. S. journalism.

I was especially pleased to be nominated by two credible "outsiders," Rob Warden, editor of *Chicago Lawyer,* which may be Chicago's foremost investigative paper, for my columns on criminal justice abuses, about which he knows as much as anyone in these environs, and author Sid Cato, financial communications specialist. Rod Warden had no special ax to grind, and some of *his* stuff on the labyrinthine ways of the law surely is worthy of Pulitzer consideration. The same goes for Sid Cato's moving book, *Healing Life's Great Hurts.*

To be singled out by such as these is something to be treasured.

More than anything, those Pulitzer nominations in 1985 told me that *News/Voice* is "winning," living up to my hopes and even expectations, making an impact, speaking out for what we believe is good and right and positive, against what we see as wrong, sleazy, mean-spirited, hypocritical.

At *News/Voice*, we find each weekly issue a very special, entirely new "event," exciting, exhilarating, rousing good fun, endlessly challenging.

WE KNOW BEYOND DOUBT that the big metropolitan dailies have no monopoly on great writing, superb reporting, astute investigating, creative thinking. Each editorial, each article, each column is finally written by a single person. Even though our resources may be less, our grit and motivation, our skills and commitment to truth assuredly are not. We are unwilling to settle for second place in the marketplace of news and ideas. We mean to earn and keep your trust.

We take pride in our strong, provocative, unambiguous stands on issues that reach from Sheridan Road to Downing Street, from the Baha'i Temple to the Great Wall, from Market Square to Red Square, from the North Shore to the South Pole, from the Skokie Ditch to the Potomac. We observe no artificial boundaries, heed no invisible fences.

You won't always agree, which is as it ought to be, but we'll do our damnedest to keep from boring you. Count on that.

As long as we're here, we'll keep making waves on the North Shore, and we'll keep trying to do what we do well enough to make you readers feel *News/Voice* deserves that elusive Pulitzer.

PART I

THIS THING CALLED JUSTICE:

Is it illusion, pomp, an impossible dream?
Do we really care?

What is this thing called Justice?

Is it mere illusion, a will-o'-the-wisp, an impossible dream?

Is it more than pomp and ritual, courtroom structure and lawbook stricture?

Is there truly "majesty" in the law as it is practiced here and now?

ARE WE IN FACT "a nation of laws" fairly and equally applied, or is that little more than the rhetoric of Law Day festivals and bar association conclaves?

Can we genuinely claim there is "liberty and justice for all" — or anything even close to those noble objectives?

Is justice, as Maurice Maeterlinck said at the turn of this century, "the very last thing of all wherewith the universe concerns itself"?

Is it true that the "one principle of justice," as Plato insisted in the fourth century B.C., "is the interest of the stronger"?

WAS NOVELIST MARY McCARTHY right when she wrote in 1971, "An unrectified case of injustice has a terrible way of lingering, restlessly, in the social atmosphere like unfinished questions"?

Or do we really care? Is our conscience, our sense of outrage, dulled to injustice?

Back again to Plato's time, Euripedes made a powerful case for justice: "We must believe in the gods no longer if injustice is to prevail over justice."

179

Many who encounter our vaunted, hallowed court system — criminal and civil alike — come away dispirited and disillusioned. They must strain to maintain their faith "in the gods."

TAKE THE CASE OF Gary Dotson, buried in a Joliet cell these past six years, convicted of a rape he didn't commit, about to be released only because his "victim," the sole witness against him, recanted her courtroom lie.

• How many more innocents like Gary Dotson crowd our mournful bastilles in every part of America?

• How many have been put to death protesting their innocence?

• How many rot in dank cells and pray for their accusers to come forward with the truth?

WE SHALL NEVER KNOW, but the numbers likely are staggering because of the flaws and cynicism which pervade our celebrated judicial system.

As it is constituted and functions today, the system is not primarily geared to produce just results.

Heresy? What I say may shatter some illusions, but harsh truth often is painful.

Our system has evolved to the point where most cases, civil and criminal, become a contest of power and money, an adversary proceeding which tolerates virtually every form of treachery, trickery, misstatement, overstatement, and outright lie under oath.

THE JUDICIAL PROCESS has degenerated into a process for stringing out verdicts in defiance of the Constitutional right to speedy justice and for enriching an ever-multiplying band of grasping lawyers.

How utterly despicable that *only 37 percent* of the expenses and compensation paid by defendants and insurance companies actually *went to the asbestos victims* themselves in the myriad lawsuits against asbestos manufacturers. The average asbestos case was concluded in two years and eight months, and 11 percent of the cases took six years or more to work their way through the lethargic courts, while the victims suffered.

Chief Justice Burger has repeatedly criticized "the high cost of legal services and the slow pace of justice," which have become a national scandal.

What often emerges, however, even after interminable delay, is not justice at all. The case of Gary Dotson is only one dramatic, if isolated, example which every man, woman, and child can understand.

IF YOU SAW THE FILM, "Places in the Heart," which won for Sally Field a richly-deserved Academy Award, you saw revolting samples of the American tradition of vigilante justice, where blacks were lynched and the Ku Klux Klan enforced its special brand of violent racism.

Our history is checkered with such examples of "man's inhumanity to man" — the savaging of Indians, the burning of witches, the incarceration of Japanese-Americans during World War II — which paint a vivid canvas of self-righteous injustice, rationalized with great conviction by its perpetrators.

What has evolved today is a system of resolving guilt or innocence which does not truly seek truth and justice, notwithstanding the pious protestations of many who are parties to this elaborate charade.

Our criminal justice system turns each trial into a game of chance, a no-holds-barred contest in which both sides go to any extreme to win. Prosecutors parlay their triumphs into lucrative celebrity status, mainly because the media glorify their exploits. Corporate lawyers string out trial proceedings to fatten their pocketbooks.

GRAND JURIES WILL INDICT a head of lettuce if prosecutors demand an indictment. The grand jury concept of protecting citizens from the Crown's excesses is long gone in the United States, where the grand jury has become a dependable prosecutorial rubber-stamp. Sensibly, the grand jury has been abolished in England, where it originated, and most other nations because it no longer fulfills its purpose.

Cynical techniques honed by ambitious prosecutors clearly undermine in many cases the *accuracy* of the verdict. How can anyone believe, for example, the testimony of a state witness scrambling himself to stay out of jail, who is granted immunity from prosecution and promised other emoluments which equate with bribery.

The prosecutor's role is to win, period, and anything else reflects adversely on his batting average and career gameplan. Yet true justice can be achieved only by balance, restraint, and an ingrained sense of fairness.

A half century ago, Judge Simon E. Sobeloff, then Solicitor General of the United States, stated eloquently the honorable prosecutor's obligation:

"The prosecutor is not a neutral, he is an advocate, but an advocate for a client whose business is not to achieve victory but to establish justice."

THAT NOBLE DICTATE is thought by present-day prosecutors to be fogeyish, unduly restrictive, and certainly an impediment to their personal ambitions.

One key reason for this blatant undermining of justice is that most prosecutors report to nobody. The Attorney General of the United States wouldn't think of putting restraints on his battery of U. S. Attorneys nationwide. They are utterly independent and often loose cannons with big egos and a high level of swaggering arrogance.

Many state and local prosecutors are elected and thus owe fealty only to the voters, who seem on the whole to favor draconian punishment for even minor wrongdoers, and who consider most judges "soft" on crime, even though U. S. jurists sentence more offenders to longer prison terms than their counterparts anywhere in the world except the Soviet Union and South Africa.

The staggering cost of our "injustice" system penalizes every taxpayer and does little to lessen the blight of crime. Since only about 5 percent of those who commit violent crimes end up in prison, our harsh approach does little to make society safer.

Our civil justice system is little better. Most citizens are excluded by the obscene level of legal fees. Law firms toady to big corporations able and willing to suffer their charges. There is a *quid pro quo:* For big dollars, lawyers buffer corporate executives from prying government agencies, tax problems, regulatory woes, criminal charges, and other such "inconveniences" for a price which is borne by shareholders and their customers. These same executives wink at endless delays, justice-obstructing ruses, and outrageous fees as the price for their personal protection.

The poor — and even middle class clients — inadvertently become part of a vast conspiracy to extract huge judgments and settlements from insurers and corporations with "deep pockets." Unconscionable sums often are skimmed by "entrepreneurial" lawyers on a contingent basis. These may range as high as 60 percent or more (as in the asbestos cases) of whatever the lawyers are able to extract from defendants. The public pays through the nose whenever outlandish judgments are rendered, often by juries understandably moved by the plight of injured parties.

Justice. It is a word we sanctify, but whose meaning is twisted and bent, distorted and invoked by those who abuse it routinely.

What often transpires in the name of justice should be more than enough to trouble, even enrage us citizens. Each of us has an enormous stake in the proper, honorable, equitable functioning of an institution of our society which we tout to the world as matchless, but which in practice malfunctions with regularity and falls far short of our expectations.

One day, God forbid, you may be caught in its web.

Part II

THIS THING CALLED JUSTICE

The Dotson case: sham, ego and Oz-like fantasy

Under a government which imprisons any unjustly, the true place for a just man is also a prison.

HENRY DAVID THOREAU
from *Walden*

Justice, many believe, was denied Gary Dotson, when he was ordered back to prison by the same judge who sentenced him six years ago.

The case of Dotson, the 28-year-old convicted rapist whose alleged victim, Cathleen Crowell Webb, recanted her damning 1979 testimony, has focused the glare of media attention on the deficiencies of a judicial and criminal justice system we tout from the rooftops as a paragon to all the world.

There are times when it works cleanly and fairly, when we marvel at its seeming equity.

TOO OFTEN, HOWEVER, as with Dotson, the "system" strenuously resists all attempts to strip away the opaque curtain which obscures from public view the Oz-like fantasy of its machinations.

The Dotson case bares sham and ego behind the curtain.

It is rare indeed when an alleged victim changes her story without a motive more compelling than conscience, which the "system" and its "players" simply cannot accept or comprehend. How can "their" star witness have the gall to tell them belatedly "their" prisoner is innocent? Sadly, their instinct is not to seek truth and justice, which is their sworn duty, but to keep from looking stupid, wrong, or unjust.

To understand why Gary Dotson *had to go back* to prison, you must understand a few basics:

1. The system refuses adamantly to admit it might be wrong.

2. The system thus is extremely reluctant to right even obvious wrongs.

3. Juries are not infallible. In fact, they are quite often conned by shrewd attorneys and/or prosecutors. Such canny defense lawyers as F. Lee Bailey have described trial by jury as the nearest thing to a lottery.

4. Contrary to what you may have assumed, many judges and prosecutors are faithful slaves to public sentiment, even though in the Dotson case everybody from Governor Thompson on down has warned against a "trial by public opinion." The hierarchy knows the public is overwhelmingly in favor of freeing the young man.

SOONER OR LATER, public opinion likely will force the system to render the justice it is resisting so vigorously thus far. A Channel 7 phone-in poll showed a whopping 94 percent of all callers disagreed with Cook County Circuit Judge Richard Samuels' re-jailing of Dotson.

Bernard Carey, the Republican State's Attorney of Cook County at the time of the original trial, told WBBM's Dick Helton he believes Dotson should be freed.

At a minimum, Carey said, Webb's testimony reinforces "reasonable doubt" that Dotson was guilty, and he's already served six years, "long enough" under the circumstances, certainly a terrible punishment if he is innocent. This would not

185

"establish" a reasonable penalty for a heinous crime like rape, as some contend, if indeed the conviction is sustained.

A wily showboat like Big Jim Thompson, after saying all the right things about the sanctity of the system, will sniff the scent of political hay and likely find some way to rationalize clemency for Dotson, even though he zealously flaunts his image as a lock-'em-up prosecutor whenever that seems the best route to more votes. In such an event, justice would be served for the wrong reason.

IT SEEMS UNLIKELY Judge Samuels will change his mind; thus far he maintains a defiant commitment to his initial sentence, new testimony notwithstanding, and it would appear his mind is zipped shut.

Dotson, he said from the bench, "has failed to sustain his burden of proof." That struck me as an odd declaration which reflects judicial precedent, yet shows how limited our concern for ultimate justice. Without Crowell's complaint and testimony in 1979, there would have been no prosecution, no conviction, no sentence. Most rapists wander the streets at will, never having been caught, much less convicted and jailed. Only a tiny percentage of those who commit violent crimes are apprehended, prosecuted, and committed to prison.

In Dotson's case, his accuser, with nothing whatever to gain except a clear conscience, has changed her story and declared him innocent.

If justice is the object of the system, as it is meant to be, every effort should be made to give the convicted offender the benefit of "reasonable doubt," which clearly exists now.

But the system is adversarial in the extreme, and what does it matter if some poor guy rots in jail even if he didn't do it?

One extra day in prison for an innocent human being is terribly wrong, an ordeal, a mental rubber-hosing. Such injustice is intolerable to men and women of conscience.

THE GREAT JURISTS and philosophers of the past have joined in a willingness to see some wrongdoers and black-

186

guards go free rather than punish an innocent person where some reasonable morsel of doubt exists. "It is better to risk saving a guilty man," Voltaire said in 1743, "than to condemn an innocent one."

The media have made much ado about the small amount of corruption exposed among a few Cook County judges in the Greylord investigation.

Yet I wonder if the affront to justice is not as great when a judge lets ego, bullheadedness, blindness, self-righteousness, or whatever bury a seeminly innocent man in prison when the only real basis for his conviction no longer stands.

If justice is to be served, Gary Dotson should be freed without further delay.

Part Two

If you sometimes think Bill's all wet, here's why

After a hard day, my father would arrive home and announce to all within earshot, "All I want tonight is a little peace, quiet, and understanding."

Shortly after dinner, he would head upstairs to the bathroom to immerse himself for the better part of an hour in a full-to-the-brim tub of steaming water. This for him was the ultimate cure-all and zenith of relaxation.

I inherited Dad's love of the hot bath, but I added another wrinkle, or perhaps ripple.

PEOPLE SOMETIMES ASK me how I manage to crank out a weekly column while tending to my other chores.

Simple. I write in the bathtub.

Cross my heart. On a yellow pad.

The setting is ideal. The bathroom is an accepted sanctum where one usually is allowed a certain amount of privacy. The warm water lapping at my neck subdues the aches and stirs the creative juices. If the phone rings for me, what better excuse than, "Sorry, Bill's in the bathtub."

The worst catastrophe thus far is a few splashes of water

189

smearing a little ink, which isn't bad considering the potential for disaster. Some of my best stuff has come after midnight straight out of the bathtub.

PLANES ARE GREAT for column-writing, too, especially if I land an aisle seat among perfect strangers. The best part is no phones. No smoking helps, too. It's best if my seatmate promptly drops off into a sound sleep and leans the other way.

Planes are by no means fail-safe for writing. I have been known in the tight confines of coach to spill a drink on my precious manuscript while rummaging for my notes.

On a flight back from Detroit recently, a Dennis-the-Menace type wriggling next to me noticed a quirk of mine.

"Hey, Mister, why do you stick your tongue out when you write."

"To catch flies."

"Yec-c-c-c-h." That was the last I heard from him.

A LITTLE TURBULENCE and a few jagged streaks of lightning just off the wing are almost sure to destroy my concentration and bring my literary endeavors to an abrupt halt. White knuckles make it nearly impossible to write legibly while attempting at the same time to assist the pilot in maneuvering through angry storm clouds. Planes, I've found, are a good deal more hazardous to column-writing than bathtubs.

I probably shouldn't admit this, but I do a certain amount of carefully-crafted scrawling while I'm alone at the wheel of my car. I keep the trusty pad at my side and, without fastening my eyes on the page, scribble at a mad pace as the words trickle out of my brain.

My mind works uncommonly well when I'm driving. The senses are especially acute when one is in command of a vehicle. One must stay alert and wary, thus sharpening the mental processes. There are few petty interruptions as I meander along the concrete ribbon of highway, and this provides the freedom to think and create.

190

STERILE, LONELY MOTEL rooms likewise lend themselves to the writer's craft, which does more to lift my spirits than late-night TV or carousing in downtown Jackson, Michigan, or Greenwood, Mississippi. In most cases, the setting, if not exactly inspiring, is fairly peaceful, unless somebody's raising a ruckus next door or the tube's blaring through a paper-thin wall.

There are other places conducive to writing. Bed, for example. The beach. The porch with rain beating a tranquil tattoo on the roof. If I had written as a boy of 8 or 9, I think I might have favored the crotch of the cherry tree in our backyard.

Oh, yes, in case you were wondering, I do type. In addition to a store of pads, I have an old IBM electric typewriter I use and cherish. I may be the fastest two-finger typist around. I once "beat" a covey of female Navy yeomen in a typing contest, humiliating them mightily.

I guess I'm the only one at *News/Voice* who doesn't write on a state-of-the-art, late 20th century computer terminal. I see it as the Editor's prerogative to choose my own "weapons." Besides, I've always been warned that people who grab onto electrical gadgets in the bathtub may wind up toasted to a crisp.

● ● ●

(For the record, I wrote this column in bed. On a yellow pad.)

HUNGER:
For him, brief pangs;
for millions, grinding daily agony

I dressed in the dark of early morning, stumbling around our bedroom, groggily picking out a tie I couldn't see, feeling for my glasses, an increasingly critical item to pursue the day's work.

For breakfast, I snatched a banana and mug of coffee, and proceeded into three meetings, one after another, leaving on my desk a stack of pink phone slips and mound of mail.

I was due by 2 at O'Hare to interview a job candidate flying in from Dallas.

By the time I arrived at the airport, nearly seven hours after groping about the bedroom, I was starving and hungrily contemplating a couple of hot dogs and glass of milk before my scheduled session.

I DUCKED INTO one of those stand-up restaurants on the concourse. The smell of hot dogs turning on the grill set my mouth watering. My stomach was growling.

At the end of the line, with food and drink in hand, I routinely dug in my pants pocket for money. Nothing. I checked the opposite pocket, then my suit jacket with the same result. No cash, no credit cards, no wallet, nothing. A more careful pocket-by-pocket search turned up a nickel, two paper clips, a felt-tip pen, and those glasses.

Even though I literally could taste the hot dogs, it wasn't to be. No money. I handed them back, a little sheepishly, to a short, squat, dark clerk behind the counter.

Sorry, I said, smiling. She just looked, I thought a little disgusted.

IN MY MIND, I began plotting. Surely I'll run into somebody I know. I *always* do at O'Hare. Not right now, it turned

192

out, as I wandered around, peering intently at passers-by scurrying up and down the long corridors. I was fully prepared to ask even the most casual acquaintance for a loan of a few bucks.

It was near 2, so I checked the Delta board for arriving planes. The flight bringing my man would be around an hour late.

That allowed me time to fidget and concentrate fully on my hunger. I was famished.

I normally skip breakfast most of the time and lunch about half the time. But this was different. Time on my hands, and a growing fixation on my grumbling gullet. I plopped down on a bench, feeling a touch sorry for myself.

As I sat for a moment or so, I shifted mental gears. I had no good reason to be so preoccupied with what for me was nothing more or less than minor, temporary discomfort.

After all, I had comforting options. I could grab a bite when my "appointment" arrived, raid the refrigerator when I got home, eat a full dinner with my family that evening, which I did. So, no big deal for me.

BUT WHAT ABOUT all those people, many within minutes of O'Hare, minutes of my North Shore home, hundreds of thousands more living in pockets of poverty all across America, millions upon millions worldwide, who face grinding, agonizing hunger day after day?

Even when they somehow find the food to live another day, there is always on their minds the overbearing dread of what happens next, how and where they'll find the bread of life tomorrow, next week. It is an unending, debilitating, frightening struggle merely to survive.

Think of the children, who bear no blame. What of them? Think of the hollow, haunted eyes, the hurt of hunger, the bloated bellies.

When people — some in the highest public places — scoff at the hunger problem, or seek to minimize its terrible toll, it would seem fitting to deprive them of food for a day or two.

193

It would be well for them to understand the panic and gnawing, painful discomfort hungry people feel.

Even on this North Shore, which is so greatly blest, there is hunger, which these newspapers discovered and why we launched in 1984 and will conduct again this Fall a "Help the Hungry *Here!*" campaign to ease the hunger of those who live, often invisibly, among us.

MY SMALL INCONVENIENCE was nothing, only a superficial reminder of the daily despair experienced by many who cannot count on "our daily bread" for themselves and their families.

Let us forego some of the exotic weapons of war, perhaps a fragment of the awesome power we possess to obliterate mankind.

Let us consider the billions of wasted dollars, the military vehicles, planes and paraphernalia idle and rusting on U. S. bases all across this country and around the world.

Let us ponder our excesses and give immediate, massive help to those in our midst who hunger.

As long as one child is hungry in this affluent land, none of us should rest easy, nor should we allow our elected leaders to forget the cries of that single naked babe.

Wednesday, October 22, 1986

DEAR GOD
be good to me
the sea is so wide
and my boat is so small

Is this a child's cry or the cry of the child in each of us?

Even the most macho, cocky, and self-assured among us feels alone and helpless at times, aching to share his fears and feelings, perhaps not daring to put aside the impenetrable façade and reveal true vulnerability.

Each of us craves and needs the reassuring word, the gentle hug, even the quiet glance of understanding, as we press on in our sometimes taxing and chaotic daily lives.

Often it is those who give outward signals of total command who are least able to cope with what is unexpected, traumatic, painful, or demanding. They may be taut and brittle, and most likely to snap when gale winds blow. We should feel for them and offer our succor.

WE HAVE NO right or reason to expect that things always will be smooth and untroubled, free of challenge, heartbreak, agonizing decisions. Nor are we better for the absence of hard choices and hard times. Adversity is the test which tells us who and what we are, whether we are made of clay or steel.

Are we able to bear life's blows and emerge the better, or are we stricken and defeated by reversals of fortune? This we'd best learn about ourselves, preferably sooner than later.

Few can go it alone. Whatever our strength and mettle, we must look outward for help and support when mountainous waves of adversity threaten to swamp our small boat. It is surely then — if not sooner and more often — we must look to our God, a loving wife, supportive family, understanding children, to good friends and sometimes strangers who appear from nowhere to render aid and solace and guidance.

Few escape all misfortune in their lives. They are the poorer for it. Steel is tempered by unbearable heat. Human beings are molded and shaped and strengthened immeasurably — or destroyed — by their ordeals.

Rather than venting our rage and wallowing in self-pity when the Lord rains trouble on us, we might best give thanks that He is offering an opportunity to know and summon the best that is in us.

195

What prouder legacy than the North Shore's trees?

Like silent sentries they stand.

Tall, resolute, resigned.

They sense from deep within it is time again for a changing of the guard.

They will appear once more in full-dress regalia and stage their matchless pageant of brief but gaudy brilliance.

IT IS BEGINNING. They invite us to wait and watch expectantly as the curtain rises slowly.

The great trees of the North Shore may be our grandest legacy.

A few were bare whippersnappers, reaching up and outward to their destinies, when Abe Lincoln was a gangling railsplitter. Mercifully, some survive.

They have been mute witnesses to history unfolding, to the violence and tranquility of weather, to countless sunsets and young lovers, to the relentless push of what we call progress, to yellow bulldozers and other fearsome mechanical monsters.

IN OUR YARD stand eight venerable, majestic trees, stately ancients which took root, starting from windblown seeds when the North Shore was more wilderness than civilization, some years before our 90-year-old farmhouse was built.

They are the crown jewels of the land we live on. They are our proudest possession. They make our patch of earth unique, different from any other in all the world. They give solitude and shade and nesting places. They exude the majesty of a natural cathedral.

Civilized man for ages has been capable of building vast structures which dwarf their surroundings, like the Sphinx and Acropolis and Colosseum. Man, it seems today, can build

196

almost anything — nuclear power plants, exotic and deadly weapons, capsules which propel people into space, glass and steel skyscrapers stretching to the heavens.

Almost anything.

EXCEPT A TREE.

Man can plant a sapling.

But man cannot fabricate or create or build a hundred-year-old oak or elm or maple, like those which grace our backyard.

Only God can do that, and it takes even Him a full century.

What prouder, richer legacy can we leave than our great trees?

Let us nurture every one and guard them fiercely.

Thursday, May 16, 1985

'Pious pornographer' Thompson presides over 'tasteless' real-life Dotson TV show

It was tasteless, degrading, hard-core pornography unfit for TV.

The ringmaster for The Greatest Porn Show on Earth was the law-and-order, tough-on-crime governor of Illinois.

"The Gary Dotson Show," as staged by and for Gov. James R. Thompson, was an embarrassing tableau which turned the painstaking search for true justice into the raunchy titillation of a seamy soap opera.

"You ought to launch a campaign to impeach the S.O.B.," growled one irate citizen in a phone call to my home last Friday night.

Uptown Saturday, a businessman-friend, who's anything but a prude, stopped me to say, "That was the most disgraceful thing I've ever seen on TV. Awful for kids. Pure, explicit, raw pornography. What's the matter with that big jerk?"

The difference is that the crude, intimate, finely traced, raw recital of sex and violence — true or false — were festering slices of real life rather than the fanciful creation of a writer of fiction.

THINK ABOUT THE impact on young children. The hearings had slipped my mind until 12-year old Hope turned on the tube Saturday morning and beckoned me to watch. I was appalled. Fortunately, Hope left. There sat the Governor, the Pious Pornographer himself, hunched over a microphone, coaxing every last nuance of explicit sexual detail out of Cathy Crowell's girl friend, then a policewoman, then his old sidekick, James Zagel, one more dependable Thompson crony appointed to high office. I endured about an hour before I switched off the TV, feeling a little sick to my stomach, and went outside into the bright, cleansing sunshine.

It was clear what was happening as those hearings droned on. The Governor was milking every last rancid drop of publicity out of a case which could have and should have been decided quietly in a tortured session with his own conscience.

It seemed clear to me last Saturday what the end result would be. Dotson would be released from prison, which he finally was last week, but should have been several weeks ago, as proposed strongly to Thompson then by Bernard Carey, Cook County State's Attorney when Dotson first was prosecuted. The cause of justice would have been far better served without benefit of the long-running TV sideshow. It was obvious Governor Solomon, a political genius ever mindful of covering his tail, would not grant a clean "verdict" of innocence, but merely would "commute Dotson's sentence" to the time served. If nothing much else, Thompson is an astute reader of public sentiment.

There was speculation Thompson would make his dramatic announcement on Mother's Day, personally delivering Dotson in a giant, beribboned gift box to his grateful Mom while the cameras ground and shutters clicked. Apparently, some members of Thompson's staff tried hard to dissuade their employer from such a typically cornball Thompsonian scenario.

THERE ARE INDICATIONS Thompson's disgraceful, embarrassing ploy, perhaps the crudest and crassest yet, may explode in his face. Street interviews by TV reporters turned up angry and cynical speculation on Thompson's transparent motives. TV commentators Dick Kay of Channel 5 and Walter Jacobson of Channel 2 seared the Governor for trivializing and exploiting the final resolution of a grave matter on the criminal justice agenda.

Only the *Sun-Times,* led by longtime Thompson cheerleader Hugh Hough, saw it as a triumphal, virtuoso performance by an old master.

Perhaps the ultimate perversion was Thompson's sappy appearance last week on the *Tribune*'s front page clad in two T-shirts presented by his fun-loving staff of juveniles on the eve of the big event.

One read "GO TO JAIL — DO NOT PASS GO," the other "GET OUT OF JAIL FREE."

To mock the gravity of such a pending decision comes close to being a good reason for impeachment.

THERE MAY BE A better way. Impeachment may be too charitable a route.

Thompson should be opposed in the 1986 primary by a strong, credible, serious, well-financed Republican candidate who treasures the proud tradition of responsible Republicanism and offers an idealistic, yet practical, vision for an Illinois still a long way from approaching its potential.

If Big Jim, using all the muscle and money at his command, survives that obstacle, the citizens of Illinois will have another chance in November of 1986.

Let's not blow it. We deserve far better.

'I lost a friend,' felled in his office by a madman's bullets

I lost a friend of 25 years Monday.

His death is sad enough, but the nauseous circumstances make it so much more intolerable.

Charley Armstrong is one more victim of America's terrible obsession with guns. His son was shot, too, and has been released from the hospital.

Any psychopath, misfit, madman, or jackass can get his hands on a gun these days in this land of ours. It's almost like buying an ice cream cone, yet the toll mounts every day of our lives like some grisly plague.

The horror and terror that guns in the wrong hands wreak on this society is unending and desolate.

LET ME RECOUNT for you a tragic tale that shouldn't have been.

Charley Armstrong, a good and vigilant father and South Side newspaper publisher, forbade one Roscoe Evans, Jr., 24, to see his youngest daughter, Patricia, 22.

It turns out Charley was unerringly right in his appraisal of the young man.

Late last summer, Evans appeared at the office of the *Chicago Metro News* at 2600 South Michigan Avenue, brandishing a handgun, and forced Patty to go with him for a ride on the South Side.

A warrant was issued for Evans' arrest, but nothing came of it. Last Friday, Evans phoned the newspaper office and made threats against the family.

MONDAY, SHORTLY AFTER noon, he appeared at the cluttered third-floor quarters with a .22 caliber rifle. Patsy was taking the day off.

200

Evans, wearing army fatigues, allegedly marched in, scattered several employees, and fired two shots at Armstrong's 23-year-old son, wounding him in the jaw and thumb.

According to several accounts, he then spotted Charley Armstrong talking in the reception area with State Rep. Jerry Washington, by coincidence another old friend of mine, and shot the publisher in the chest, cursing and taunting Armstrong as he lay dying.

A common, everyday sort of tragedy in America these days, yet so painful when one knows and perhaps loves the victim.

I ADMIRED CHARLEY ARMSTRONG. His *Metro News,* probably the major black-oriented weekly in Chicago, with a circulation near that of the *News/Voice* group, was not always artistic, but it took strong, plain, unequivocal positions which mirrored the personality of its publisher of two decades.

Charley was the sort of guy who gave unswerving support to those people and causes he supported and took off with equal vigor and venom after his adversaries. When he chewed somebody out, they stayed chewed for awhile.

Big, burly, bold, blunt, and bellicose, he was refreshing in a world seemingly overrun with smooth stones and cautious bureaucrats. He had the marvelous quality of being totally outrageous at times.

If Charley was your friend and backer, you could count on him. A staunch, but selective Republican, he gave me all-out, unblinking support when I ran for the U. S. Senate against the wishes of some dominant GOP pols.

I understand he didn't back Ronald Reagan last November.

I'll remember Charley fondly. They don't make many from that mold. What an unthinkable tragedy! What a blight are those inhuman, unthinking types who believe violence can solve their problems and ease their twisted minds.

God bless you, Charley.

Morality demands that Marcos must go, with push from U. S.

Where has our morality gone?

How can we continue to bed down with a scheming, murdering blackguard like Ferdinand Marcos?

How can this nation, rooted in idealism and founded on revolution, continue to tolerate the killings, the brutal intimadation, the massive vote fraud, the myriad abuses in the farcical Philippine election which seems almost certain to have thwarted the will of a majority of Filipinos?

How can our President call for reconciliation and be anything but appalled by the harsh truths which are being reported to him from countless legitimate sources, ranging from the Catholic bishops of the Philippines to hundreds of news correspondents to his own election watchdog team, headed by U. S. Sen. Richard Lugar (R., Ind.)?

HOW CAN PRESIDENT Reagan give aid and comfort to the brutal Marcos regime with his offhand remarks, hopefully careless rather than studied, and thus undermine a spontaneous uprising of Filipinos?

In response, it is not enough merely to mouth once again the tired, tattered lines about our vital strategic stake in the Philippines, our reliance on two key military bases there, and the Communist threat to our interests if Marcos is toppled.

Each is an important consideration, to be sure, but they have become rationales for our bowing and scraping, for our cozy liasion with Marcos. They are the lame cop-outs for our disgraceful, immoral course of conduct in blithely rubberstamping the Marcos brand of despotism and corruption.

There are ways to deal with the likes of a Marcos that will uphold U. S. integrity and free us from an intimate alliance with this corrupt, cunning dictator who, seemingly with our blessing, has oppressed and pillaged and savaged his own countrymen both in the election two weeks ago and through many years.

The U. S. does indeed maintain two vital bases in the Philippines, key outposts of our Pacific defense. These must be declared untouchable and non-negotiable no matter who rules the Philippines.

LET US MAKE unmistakably clear that we are not some helpless Gulliver rendered impotent by Lilliputians, that we will defend our bases against enemies inside or outside the Philippines with military force, if force becomes necessary.

Further, we should provide our eagerly-sought aid funds for both military and civilian purposes only to those foreign leaders who side with us and allow their people to pursue their destinies in peace and freedom.

We have at our ready disposal both the military might and wherewithal to aid our friends.

But we seem bereft of will and a sense of what is right.

Our leaders have toadied far too long to the murderous tinpot dictator Marcos and his beauteous, jet-setting, 'dragon lady' spouse.

If we continue to do business with the Devil incarnate, it will be obvious to the whole world, to all who look to us as a bastion of freedom and idealism, that we have sold our soul and are in fact no better, no more honorable, no more committed to virtue and truth and liberty, than those villainous types we embrace.

After a puppet parliament declared Marcos the electoral victor, President Reagan, treading gingerly, said: "At this difficult juncture it is imperative that all responsible Filipinos seek peaceful ways to effect stability within their society and avoid violence, which would benefit only those who wish to see an end to democracy."

ALL WELL AND GOOD, but not enough. How, pray tell, can democracy "end" where it exists only in name?

Before it is too late, we must take a stand for justice in the Philippines. We cannot accept a fraudulent outcome in what was touted in advance as a free election.

Yes, there are risks, as there is always risk with bold action, but risks we must take without cringing or political grandstanding. We must stand up for what a sizeable majority of Americans, viewing the outcome from afar, know from their own good instincts is the right course for this nation to pursue.

We must denounce the Marcos regime and cease our dealings with him. We must assure that he is carted off to exile, just as we arranged such a fate for Jean-Claude "Baby Doc" Duvalier, deposed President of Haiti. We must support the aspirations of a majority of Filipinos for a rebirth of freedom in their land.

Let us heed the influential Catholic bishops of the Philippines:

"In our considered judgment, the polls were unparalleled in the fraudulence of their conduct. . . . The people have spoken. What they attempted to say is clear enough."

RETAINING POWER through fraud, the bishops said of Marcos, is "tantamount to forcible seizure" with "no moral basis."

I spoke a few days ago with two Filipino Americans, both working on the North Shore. The first, a deliveryman, told me simply, "The lady won." The other, a waitress, said the election was "disgusting, it would not be just if Marcos wins."

President Reagan has condemned communist Russia as an "evil empire."

Yet he seems largely blind to the fact that Ferdinand Marcos is an evil emperor. He appears reconciled to Marcos' survival and continued dominance in the forseeable future.

The President quite implausibly suggests the election may mark the beginnings of two-party government in the Philippines. In present circumstances, this is the height of unreality, from which, if precedent prevails, Mr. Reagan, at some point, will recover.

He should listen carefully to the words of Corazon Aquino, Marcos' courageous foe, who claims unequivocally she has won the election. It was her husband, remember, who was gunned down 30 months ago as he returned from exile to his Philippine homeland, where he was considered the prime threat to Marcos' continued rule.

"It would be a delusion of policy," Mrs. Aquino said last week, "to believe that an opposition whose leaders and followers have been and are being killed can suddenly settle down to a Western-style opposition role in a healthy two-party system.

"I would wonder at the motives of a friend of democracy (President Reagan) who chose to conspire with Mr. Marcos to cheat the Filipino people of their liberation."

Strong words. We cannot, in good conscience, ignore them.

December 1, 1983

Can a poor man win high office?

He was a homely baby, but engaging even then, and his parents were poor as church-mice.

He grew up a very plain man, maybe even ugly, with big protruding ears, a wide gap between his front teeth, and the loping, awkward gait of an Ichabod Crane. But he was engaging still and possessed of bold opinions, deep commitment to his beliefs, and the urge somehow to serve his fellow man.

He became a school teacher. He married and had children.

He moved on to teach history and a bit of economics in a small college. He captivated his students and made the dusty past come alive to them. He had the rare ability to bring the present into focus by drawing on the lessons of history. He breathed fire into his lectures, and his circle of influence expanded quite rapidly.

IT WAS INEVITABLE that one day he would enter the political arena. After a bruising battle with a lacklustre incumbent, he was elected by a slender margin to a seat in the state legislature.

It was a rugged, continuing struggle to make ends meet, but somehow he scratched along and kept his family together and his own head above water.

He began to make a name for himself, and he was elected to three more terms from his relatively safe district. His pungent, often controversial, statements earned him reams of newspaper copy and growing influence in the affairs of the state.

When his party began to cast about for a candidate for governor, his name entered frequently into the speculation, and a small but insistent clamor arose for the young legislator to get into the race.

And so he was confronted by crisis.

HE WAS FORCED to look hard at his personal situation; to take a careful, realistic inventory of his assets and liabilities; to make the agonizing decision that could project him into national prominence or relegate him to a measure of local fame.

The balance in his savings account, shrinking steadily since he first took office, was down to $5,500. He had another $11,000 in listed common stocks, the modest residue from his grandfather's estate. He was almost solely dependent on his fairly meager legislative salary, plus part-time teaching jobs, to maintain his growing family.

Here is a man the nation clearly needs in public life. Which way should he turn?

• • •

The situation is strictly hypothetical, but all too typical.

CAN A MAN like this — able, dedicated, engaging, but poor and plain of face — be elected to high office, like Governor or U. S. Senator, from a major state in this ninth decade of the 20th Century?

Possibly, but highly unlikely unless he sells his soul to the ever more voracious special interests whose Political Action Committees (PACs) spew dollars to advance and protect their interests.

Could a latter-day Abraham Lincoln win his way to the White House in 1984?

Probably not.

Stewart Alsop, writing 15 years ago in the *Saturday Evening Post,* went even further: "There are very few ugly politicians left," he said, "and soon there will be none . . . To have any chance of being elected to high office from a big state in the television era, a man must be either rich in his own right, or willing to be beholden to rich men. The poor politician . . . will soon be as extinct as the ugly politician . . ."

Without the support of an incumbent political machine, it takes three to five million dollars to run a full-scale successful campaign for Governor or U. S. Senator from Illinois.

The defeated Republican candidate for Governor of Texas spent fifteen million dollars, much of it his own money, in 1980. The U. S. Senate today includes names like Heinz ("57 Varieties"), Danforth (Ralston Purina), Pell (old money), Kennedy (Merchandise Mart, etc., etc.), and Goldwater (department stores). Governors bear names like Rockefeller, DuPont, and, until recently, Brown (of Kentucky, aided and abetted by fried chicken and spouse Phyllis George).

SOME OTHERS, not necessarily rich, like Senators Glenn (astronaut) and Bradley (New York Knickerbockers), and Congressman Jack Kemp (Buffalo Bills), had the enormous advantage of celebrity status, which attracts dollars and creates widespread name recognition.

Increasingly, politics at the highest level is the private preserve of the man with bottomless moneybags, flashing white teeth, disarmingly sincere grin, resonant "anchorman" voice, and the assorted virtues of an Eagle Scout.

If this be so, the very essence of the American concept of a people's government has somehow been destroyed.

December 8, 1983

Can this be justice? A portrait of 'failure'

"Our failed criminal justice system."

Those are my words, and they contain uncomfortable, unsettling, disturbing implications which all of us need to confront.

When I say "failure" and use the term "failed," I do not mean to imply that it never works. We all know better. We all have seen times when its verdicts are clean and decisive and just. But surely not often enough.

What I do say emphatically is that our criminal justice system cannot be trusted in any given case to produce an equitable result, and that its performance is erratic, uncertain, inconsistent and not infrequently wrong.

IF OUR CRIMINAL justice mechanism is to be judged by its progress in reducing crime — and this surely must be its main objective — then overall it clearly is a dismal failure. As sure proof, our prison/jail population has soared well above 600,000, its highest level in history, greater than the combined populations of Cincinnati and Des Moines, even as crime has leveled off and we continue to resist the promise and economy of proven alternatives to incarceration.

When I speak of the failure of our criminal justice system, I refer in part to its failure to adhere to the benchmark set by former Solicitor General Simon Sobeloff, when he stated three decades ago that the system's business "is not to achieve victory but to establish justice."

Yet the obsession to convict at all costs is part of what undermines the quest for justice. Former United States Attorney Tom Foran of Libertyville puts it this way:

"Nobody alive's a striped-ass saint, and if a federal prosecutor decides to get you, you're a goner, no question. If he ignores his oath, watch out! We've got some real hot-eyed types these days looking for blood and headlines and Wyatt Earp-type justice. String the bastards up and to hell with the Constitution."

When I speak of the failure of our criminal justice system, I am not isolating or focusing on any narrow segment of the system. I am ranging across the whole sweeping spectrum of Americans touched by the system, from the young black who is poor, undereducated, unemployed and powerless, to the mature board chairman and visible politician who are rich and educated and powerful.

THE SHOCKING FACT is that the system too often works well for neither.

Let me make my case.

• Take Wharton Shober. Mid-50s, Princeton, Philadelphia Main Line, old money, Social Register, president of an inner-city hospital, indicted for bribing former Congressman Dan Flood of Pennsylvania. Here's what Shober told me: "On Jan. 5, 1978, the Federal prosecutor, Alan Lieberman, offered me use and transactional immunity if I would testify that the political contribution to Flood was indeed a bribe. He said that if I did not accept his offer, he would indict me, prosecute me and place me in prison as a convicted felon. He did indict me, but he had absolutely no case. Indeed, the matter was thrown out of court by the judge before a defense presentation, or before it went to the jury. Nevertheless my lawyer bills totalled around $650,000 and I lived under a cloud for 21 months. Is this reward adequate for refusing to be bribed by immunity?" Shober asks rhetorically. "Lieberman now," Shober continues, "as a result of great publicity connected with his indictments, has a cushy private law practice."

I ASK YOU, can this be justice?

• Take Mario Urioste. Poor Mexican from the state of New Mexico, mid-20s, frail, 125 pounds, convicted of stealing a couple of shirts and record albums. Sentenced to serve time in the maximum security prison in Santa Fe. Repeatedly raped and beaten by violent fellow inmates. Finally, in the grim riot of February 1980, tortured and murdered. For a few shirts and record albums, Urioste was given what amounted to a death sentence. Can this be justice?

• Take the late Otto Kerner, governor, general, judge at three levels, United States Attorney, legal scholar, staunch fighter for civil rights and prison reform, graduate of Brown and Northwestern Law School, student at Cambridge. Convicted by a jury of his "peers" — heavens, no! — on the testimony of two race track owners granted total immunity from prosecution and thus spared prison themselves. The ambitious prosecutor rides the Kerner prosecution and other political convictions to the Governor's mansion in Illinois. Kerner flatly accuses his accuser of "influencing" the key witnesses against him "to commit perjury," a criminal offense if true.
Can this be justice?

• Take the Pontiac 10, on trial for murdering three guards at Illinois' Pontiac state prison. A heinous, vicious, unforgiveable crime. The investigation botched, virtually no physical evidence available. Under intense pressure, the prosecutors piece together a case after the fact by granting so-called "eye-witnesses" immunity, promises of reduced sentences, cash payments, protection, changed identities. Almost three years after the riot, all 10 defendants are acquitted by the jury. Can this be justice? How can we really know if the accused are truly guilty, that the prosecution witnesses, liars caught in repeated lies, aren't bribed by favors rather than committed to truth? Why do prosecutors indict when they have no hard evidence? What has happened to the sacred concept of "reasonable doubt"? Would we rather convict somebody, anybody, than those truly guilty? How, in cases like this, can we know that a grievous wrong has not been prepetrated?

Can this be justice?

• Take the Menard 3, three inmates who died of suffocation four summers ago in their tiny, crowded, airless cells when temperatures soared above the 100 degrees mark in this southern Illinois prison. Did society have any right to "kill' these three who were sentenced to prison? How about thousands of others subjected to impossible, inhumane jail and prison conditions?

Can this be justice?

• Take Paul Luftig, former president of the Franklin National Bank, indicted on 14 counts of fraud for falsifying documents, presumably to conceal $7 million in losses before the bank folded, sentenced to a 3-year prison term. The American Lawyer's Steven Brill, intrigued by the claims of Luftig friends that the banker has been convicted unjustly, writes: ". . . a review of the 6,099-page record of Luftig's trial, combined with interviews with five of the twelve jurors, provided compelling evidence that in Luftig's case our system misfired."

Says Luftig's lawyer, Harold Tyler, Jr., former Federal

judge and deputy United States Attorney General now in private practice in New York: "I'm so angry about this case that I almost can't speak."

Can this be justice?

• Take the black man who murders a white man in the states of Ohio, Florida, Georgia, and Texas. He is sentenced to death 19 times more frequently than a white man convicted of murdering a black. It is a sad fact that the black, the poor, the alien, the unappealing are those who fill death row.

Northwestern University law professor Jon R. Waltz says it is "an open secret that prosecutors in Chicago and other large cities have been using their peremptory challenges to systematically eliminate all blacks — or all but token blacks — from juries in criminal cases involving black defendants."

Can this be justice?

I could go on . . . and on . . . and on. But that would serve no further constructive purpose. My point is made.

SUFFICE IT TO SAY the foregoing, in my view, is compelling, depressing evidence that our criminal justice system has failed in far too many instances, on far too broad a scale, to brush off its failures as aberrations or freaks or isolated happenstances. They are, rather, daily reminders of a malfunctioning apparatus which is critical to this nation's credibility as a lawful society.

What shall we do? Let us consider. Nowhere has this nation failed in its mission more dismally than in reducing or even controlling crime. Nowhere have we squandered more billions with fewer obvious results. Nowhere have we sallied forth with a more ill-defined, outdated roadmap.

Our presumed leaders, elected and appointed, have shamefully ducked the hard questions about crime and punishment. They have pandered shamelessly to the fears and concerns of the public. They have permitted the urgent crisis of criminal justice to fester, worsen and get completely out of hand.

We need radical changes in our approach, changes which can save billions of tax dollars at every level of government, salvage countless salvageable human beings, and yield vastly better, often dramatic results in reducing crime.

LET US TOLERATE no further demagogy and delay.

The whole nation will benefit if somehow we can begin to turn around for the better our failed criminal justice system. This should rank among the highest of all priorities on our national agenda. If we do not act soon and seriously, we may find that our goal of a truly just and lawful society is beyond our grasp.

Thursday, March 6, 1986

Ron & Rosty: Think again before you scuttle tax-free bonds

House Ways & Means Chairman Dan Rostenkowski (D., Chicago) is agin 'em.

President Reagan is agin 'em.

What are they, and what's so bad about 'em?

They're tax-free municipal and industrial revenue bonds, which, if used in the right way for the right projects, may be the most vital, widely-employed financing instruments ever devised.

Tax-free industrial revenue bonds, used for labor-intensive projects with significant investment in fixed assets, are an enormously effective tool for creating jobs and developing new industrial enterprises, the very sort which have suffered grievously in the so-called "Rust Belt" and especially our big cities from the inroads of foreign buccaneers, aging facilities, and the merciless demands of fast-changing technology.

WITHOUT TAX-FREE municipal bonds, America's hometowns, from the great metropolis to the small village, and embracing the school district, sewer/water authority, and recreation board, would be deprived of their surest, most economical mode of financing critical capital projects of every shape and dimension.

President Ron and Chairman Rosty bemoan "lost" revenues from tax-free bonds at a moment in time when the budget is desperately out of balance. But excising incentive is the worst possible way to narrow the gap. The compelling counter-argument is that tax revenues lost by giving tax-free bond-buyers a break are more than made up by fresh tax dollars generated through new and expanding business, thousands upon thousands of new jobs, revitalization of struggling communities, and other diverse benefits from the bond proceeds.

I don't profess to be an expert in sophisticated financial instruments, so I picked up the phone and called New York for Jim Lebenthal, longtime friend, college classmate, and nationally-prominent purveyor of tax-free municipal bonds, which he calls "the workhorse of investments."

What would happen, I asked him, if the President and the Chairman prevail on the Senate to join the House in killing tax-free municipals?

"Everyone," he told me, "is going to pay more — and get less — from their state and local government."

THEN HE RATTLED off a list of "a few of the changes" we could expect in our everyday lives:

- More slums

- Fewer jobs

- Less housing

- Higher rents

- Higher electric bills

214

- Higher property taxes

- Higher airfares

- Costlier tuitions

- Bigger hospital bills

- Scarcer parking

- Fewer buses

- Browner water

- More garbage

- Dirtier air

You scoff? Ask your own local officials, your mayor, village president, council members, school boards, recreation officials. See if they don't agree.

President Reagan frequently demonstrates a certain disdain for America's big cities. But Dan Rostenkowski is a lifelong Chicagoan, a deep-dyed city boy. How can he possibly rationalize such an outrageous assault on cities large and small, on our school systems, on the capital needs of the nation at a time when our entire infrastructure is in woeful disrepair and daily disintegration?

To wipe out *the* primary tax incentive which enables this nation to finance its schools and gyms, roads and public buildings, plants and warehouses, and thus create countless jobs, makes not a grain of good sense.

If you agree, you'd best register with the President and the Chairman (and your Senators as well) your outrage before this improbable pair wreaks damage that may be both devastating and undoable.

The stuff of fantasy: Being a boy again

Wednesday, January 15, 1986

Old ballplayers never die, they just swing away

The excitement began building weeks before the looming great event. I'm finding it nearly impossible now to contain my anticipation and keep my cool.

Of course you think I'm talking about the Super Bowl, which has ignited all Chicagoland like nothing since Mrs. O'Leary's cow kicked over that lantern.

Well, I'm not.

My personal "great event" starts the Sunday *after* the Super Bowl, when I take off in the early morning from O'Hare for the flight to Tampa.

THERE I'LL BE reunited for a week with my faded youth, the happy days of growing up in a southwestern Ohio mill-town where *baseball* was my teenage passion.

It was then and there I developed a lifelong love for what easily is the ultimate of all sports played by civilized folk, notwithstanding the giddy, unprecedented euphoria over the lovable, fearsome, crazy-quilt Chicago — really North Shore — Bears.

217

How many of you male readers — maybe even a few fe-
males — aspired for one brief shining moment to break into
the big leagues, to save the key game with a leaping, back-to-
the-wall catch, to blast the game-winning home run before
thousands of delirious, adoring fans in the decisive game of
the World Series?

I did. That fervent desire burned deep within my breast
despite middling skills on the playing field.

FOR THE FIRST week of February, I'm going to be closer
to that fantasy than ever before in my lifetime, surrounded
by some who tasted the heady wine and others, like myself,
who aspired to do so.

You see, faithful readers, I'll be headed for Tampa as a full-
fledged member of the Cincinnati Reds' "Dream Week" roster
to play baseball under the watchful eyes and expert tutelage
of real-life major leaguers, past and present, some of whom
were among my idols.

You true fans will remember the rippling muscles of Big
Klu — Ted Kluszewski — who ripped the sleeves off his T-
shirt, the better to display his Herculean biceps, who hit many
a baseball out of sight for the Reds, and who, in the waning
days of his career, lofted two long home runs in the opening
game of the 1959 World Series as a first baseman for the Chicago White Sox.

Klu will be there all week in Tampa to see if he can induce
the likes of me to hit one out of the infield. Pete Rose, they
tell me, may be a drop-in.

KLU WILL BE there, and so will former Reds like Joe
Nuxhall, Tommy Helms, Jim O'Toole, Ed Bailey, and Jim
Kaat, names that will ring a bell with all genuine baseball de-
votees, but will mean no more to the rest of you than President
Chester A. Arthur's Vice President, old what's-his-name. Yes,
Virginia, the U. S. did indeed have a President named Chester
A. Arthur, who guided us through the critical years of 1881–
85 following the assassination of James A. Garfield.

218

At my age, this Tampa venture may seem at best a risky, harebrained mission. Martha, though jauntily supportive, views it with apprehension.

So be it.

I know guys older, paunchier, creakier than I who climb tall mountains, ski the Alps, shoot whitewater rapids, drive daily to Chicago from the North Shore, and otherwise defy death and debilitating injury, so why should I shrink from engaging in a bucolic pastime like baseball?

AT NO POINT in my checkered hardball career was I in serious danger of making the big leagues, no matter how glorious my dreams at the time. I did hit .302 in my final year before the Navy and college, and broke up a no-hitter in the eighth with a triple after striking out in three prior at-bats. The opposing pitcher was denied immortality only because he managed to hit my bat with a fast ball at the zenith of my wild swing.

Still, my odyssey with baseball lives on and has not even flickered along the way.

As a stringy kid in Hamilton, Ohio, I pursued baseball with a religious zeal. I started playing in the street outside our house, where our raggedy bunch overcame such formidable obstacles as overhanging branches, a water-soaked, lopsided ball with the cover dangling loosely, gaping potholes, neighbors who took exception to foul balls landing in their flower beds and on their front porches, and the genial cops in cruisers who broke up our games temporarily with a wink and drove on.

Somehow, no matter what transpires later in life, one clings to that childhood bond forged with a favorite team. It's somewhat like wispy, idealized memories of your first love.

At about 11 or 12, we "graduated" to ball diamonds out near the local Ford plant, and played in Knothole Leagues sponsored by the Reds in communities like Hamilton which ringed Cincinnati.

At 14, I remember hearing vague rumors of a super-athlete,

younger even than we, a fledgling Dizzy Dean, who could throw a baseball through a brick wall and hit it to the far reaches of our fenceless playing fields. All of it was true.

HIS NAME WAS Joe Nuxhall, lifelong friend and fellow townsman, who at 11 made us older boys look both inept and scared stiff as he blazed his fastball past us, both in front and back, which kept us jittery and loose. At 15, he became the youngest player ever to appear in a major league game, when the Reds brought him in from the bullpen in the eighth inning of a game that was long gone. He was shelled by the great Stan Musial and other St. Louis Cardinals, briefly abandoned baseball to finish high school, and later returned to the major leagues as a first-rate southpaw pitcher who won 135 games in a 16-year career.

"Hamilton Joe," to this day the Reds' "color" broadcaster, will be on the "faculty" at Tampa, which for me will be more than a little special. I'm praying he'll show me a little more mercy now than then.

Something else will be special about this idyll. One of my teammates will be my son, Peter, himself a lifelong Reds' fan even though he's never lived a day in Ohio. I guess my affection for the Reds somehow has rubbed off on him, because he's at least as excited as I.

It will be a lasting memory, I suspect, as we trot out onto the field together for the first time, each wearing the authentic home white uniform of the Reds, successors to the old Cincinnati Red Stockings, the team that launched America's national pastime in 1869. I can hardly wait.

A FEW WEEKS AGO, I ran into Jack Brickhouse, the renowned Hall-of-Fame broadcaster and celebrated man-about-Chicago, and told him of my upcoming adventure.

"Bill, you'll fly down to Florida on a commercial plane," he told me, "but I guarantee you'll soar all the way back home under your own power."

I may even "soar" *to* Tampa.

220

'THE STUFF OF FANTASY':

A true baseball buff relives dreams of glory at Reds' camp in Tampa

This is the stuff of fantasy.

● ● ●

Elongated Jack Billingham, premier pitcher for the Cincinnati Reds and Houston Astros, looking at least a foot taller than his actual six-three, glowers down from the mound toward home plate. The batter, waggling his Louisville Slugger, peers intently at Billingham, hoping to catch at least a glimpse of the ball he's about to throw.

Billingham winds and fires. The anxious batter makes enough contact to send a looping foul into the stands behind first base. Then a ball, low and outside. The third pitch, hard and fast, heads straight down the middle, but, at the last split second, dips to the outside corner. The batter, off stride, makes good contact and raps a sharp grounder wide of first base toward right field. The first baseman, former Cincinnati catcher Ed Bailey, moves over to stab the ball, tosses underhand to Billingham covering first, and nails the heavyfooted runner by a long step.

● ● ●

A routine baseball play, one of thousands like it in the season ahead and 100 seasons past since The Great American Pastime made its debut in 1869.

A routine play, but not for me. I was the batter, you see, taking my licks in Tampa two months ago against a real-life major league pitcher for the first time ever in my checkered, very ordinary, long-ago baseball "career." As for that "sharp" ground ball, I will claim to my dying day it would have been a sure infield hit in my "prime," when I was considerably fleeter of foot.

For me, this head-to-head, eyeball-to-eyeball — call it what you will — confrontation with an All-Star team of authentic former Cincinnati Reds was the climax of "Dream Week," which is how it was properly billed when I decided last Fall to risk it all and take along for moral support my son, Peter, giving him what for both of us was a memorable, once-in-a-lifetime Christmas present.

ALL THE GUYS I played ball with when we were kids hungered to be major leaguers, and this was as close as I — and all but one of them — would ever come.

It was indeed Dream Week, all that and more for me, a solitary, special week carved out of my usually chaotic schedule that stopped time and spirited me away from all the daily cares and demands of everyday life.

I spent my boyhood in Hamilton, Ohio, 25 miles up the pike from Cincinnati, home of the Reds, who were my idols during those impressionable years from nine to fifteen, when undying loyalties are forged. They linger undimmed to this day.

One night last summer, I heard the familiar radio voice of my old Hamilton friend, Jos Nuxhall, onetime great Cincinnati Reds pitcher and now broadcaster par excellence, who was touting Dream Week. The very next day, I started the ball rolling. It didn't stop until Jack Billingham beat me to first base in Tampa two months ago.

THE LETTER arrived last October 7: "We are pleased to inform you that you and Peter have been selected as members of the 1986 REDS DREAM TEAM, and we have reserved lockers for you . . ."

I presumed that meant my check had cleared and they somehow had determined I wasn't immobilized in a body cast.

222

The tension mounted as February 2 approached. An "official roster" arrived in the mail. Sheer dread supplanted anticipation. Fifty-two of the seventy Dream Week "players" were 49 or under, half the total in their 30s, and only 18, myself among them, over 50. We sprang from 10 states, mostly Ohio, of course, but including New York, California, Indiana, Kentucky, Illinois (me), and Mississippi (Peter).

I didn't take the "team plane" from Cincinnati, but flew direct from O'Hare to Tampa and rode in a motel van to the Airport Hilton, our "team headquarters" for the week, where the real Reds stayed during spring training.

I was greeted effusively in the lobby by two Dream Week aides, the exuberance of whose welcome suggested they must have had me confused with Henry Kissinger.

THAT DID LITTLE to buoy my spirits, for I knew in my heart of hearts I hadn't looked at a fast ball from the batter's box in 30 years or so.

First on the agenda was a short trip to the training complex where we would try on our uniforms, a highlight we could enjoy before being tested in the crucible of combat. Peter, flying in from Memphis, wouldn't arrive for several hours.

In mid-afternoon, the troops began to assemble in the lobby. We were a motley crew of varying dimensions, degrees of fitness, and general demeanor. There were polite, tentative greetings as we pawed the turf, exchanged pleasantries, and eyed each other suspiciously. On the bus, I sized up the group with a mixture of distrust, skepticism, awe, and good feelings, since we were, after all, blood brothers.

Too many, I thought, seemed sleek greyhounds who could outrun a speeding bullet or muscley bulldogs capable of hitting a bowling ball out of the park, surely superior ballplayers who would heap shame on my pathetic rendezvous with the past.

One fellow about my age sported a nose which had obviously been broken three or four times and badly set. I had him pegged correctly, it turned out, as a lifelong jock who would be nothing but trouble. Fortunately, I wound up on his team.

MY SPIRITS ROSE a notch or two as I counted a half-dozen or so good-sized bellies and mounds of badly distributed flab. These guys can't do much, I muttered silently by way of consoling myself.

Good Lord, what was I thinking of when I signed up? Damn fool, I should have paid the freight for Peter and stayed home. But no, you big jerk, you've got to go out and get yourself brained, just like Martha said. Then why did she encourage me, instead of stopping me cold?

The bus ground to a halt at the Redsland training complex, where the greats, near-greats, not-so-greats, and dead busts of the Cincinnati Reds had worked out winter kinks, worked off winter pounds, and worked themselves into respectable spring shape for many a long, long season past, and where they would do so again a few weeks hence.

It was a rambling, ordinary-looking, yellowish, concrete-block structure. I bounced off the bus, feigning a cockiness I didn't feel, implying I ran seven or eight miles daily in the pre-dawn to stay fit, and proceeded with my newfound teammates somewhat uncertainly into the building.

There it all came together. We found ourselves in the ultimate inner sanctum — a genuine major league locker room — complete with the trappings of the trade, from rolls of tape and jars of liniment to doorless chickenwire-and-wood lockers which don't lock.

IN THE MIDST of that splendor, I found a locker with my name on a card taped across the top. Hanging neatly inside was *my uniform,* a faithful replica of the Reds' home whites, thigh-hugging stretch pants and pullover jersey with "W. RENTSCHLER — 20" emblazoned in brilliant red letters across the back.

There was also a thin nylon windbreaker, bright red stirrup stockings, and a jaunty cap with the distinctive Reds' C. We athletes jostled each other for position in front of the several full-length mirrors and then took turns posturing and preening as we ogled ourselves in these coveted major league ensembles. This set the juices flowing. We were told solemnly to be ready at 9:15 sharp the next morning for our first day of serious baseball.

• • •

A good month before I left for Tampa, I bought myself a magnificent "Keith Hernandez" first baseman's mitt at Kiddle's, our local sporting goods emporium. It was hard as a wood plank when it came out of the box, and there was precious little time or inclination to engage in the time-honored ritual of "breaking it in." When I arrived in Florida, the massive mitt, twice as big as any I'd owned previously, had all the resiliency of a brick wall, and I could envision balls bouncing out of the pocket for embarrassing errors. I could tell I needed help.

Right off the bat that first Sunday night, I spotted Joe Nuxhall, who was a member of the Dream Week faculty and manager of one of six teams at the Tampa camp. He was parked in the lobby with his charming, tolerant wife, Donzetta.

NUX EMERGED FROM Hamilton's sandlots and became at 15 the youngest player ever to appear in a major league game. His whole life — a span of a half century — has been baseball.

He is a rugged, easy-going, gentle giant of a man, around 250 or so pounds these days, standing six-four, and he still pitches batting practice on occasion for the real Reds. I think I can outrun him over 50 yards. His massive head might have been carved out of an oaken stump. Despite his mild disposition today, he had a tendency as a young hurler to blow sky high without warning. I remember once when he slipped on the wet grass at Wrigley Field trying to field a bunt. He went down hard and never got out of the inning, hitting a batter, walking several, stomping around on the mound, and shortly cooling off under a locker room shower.

• • •

"Nux, you've gotta help me. I'll never catch a ball in this new glove," I lamented. He gave it a quick look and a couple of pats, and agreed.

"I'll see what I can do."

• • •

(To be continued next week)

Wednesday, April 16, 1986

'THE STUFF OF FANTASY 2'

Old master Klu lends Bill a mitt, dispenses hitting tips

Baseball, I've always thought, is the sport supreme, the ultimate civilized game, absent the tyranny of the clock, a game slow to unfold, somewhat like life itself. It is the diversion which binds in common cause bricklayer and heart surgeon, stately dowager and swaggering Casanova, Harvard professor and tattered urchin, grizzled cabbie and corporate czar.

Baseball is a summer sport, meant to be played by boon companions on growing grass under a merciless sun which turns a cold drink into the nectar of the gods.

Baseball is a game for boys, some grown older, but boys still, lighthearted, mischievous, unrestrained. As men, they may play golf or tennis, but baseball endures chiefly in their

226

memories. For all but the chosen few, baseball as serious business ends in the late teen years, and only a scant handful go on to play in college or beyond.

That, perhaps, is why Dream Week last February was so very special for me. It gave me the unrepeatable chance to leap the wide chasm of years and return, for what Jack Kennedy called "one brief shining moment," to the carefree role of a Midwestern boy playing baseball one more time.

• • •

OLD FRIEND Joe Nuxhall remembered. When we arrived at the Reds' training spread in Tampa that first Monday morning, Nux spotted me, yelled, "Hey, Rentsch," and tossed me a supple, red-brown, broken-in first baseman's mitt, one that clearly had seen its share of action through seasons past. I put it on and pounded it. It felt right and a certain relief spread over me. I could catch a ball most of the time, I thought, with this mitt, which was as special in its way as a precious antique.

Indelibly printed on the thumb in block letters was "KLU," which obviously meant it was the property of baseball great Ted Kluszewski, of Cincinnati and later White Sox fame, a prodigious home run hitter with celebrated biceps he exposed to adoring fans by cutting off his shirts at the shoulder.

This was Big Klu's mitt.

"Klu's glad to lend it to you, Bill," Nuxhall said. I was elated.

During the week, I got acquainted with Kluszewski, who looks about the same as I remembered him. He was on hand daily to give us hitting tips and josh with us in his low-key, matter-of-fact way.

After watching me flail away in the batter's box, hitting several balls painfully on the handle, Klu stepped in and told me, "Rentsch, you're overstriding and not holding tight to your bat after you make contact. Move back in the box a little and keep a firm grip on the bat when you follow through."

227

ADVICE FROM A pro. It helped. Sadly, I read last Sunday that Klu had suffered a heart attack in Florida and was in intensive care in a hospital there. I'm pulling hard for a friend.

I assumed that first day would be leisurely and devoted mainly to getting the feel of that rock-hard pellet with red stitches, bending down to pick up grounders, taking some practice swings at soft pitches, and the like. I was dead wrong.

Our major league tutors summoned us into a circle outside the main building for our initial briefing. We stood there, all shapes and sizes, self-consciously resplendent in our uniforms, and got the word from the baseball faculty, among them Nux, Klu, former second baseman Tommy Helms, the Reds' first base coach who hugged a sobbing Pete Rose last season after Rose stroked his all-time record breaking 4,192nd hit; catcher Ed Bailey, out of Strawberry Plains, Tennessee, now city councilman from Knoxville; southpaw pitcher Jimmy O'Toole, Chicago native and father of 12; George (Skunk) Culver, a droll, leathery pitcher who tossed a no-hitter against Philadelphia in his heyday; Jimmy Stewart, premier utility infielder/outfielder/pinch-hitter and salty raconteur, and Wayne Krenchicki, a current major leaguer who was traded after Dream Week to the Montreal Expos.

Presiding over the camp was Jim Hoff, the Reds' personable, sharp-as-a-tack minor league coordinator, who gave us our marching orders.

- "Do what you can do," he told us, "and don't overdo."

- "We're here to help you. Call on us. This ought to be fun, and we expect to have as good a time as you fellows."

- "We give awards every day. A gold rope for great fielding plays, brown rope for real bad goofs."

- "You get fined a buck for breaking the rules. You don't

wear a helmet up to bat. That costs you a buck. You wear jewelry — watch, ring, chain — on the field, that's a buck, too. You call your manager 'Coach,' and that's a buck. Call him Skip or Jimmy or Nux, that's okay. Not coach."

THEN WORDS of wit and wisdom from each of our big league bosses — managers, not coaches. Pro ballplayers, I've found from a week in close proximity, are the greatest of story-tellers. They seem to possess near total recall. They can re-count the exact location and nature of the pitch, the direction of the wind, and the ultimate resting place of the ball for a key home run they hit two decades earlier. As with fish, the stories get bigger and the home runs longer with each telling.

First on each day's agenda came the calisthenics conducted by Reds' longtime trainer Larry Starr. I'm no great exercise fan, especially the regimentation of day in, day out running or formal conditioning.

But Larry's regimen was tolerable, even sensible — not ex-cruciating — consisting mainly of reaching and stretching and limbering up with neck rotations, shoulder shrugs, arm ex-tensions, trunk twists, leg stretches, and the like.

For me, they worked. At the end of the week, I felt great. In between, I thought death was imminent.

After the third day, the only parts that didn't hurt were my hair and the roof of my mouth. That's another story.

● ● ●

'THE STUFF OF FANTASY 3'

A week of being a boy again

The time had come to play ball.

I assumed that first warm, hazy, early February morning in Tampa would be devoted to "getting the feel" of the ball, bat, and glove, to some casual throwing, hitting and infield practice.

After all, even the youngest among us had been removed from the rigors of competitive baseball for eight or ten years. For some of us, like me, it was thirty or so.

I was quickly proved wrong.

After loosening-up exercises and a bit of small talk and salty advice from our major league mentors, we were summarily divided up, twelve to an informal "team," and sent off, resplendent in our official Cincinnati Reds home uniforms, to one of four playing fields, laid out like four 90-degree slices of pie with home plates clustered at the center and separated by chain-link backstops and fences.

THE DIAMONDS were literally impeccable, better than Wrigley Field, the best I'd seen, meticulously manicured by some wondrous ground crew. The infield grass was of putting green quality, the red clay soil was tamped to smooth perfection.

There would be no bad bounces, I thought to myself, thereby ruling out one common excuse for infield miscues.

Twenty minutes after arriving at "our" field (son Peter was assigned to another), I found myself stationed at first base and ready, I guessed, to play ball. I took a small measure of comfort from Klu's pliable, broken-in mitt, which, I prayed, still contained enough leftover "stuff" to get me through at least the first day.

230

It seemed more than passing strange, unreal, a little eerie, after all the years that had sped by.

It was now, but it was then, too, a long time ago. A flood of memories enveloped me.

WHAT IS IT that motivates the athlete, whether an unsteady 10-year-old sandlotter, accomplished major leaguer, or all who fall in between? What truly is it? There are the dreams of glory, of course, for each longs to play the hero's role, get the key hit, make the game-saving play, but there is something more immediate, lurking near the surface of buried emotions, gnawing and unsettling.

I felt it this very moment as the tension built toward the first pitch of my latter-day "reunion" with a game I still love.

What mattered most at the moment? Simply, I didn't want to embarrass myself in front of my peers, teammates, friends new and old, even my son.

Every athlete, actor, speech-maker, performer of every description and degree of skill wants almost desperately to avoid that moment when he muffs the ball, fluffs the line, "makes a friggin' ass" of himself, as old-time Red Jimmy Stewart put it to us in the indelicate vernacular of the gnarled major league veteran.

Playing ball in pick-up games in the streets outside my childhood home, on the sandlots of my native Hamilton, Ohio, in prep school, I caught hundreds of balls and made hundreds of putouts routinely and with increasing consistency at first base, the only position I ever played. What I remember vividly of my fielding prowess is a couple of bloopers, one of which didn't matter a lick, while the other cost a game. The harmless goof was on a ball the pitcher shovelled to me from a few feet away. I dropped it, that's all, and nothing came of it. The other was devastating at the time. I was a senior at Berkshire School in Massachusetts, and we were playing arch-rival Kent. In the very first inning, with two on, their batter rapped a sharp grounder which I bobbled, kicked, picked up, and hurled over the catcher's head. Three runs scored, and we lost,

231

5–3. Both incidents flashed through my mind this day in Tampa as I "warmed up" my fellow Dream Week infielders with lazy bouncers across the rich red dirt.

THEN I ROLLED the infield ball in toward our bench, gritted my teeth, moved deep and away from the bag as "their" leadoff man, a short, stocky redhead batting left-handed, stepped into the box. He looked young and deadly serious. He was. He drilled the first pitch far over the right fielder's head and coasted into third with a stand-up triple.

I gulped and wondered if I was in far over *my* head. Maybe Martha *was* right.

That first hitter, Dave King, 37, the baseball coach at Sidney, Ohio, High School, had borrowed the money, I learned later, to cover the costs of his "dream" in Tampa. That triple was no fluke. He played brilliantly all week and ended up batting over .600. Nice guy, too.

I came up for the first time in the third inning. The pitcher, in his mid-30s, whom I had been "scouting" intently from the bench, was fast, wild, and, as be glowered in from the mound, reminded me of King Kong or at least Goose Gossage.

With blood in my eye, determination in my soul, and fear in my heart, I marched to the plate.

"Hey, Rentschler, that'll cost you a buck."

I'D FORGOTTEN THE required batting helmet. My first fine. I got another for wearing my watch and ring. No jewelry allowed.

For the first time ever, I was wearing batting gloves, soft and clinging like the brown kid gloves my mother used to wear when I was a small boy. They are standard equipment these days.

The first pitch sailed high and behind my head. I edged nervously away from the plate. The next was a foot outside. I swung wildly anyway and missed. Then called strike two. I dug in and glowered back, took a healthy swing at an inside pitch, caught it on the handle, and popped it feebly between pitcher and first for the third out. No damage.

232

After seven innings, we broke for lunch in the locker room, a straggly crew, spent and aching.

"All right, guys," yelled camp czar Jimmy Hoff, the Reds' Minor League coordinator, "Eat up and let's get back out there by one."

Maybe for a skull session and light workout before we called it a day. Not on your life. We would play a second seven-inning game, which the old pros — Joe Nuxhall, Ted Kluszewski, Ed Bailey, Jim O'Toole, Tommy Helms, George Culver, Jimmy Stewart, Wayne Krenchicki, and Hoff — would use to evaluate the abundant talent before conducting a "draft" that night and assigning us to our teams for the week.

THE AFTERNOON GAME, for those of us still up and about, was fun. Most of the "hotshot" Dream Week pitchers had worn out their arms in the morning affair, so the former Major Leaguers took to the hill in the afternoon.

Nux, the crafty, hard-throwing southpaw of yore, who still pitches batting practice for the "real" Reds, started for us. At 57, he nurtures a wicked assortment of junk, including a knuckler, screwball and roundhouse sandlot curve, which baffled our opponents. He set down the six men he faced with ease, and then turned over the pitching chores to Helms, Bailey, and Krenchicki, who were working on a joint no-hitter going into the seventh inning. Jim Hoff surrendered two harmless singles, took a lot of guff for losing the no-hitter, but preserved the shutout, and we won by something like 17-0, with some of our hitters having big days. I kept one rally going with an infield single.

The long, demanding day left most of us happy, hurting, drained, and eager for more. The Reds' training room was the most popular place in Tampa, and the hot tub back at the Hilton was akin to Nirvana. Most of us, I'm sure, slept the sleep of the innocent.

Next morning, the teams were posted. Peter and I found ourselves, happily, playing together. Our manager was Krenchicki, only then-current member of the Reds, since traded to the Montreal Expos. I felt a flicker of disappointment, since I'd hoped to be tutored by one of my heroes from a bygone era.

'Chicki's team was balanced and talented. The left side of the infield, Tip Tipton, 36, a dentist from near Toledo, and Steve Hussey, a Cincinnatian, fielded brilliantly all week, while both hit well, with "Huss" leading the league. We had two solid, gutty pitchers, Riley Sorrell, 50, an imperturbable farmer from Eaton, near my old hometown, and Menis Ketchum, 42, a contentious lawyer (what else?) from Huntington, West Virginia. A watch-charm cardiologist, five-two Dave Joffe, 40, played a gritty game in the outfield and made one memorable catch with overtones of comedy. Lima realtor Jim (Shoe) Schomaeker alternated between first and third while nursing a pulled hamstring. Team godfather was John Shafer, 57, the casting director's choice for a rugged, no-nonsense catcher who kept us fired up and on our toes.

IN OUR OPENER against a team co-managed by Nux and Stewart, we started fast and took a seemingly safe 5-1 lead into the final inning. No lead is safe. Their leadoff hitter hammered a line drive home run to the fence in distant left center. An omen, but not by itself worrisome.

Then things began to unravel. A couple of walks, a solid hit, bases loaded, and they were down by only two. Gene Monnin, 49, with flattop hairmow and potbelly, didn't look too menacing. All he did was hit a skipper down the third base line past the limping Schomaeker to clear the bases and win the game, 6-5, for the bad guys. A crusher! It would be our only loss.

On Wednesday, we weren't to be denied, trouncing Tommy Helms' team, 9-3, on a good combined pitching performance by Sorrell and Ketchum.

Thursday would be a big day, with a doubleheader against visiting Dream Week teams representing the Baltimore Orioles and the hated New York Mets. Excitement was high, and we were primed. The Orioles looked awesome, jaunty, and professional as they filed off the bus in their orange-and-black uniforms. But their pitching proved mediocre, and we jumped off to a big lead, as was our habit, on a string of walks (two to me) and some clutch hits.

Which brings me to Peter.

Peter had a good week. He hit tolerably well, getting several key blows to keep rallies alive or drive in runs. He was robbed of one solid hit when the ump belatedly called time, but then he came right back and did it again. He fielded respectably, even though a sore shoulder forced him to "shot put" the ball rather weakly to first. He led the league in "pounds of ice applied to aching anatomy."

Like Willie Mays' great over-the-shoulder, back-to-the-infield World Series catch, Peter made one play that ought to be engraved forever on a bronze tablet somewhere in Tampa.

OUR TEAM WAS rolling to victory over the visiting Orioles, leading 10-2 as the demoralized Dream Weekers from Maryland came up for their last chance. That final inning, as you can tell, always gave us fits!

Their rally started mildly, but soon they were pounding the ball to all fields, and the score had tightened to 10-8 with two on and two down. The Orioles sent up their cleanup hitter, a burly, bearded giant who strode to the plate with a decided long-ball glint in his eyes.

The count went to 2-and-2, and he did indeed hit the ball a long way, but mainly up, soaring almost out of sight toward the clouds, a towering pop fly that seemed likely to come down somewhere behind Peter in the vicinity of second base.

Peter first glanced nervously at Tip Tipton, the smooth-fielding shortstop, who shot Peter a "Sorry, pal, it's all yours" look. A bit frantic now as the ball started its descent from on high, Pete looked at me with imploring eyes and once again met only a chill rebuff.

He had no choice. It was his to cope with. The runners were circling the bases. The game was on the line. Watching the arc of the ball from my vantage point, I guessed it would fall to earth about fifteen feet behind "My Son the Staggering Second-Sacker," tying the game and putting us in imminent danger of ignominious defeat.

As the ball descended, Peter circled, did a little jig, and back-pedalled, desperately trying to catch up with the ball. At the last possible moment, he lunged backward, reaching over his head and behind him, and fell with a crash to the turf on his back, banging his head a nasty blow. His teammates, myself among them, watched intently for the ball to trickle free as he hit the ground.

But it didn't. He hung on somehow. The game was over. The Orioles were vanquished and Peter was literally mobbed by his ecstatic cohorts. Another great moment in sport!

• • •

THE METS WERE different. Some, like Hofstra Law School dean Eric Schmertz, were debonair and composed. More conveyed the scrappy, cocky, caterwauling image of an Eddie Stanky, of Noo Yawk and Noo Joisey, which they represented. We were dying to beat them. The game settled down to a tense duel. They took a 1-0 lead off Riley Sorrell which they held into the fourth inning. Still not hitting, I drew a walk, moved up on a single and an error, and came home with the tying run on another walk. Riley broke the tie himself, hitting a long triple and coasting home on a sacrifice fly, for a 2-1 margin which we carried into their final, dangerous time at bat.

The tension mounted. It came down to runners on first and second, two outs. Oh, how we wanted that game!

The batter rapped what appeared to be a game-ending grounder on two bounces to Tipton, who gobbled it up and fired a perfect strike, just above the belt, to me at first.

As the ball came at me like a speeding bullet, it seemed my whole life passed before my eyes, but especially every error I'd ever made as a kid. I thrust my glove forward to grab the ball, which unaccountably eluded my grasp, caught me amid-

ships, and, horror of horrors, dropped at my feet. I snatched
it up, and ran halfway across the diamond to keep the front
man from dashing home. The bases were loaded. I was morti-
fied. I wanted nothing more than to crawl into a deep, black
hole.

SOMEBODY YELLED, not too convincingly, "All right,
Rentsch, let's get the next one."

I prayed a little. Sorrell, pitching brilliantly, seemed un-
ruffled. The count went to 0-and-2. The sawed-off batter, sent
up to coax a walk, took a vicious cut, the ball popped into
John Shafer's big mitt, and the game, as they say, was history.
We'd won.

I literally bounded to the mound and hugged a grinning
Sorrell.

The Krenchickis ended with a 3-and-1 record, second
among the six teams. As old ballplayers are fond of saying,
"We shoulda won 'em all."

• • •

ON THE FIFTH day, the Lord showed His mercy, and the
heavens opened up. Our games were rained out, and we headed joyfully for the whirlpools and our downy beds, waiting
expectantly for *the* BIG game tomorrow at Al Lopez Stadium,
where we would take on a team of former Cincinnati Reds
stars.

Saturday dawned no brighter, and the deluge continued.
The field turned to pea soup, and the game was postponed
to bright and early Sunday morning. I've written of my turn at
bat and near-hit against Cincinnati hurler Jack Billingham,
my best trip to the plate all week.

Because Schomaeker was still limping, Krenchicki put him
at first and sent me to right field, unfamiliar territory. The
very first batter was the vaunted Klu. I felt I was looking down
the barrel of a cannon and he was thinking right field as he
measured our pitcher. Please, God, let him hit it out of the

237

park, anywhere, but not to me. Klu obliged, tapping the ball to second for an easy out.

It gave me some comfort to observe that the prowess of even the great ballplayers diminishes with age just as it does for us ordinary mortals.

Klu and Nuxhall are in my age bracket, and while I threw down no gauntlets or even batting gloves, I saw enough to convince me I could outrun either for 50 yards or so. In our all-star game, the utterly reliable Tommy Helms of my memory dropped an underhand flip to second, and a routine grounder skittered between the legs of third sacker Darryl Chaney. Just like us guys.

I had a plane to catch. Our ranks thinned. By the sixth inning, with four Dream Week teams yet to play their three innings each against the All-Stars, the major leaguers led by only 2-1. As I left, I sensed the eruption was waiting to happen.

• • •

HOW WOULD I gauge my performance? Charitably.

Best of all, I made it through the week unscathed, without mishap, and emerged feeling better than when I left dreary Illinois in late January.

The pain was good pain. I didn't make a single trip to the immensely popular, usually crowded trainer's room. I didn't pull a hamstring or snap an Achilles tendon, like one fellow my age, who was emphatically out for "the season." My throwing arm, which also holds my tennis racquet, gave me no trouble. No tennis elbow, no baseball shoulder, no pain, no strain.

Despite one humiliating error, and a couple of minor misplays, my fielding, aided by Klu's big mitt, was better than I expected. I made most of the required plays, handled several low throws on the short-hop, and made the putout on a rare pickoff play at first. One teammate put me down as "good field, no hit."

That hurt. "Good field" was a compliment of sorts, but everybody wants to hit.

My hitting left much to be desired. At the plate, I inflicted little pain and suffering on the ball, which I wasn't "seeing" well, and which often looked not much bigger than an aspirin tablet. I went 2 for 8, both infield singles, and walked four times. When I wasn't lunging at pitches, I was hitting balls on the handle rather than the "meat" end of the bat. I struck out three or four times.

AS THE WEEK wore on, I felt more comfortable at the plate, saw the ball better, and drilled a few good shots in batting practice. The bat supply kept shifting and dwindling and I was unable all week to find and keep a bat I liked.

Baseball, like the Navy, is a waiting game. You wait to get up to bat, you wait for the right pitch, you wait for the ball to be hit your way. As in military service, you wait for chow, for commands, for assignments, for the call to duty.

I was even reminded of summer camp, especially the fact that your name is written in permanent magic marker into every stitch of gear you wear.

• • •

IT'S OVER NOW for me. I treasure every minute. It was a lark which I took seriously while I was immersed in it. We played 41 innings in five days, a quite incredible test of stamina which far exceeds for me any prior marathon of endurance. At age eighteen, I don't recall playing more than three games — twenty-seven innings — in a single week, and then only once.

This was indeed the stuff of fantasy, something to tuck away and savour for all time. It was one brief moment, *my* brief moment, to partake of the legend and lore, the reality and romance, of every kid's dream, a chance to play in the big leagues.

For me, lt was a week of being a boy again.

The 'boys of summer' herald spring's coming

With the Illinois prairie still barren, and looking its scruffy, gray-brown worst, the boys of summer are drifting south and southwest to engage in the annual rite of spring.

It's baseball time again, a time of year which brings groans of distress and disbelief from those who disdain the sport, but which stirs the embers of youth and the tingle of anticipation in us passionate diehards who love baseball like no other sport.

TO ME, SINCE I was eight or nine, baseball has been a very special game, the ultimate of all team sports we play and watch, the quintessential spring tonic to rout the nagging aches and bleak shadows of winter.

Such a simple affirmation elicits howls of rage and pain from the devotees of football, basketball, and other team diversions.

But football has become a ritual of savagery, of cutting up and pulverizing, knocking senseless, inflicting injuries that will linger and worsen over a lifetime. It is a game for young men whose necks proceed straight down from their ear lobes and measure the circumference of a stout oak.

On their shiny, hardwood field of combat, the ebony trees of basketball, Masai warriors standing close to or above seven feet, make the game seem all too easy as they soar up near the cloud-banks, stuff an inflated orange sphere down through a steel rim and shatter plexiglas backboards.

Ah, baseball, a game where even the scrawny and under-sized can excel, where there's a place both for pure talent and grace, like Musial and Clemente, and for sheer will and guts, as with Pete Rose and Eddie Stanky.

Yes, there are a few "small" basketball players, six-two or so, and a handful of football "runts," weighing in around 175, but both games discriminate cruelly and effectively against talented athletes of more "normal" or average dimensions.

BASEBALL IS NOT without its blemishes, as both its fans and critics will attest. A baseball game can and often does drag. The season is too long. It's no fun sitting out there on a frigid April afternoon. Flame-throwing pitchers often put hitters to shame. The sport is largely devoid right now of colorful crowd-pleasers.

Baseball to many appears tame, dull, slow, even anemic.

But they neither love nor understand baseball, and baseball, above all else, must be understood to be loved. Its nuances are endless and intricate. To those who grasp the nuances, baseball is the sport supreme; to those who do not, baseball can be an interminable bore.

The true baseball buff agonizes with each pitch. He knows the players, their strange quirks, their special capabilities. He is quick to note that a superb pitcher for seven innings is losing his stuff in the eighth. He spots every momentary flaw or hitch in the swing of each batter. From his seat beyond third base, he calls every pitch more accurately than the umpire crouching directly behind the catcher. He knows just which pitcher to summon from the bullpen in time of trouble, and precisely which pinch-hitter to insert in each situation. He is indeed a student of the subtleties of a game he loves.

To this fan, baseball is still king. Baseball is a game that remains largely unchanged, unreformed. Perhaps this explains in part the fierce loyalty of its partisans, whose expertise, like mine, dates back to their own days as aspiring major leaguers.

We played ball as kids on narrow asphalt streets, contending as much with overhanging branches, cast-iron lamp posts, and cars, both parked and moving, as with our ragged foe. We played, too, on vacant lots where the obstacles included stones and broken bottles, uneven terrain and weeds in clumps and tall grass that not infrequently turned routine grounders into extra base hits.

241

THE BALL ITSELF was generally lopsided and water-soaked, and we continued to play when the seams gave way and the scarred and blackened cover parted from its core.

A foul ball sliced into a tulip bed or against the façade of a frame house invariably brought a police cruiser to break up the game — amiably and temporarily — while the crotchety complainant watched from behind drawn drapes to make sure justice was done.

This Spring, there will come an afternoon when the lure of bright sun and cottony clouds will overpower me, and I will steal off from my cares and chores to Wrigley Field or White Sox Park.

Baseball will continue to thrive. There are too many like me to let it die.

Thursday, September 27, 1984

You were there, Emil Verban, when we needed you

The authentic patron saint of the Chicago Cubs' remarkable resurgence to baseball respectability and possibly even supremacy may well be Emil Verban.

Emil Verban. How's that again? Emil Verban?

Maybe Dallas Green. Or Jim Frey. Perhaps Andy McKenna. How about Sandberg and Sutcliffe? Or the Bull, the Penguin, and the Sarge?

But Emil Verban?

YOU BET. And thereby hangs a tale.

Five or six years ago a group of zany, wild-eyed, diehard, lifelong Cub fans met secretly in a Washington, D.C. phone booth one foggy night to establish an organization devoted to utter futility.

242

Even though they professed a commitment to the notion that "hope springs eternal," they were dedicated in truth to the proposition that the Cubs are born losers — and "we love 'em for it."

They needed a shining symbol for their endeavor, a true Cub whose radiance in major league baseball was roughly akin to the glitter of Millard Fillmore in the annals of the American presidency.

SEARCHING THE ARCHIVES, they came upon the name of Emil Verban. They went no further. Beer had numbed their brains, and for their own yet undisclosed reasons, they anointed Emil Verban on the spot.

Assuming, with cavalier disdain for fact, he had long since gone to his reward, they christened their thing, their baby, their creation, grandly, The Emil Verban Memorial Society.

For a while, nothing much happened. The Cubs continued to make losing seem like the only way. But the founders, including such old and good friends of mine as Bruce Ladd, Tom Houser, and Dick Wiley, former Illinoisans seduced by the heady elixir of the muddy Potomac, endured and let nothing impede their acute addiction to the hapless Cubbies of Chicago.

A few years back, to their acute embarrassment, they discovered that Emil Verban, the object of their memorial, was alive and well and damned unhappy, not to mention wounded in the psyche, about being the butt of their amusement and the symbol of Cub frustration.

AT JUST ABOUT that time, strange things began happening, a renaissance of sorts on the North Side. There were stirrings at Wrigley Field and some small scraps of evidence that the Cubs might even have a promising future, that next year might be just around the corner, a panicky prospect.

The Society leadership, such as it was, scrambled for the record books to reappraise Emil Verban, who to their horror, turned out to be a successful downstate banker, landowner, and country squire from Lincoln, Illinois, near Springfield, and even more astounding, a helluva ballplayer.

You heard me: This was no run-of-the-mill, journeyman major leaguer, but a slick fielder, line-drive hitter with a .280-plus lifetime average, three-times All Star, wearer of a World Series ring, one of the toughest in history to strike out.

How do we make amends, the founders wondered uneasily? Aha. Throw a terrific party! And eat crow. So they would put on a genuine spectacular in our nation's capitol, a luncheon at which the guest of honor would be none other than Emil Verban.

NOTWITHSTANDING HIS pique and lingering hurt, he graciously accepted, bringing along his wife, son and namesake, and other relatives for what had to be one of the great moments of any man's life.

There on the dais with him were Baseball Commissioner Bowie Kuhn; Presidential press secretary Jim Brady, who rose briefly from his wheelchair with help from wife Sarah to pay homage; U. S. Senator Alan Dixon, who recited a litany of Emil's impressive statistics during a notable 10-year career; U. S. House Minority leader Bob Michel, a Peoria Republican, and Jim Finks, new president of the Cubs.

Before the luncheon, old friend Ladd, the main miscreant and keeper of the flame, escorted the Emil Verban clan to the White House for a clubby visit with The Gipper himself, a come-lately member of this august society.

I said something earlier about patron saint. I meant it.

THE CUBS DIDN'T really start to jell until those guys who met in that phone booth finally recognized talent and made their amends to Emil Verban, who shed a few tears on that memorable day last April and said without batting an eye:

"This is *the* year. The Cubs are going *all the way!* Nothing can stop them."

You doubters ought to be ashamed of yourselves.

Those of us who are members of this select body are truly ill-equipped to live with the fruits and responsibilities of sudden success after all those years of failure and ignominy.

Anyway, it's a great feeling! Go, Cubs. You've lifted our spirits.

Let Emil Verban throw out the first ball next week.

Hope for the 'Hopelost'...

December 20, 1983

Who shall care for the poor and oppressed?

For the poor and oppressed, for the unemployed and the destitute, and for the sick and the suffering, and for all who remember and care for them, let us pray to the Lord. Lord, have mercy.

— From the Book of Common Prayer

• • •

An endless debate rages over who should bear the main burden. Shall it be the federal government, the states, business, churches, private agencies, each of us individually? Who shall "remember and care for them"?

Where the help comes from matters not a whit to those most desperately in need. The argument itself often is an excuse for doing nothing at all or as little as possible to alleviate hardship and despair.

At least as irrelevant is all the overblown rhetoric about welfare queens and foodstamp ripoffs, which are repugnant, but which offer no valid basis for depriving needy youngsters, or the old, ill, infirm, retarded, and all who are truly destitute.

Nor do the ripoffs diminish our personal responsibility toward those who suffer and bleed and cry out for help.

247

We churchgoers of all faiths sit in the pews and gaze up at the pulpit, listening or pretending to listen as the clergyman intones words of deep meaning.

• • •

In peace, we pray to You, Lord God. For the just and proper use of Your creation; for the victims of hunger, fear, injustice, and oppression.

• • •

Do we actually *hear* those words? Even on the North Shore, there is hunger. In what way have we changed our lifestyles or stepped up our contributions in time of widespread distress? With a deep, dreary recession giving ground grudgingly for many, what have we done to help? Have we responded to the pleas of a dozen worthy charities — our own churches and temples — trying desperately to close the gap between the dollars they have and those they need?

• • •

For the poor, the persecuted, the sick, and all who suffer; for refugees, prisoners, and all who are in danger; that they may be relieved and protected, we pray to You, O Lord.

Are we listening to that priest? Who gives a damn about the wretched street people of Chicago? About migrant workers living in intolerable conditions, some in our very midst? About refugees imprisoned, often without cause, by our own government? Does it matter to us that callow first offenders sentenced to prison in many cases for non-violent crimes are confined this day in sub-human cells side by side with vicious, hardened career criminals?

• • •

I ask your prayers for the poor, the sick, the hungry, the oppressed, and those in prison. Pray for those in any need or trouble.

• • •

So often the words touch us for the moment, but are quickly lost. They trickle down and disappear like drops of water on the sand. We have jobs and warm homes and good food. We are blest. But that does not make us better or more deserving. Nor does it make the unemployed lazy or shiftless or less worthy. Perhaps less fortunate. What can we do to help those we know in "need or trouble"? Can we spare a few minutes or hours from our pursuit of pleasure and wealth? Can we spare a few dollars or many dollars? Can we take time to visit someone who's hurting or bleeding or needing solace? Will we?

• • •

For those in position of public trust, that they may serve justice, and promote the dignity and freedom of every person, we pray to You, O Lord.

• • •

Do those words sink in and have meaning for you? How do our public servants measure up? Do the candidates you expect to vote for next November truly "serve justice, and promote the dignity and freedom of every person," or do they merely mouth hollow, hypocritical words? Are they cold and insensitive to human need and deprivation? Should you consider anew your choices?

• • •

For the aged and infirm, for the widowed and orphans, and

249

for the sick and the suffering, let us pray to the Lord. Lord, have mercy.

• • •

We are told again and again we live in a self-centered me-era, a time of getting ours above all else, with little true concern for the needs of others. How many of us do what we perceive as the acceptable minimum? Each of us can do more and better. On all of us, Lord, have mercy.

Thursday, November 28, 1985

An Editorial

Search your heart to Help The Hungry HERE!

The season of giving is at hand, and as you search for the perfect tie or scarf or toy, it is wise also to search your heart. We're sure you'll find, in addition to the joy of the holidays, a compassion for those unable to provide daily bread much less than a feast.

Some few will scoff at the notion of hunger within a short drive of their homes. Although there seems to be no excuse for such deprivation amidst plenty, let us dispel any doubts that there are poor and hungry families in some Lake and Cook County homes.

Whether the cause of poverty is misfortune or ill health, the result is a feeling of helplessness, a shyness against revealing a dire situation.

But it's so easy for you to help. Take a minute right now and simply mail your check or money order in any amount, pennies or hundreds of dollars to *News/Voice's* **Help The Hungry** *HERE!* **campaign.**

250

Footprints across my mind

Thursday, January 10, 1985

Of still water, Yuppies, bigness, Blake Carrington and Lee Iacocca

The conventional wisdom is usually wrong.

• • •

The most overpaid Americans are lawyers, the most underpaid, nurses.

• • •

If the U. S. continues to stress the growth of service industries, one of our major sources of new jobs may be for people willing to wash and wax and service Japanese and German cars.

• • •

Still water runs more often dumb than deep.

• • •

251

After reading *Newsweek's* cover story on the Yuppies, I only hope they amount to something when they grow up.

• • •

Have you noticed that the garish, new, blue State of Illinois building is built along the lines of its sugar daddy, Big Jim Thompson?

• • •

Money and wisdom are not natural partners.

• • •

A banana is a good example of superb packaging, second only to an egg.

• • •

Practically no one achieves his full potential who doesn't make some mistakes along the way.

• • •

No nation which does not concern itself with its poor and disadvantaged can claim greatness for itself.

• • •

Baseball is the ultimate sport. Unlike football and basketball, baseball gives equal opportunity to players of all physical dimensions, short and tall, scrawny and powerful, fast and slow.

• • •

The most perfectly cast TV star today is John Forsythe as Blake Carrington in "Dynasty." He comes across more as Carrington than Forsythe, which is the ultimate triumph of acting.

● ● ●

Can you imagine anything much worse than working underground in the dank, dark confines of a mine?

● ● ●

Calling homosexuals "gay" distorts the original meaning of a perfectly good word.

● ● ●

Bigness in and of itself is not bad, yet big companies are mainly responsible for many of America's ills: pollution, unemployment, inefficiency, compliant politicians, tax inequity. Small companies, by contrast, have created more than 75 percent of all new jobs over the past 15 years.

● ● ●

My idea of a modern American hero is Lee Iacocca, the saviour of Chrysler and a role model for stereotypical, bureaucratic big-company executives who have led this nation backwards into industrial mediocrity.

FOOTPRINTS ACROSS MY MIND:

Losing a daughter, attacking the shrimp, tuning out the Series, seeking a happy jogger

• No matter what their upbringing, people turn out to be pretty much what they make of themselves.

• • •

• Do you male readers remember secretly pasting your girl friend's picture inside the door of your school locker?

• • •

• Nothing beats bacon and eggs at any time of day or night. Very crisp bacon, please.

• • •

• Do you have as much trouble as I do figuring out how to work the fixtures in hotel bathtubs? Have you been scalded lately?

• • •

• One of life's small excitements for me is to see a "wild" animal — deer, fox, even racoon or skunk — in its natural habitat.

• • •

• *Tribune* columnist Bob Greene got to wondering the other day how old is elderly. To me, elderly is a state of mind, but certainly it's 10 years older than you are, even if you're 90.

• • •

• If ever you happen on a jogger who looks happy, please let me know.

• • •

• Are jeans fading, or is it only my imagination?

• • •

• Even at an elegant affair, people attack the shrimp tray like hyenas ravaging a carcass.

• • •

• Whatever happened to Michael Jackson, and will he have as many lives as Frank Sinatra?

• • •

• If you're the father of the bride, as I was last Saturday, gaining a son doesn't quite make up for losing a daughter, even if he's a great guy, as my new son-in-law is.

• • •

• It's gotten so I prefer Colgate's blue gel in a pump to any other toothpaste in a tube.

• • •

• On a good Sunday, the Bears can lick anybody.

• • •

255

- It's reassuring to know how many good, kind, caring people take the time to write to these newspapers.

• • •

- A wedding is the ultimate festival of family and friends.

• • •

- Ed Meese is turning out to be just as bad as I feared when he was scrambling to salvage his nomination as U. S. Attorney General.

• • •

- Few occupations outside the theatre put as much spotlight on their practitioners as our churches, which make stars — in some cases, superstars — of the clergy.

• • •

- Quite a few baseball fans tune out the playoffs and World Series because their team didn't make it. Wait 'til next year.

Thursday, May 30, 1985

FOOTPRINTS ACROSS MY MIND:

Good decisions, bad advice, new ties, hot baths and mice

- Most good decisions are made by having the guts and good sense to ignore bad advice.

• Among baseball's attributes as the ultimate sport is that it is not ruled by a clock like football, basketball, hockey and soccer.

• • •

• The written word is the only immortality.

• • •

• I'm told the reason they're starting to use lawyers instead of white mice in medical experiments is that the lab technicians don't get so attached to them.

• • •

• Why anybody leaves the North Shore for a summer vacation is beyond me.

• • •

• I get a lift out of a new tie, which costs a good deal less than a new suit.

• • •

• You can usually tell a home "done" all at one time by a decorator from one put together lovingly over many years by the people who live in it.

• • •

• As political campaigns get more and more costly, our elected officials move further and further away from the people.

• • •

257

- One of the foremost luxuries to me is a hot bath.

• • •

- Before we honor the work of a "great" abstract artist, he/she should be required to paint a cow which looks like a cow.

• • •

- The current crop of corporate "takeover" artists has done more to undermine U. S. strength than anybody else, with the possible exception of the bankers and other lenders who literally throw money at them.

• • •

- I'm becoming somewhat addicted to those new toothpaste pumps.

• • •

- Every time somebody misuses the word "at," as in "Where's he at?", I cringe.

• • •

- Among the regulars who park underground in our office building, the "vanity" license plates are a little wild: YUPPIE 1, SUNTAN 2, DANGRUS, ILUV U 2.

• • •

- Whatever happened to Michael Jackson?

The predatory sharks of big banking

August 18, 1983

Price fixing OK for big banks

Price fixing is illegal.

Right? Wrong. Well, it depends.

BEFORE OUR very eyes, the big banks, usually starting in New York, fix prices, which means the prime rate, which is the "base" price of borrowed money, presumably that rate the banks charge their better credit risks.

Other banks around the country, sheeplike, following the lead of Big Apple and other money center banks, scurry into line, usually in a matter of hours. That process, by any gauge, is legalized price fixing.

Murderous, Mafia-level, juice-loan interest rates deepened and lengthened the slowly waning, 2½-year recession, which bankrupted many small companies, wiped out life savings, sent layoffs and unemployment soaring, and created untold hardships.

Now, interest rates are creeping up again.

EARLIER THIS month, the big bankers struck, fixing the prime rate at 11 percent, up half a point, but ominously pointing the way to further increases.

Why? Good question.

A banker in Iowa last month told me loan demand was "flat most everywhere." He couldn't understand why interest rates should be rising.

Could it be the result of price fixing? Of course.

What does "prime rate" really mean?

FIRST OF ALL, you need to understand that the prime rate is — excuse the expression — phony as a three-dollar bill. It is nothing more than a kind of public code which signals to members of the banking fraternity a starting point for setting their own rates.

The really big, blue chip corporate customers often cut deals with their banks below the prime rate, while ordinary people, when they borrow, usually get stuck for a rate well in excess of prime.

The prime rate has little relation to reality. It amounts to an artificial pegging of rates to control bank profits and loan volume. By historic standards measured against the rate of inflation, the prime rate should be two or three points lower than the present 11 percent. With demand for money slack, as that Iowa banker noted, rates should be soft rather than rising.

So? So the big banks, nervously eyeing the monstrous federal deficit, which neither the Congress nor the President is willing to tackle in earnest, nudge the prime rate up to cover their collective fannies, which just might stop the recovery stone cold dead.

Business Week fingers an accomplice in this carefully-rigged scenario: The Federal Reserve Board, whose chairman, Paul A. Volcker, was reappointed recently by President Reagan.

"The Fed," says *Business Week,* "has made a dismaying swing from monetary accommodation to credit restriction." This "swing" none-too-subtly suggested to the big banks they damn well better fix the prime rate at a higher level to keep the brakes on inflation.

WHICH COULD kick in the head the resurgence in housing, construction, and new car sales; "exacerbate" our worldwide trade deficit and "reduce U. S. competitiveness"; stop the return to jobs for many unemployed workers, and blight the fragile recovery.

A few questions:

Is the Justice Department moving to prosecute such price-fixing by the big banks? Do we hear threats from regulatory agencies to assure that rates are dictated by the free market? Are the banks themselves cutting money prices to compete for business with their fellow banks, except perhaps for the corporate giants they can't afford to lose? Is anything being done or even proposed to protect the little guy from the unfairness of it all?

No, no, no, and no. Not on your life.

THERE IS no tolerance in financial circles for price cutters. There's no room for grubby discounters in commercial banking — at least not above the table.

The bankers have a ready answer: When they raise the prime, they tell you they're paying more for money, which is what the Fed wants them to tell you. Business people will tell you the very same thing, that they, too, are paying more for their raw materials and other needs. But if they sit down and try to hammer out prices with their competitors to guarantee an adequate level of profit, they'll find their offices crawling with federal investigators.

Price fixing? That's a crime for everybody but the big bankers.

Big banks lead the backward march into economic chaos

Let me tell you why I believe we are marching resolutely backwards into economic chaos and distress.

You probably read of the $4.9 billion (that's $4,900,000,-000) offer made last week by an investment group to buy Beatrice Cos., Inc., the Chicago-based, multinational food and consumer products giant.

The offer was rejected Sunday by the Beatrice board, but you may count it as near certain that this corporate colossus will be peddled soon for $5 billion or more and thus become the largest non-oil buyout of all time.

This deal, like other massive takeovers and leveraged buy-outs, will benefit the *few* richly, but have a devastatingly negative effect on the *many* and on this nation's future.

IN NO TIME FLAT, with a few phone calls and meetings, the would-be buyers of Beatrice were able to arrange a $3.5 billion line of credit with the same big banks which are lobbying feverishly and aggressively in Springfield for wide-open interstate banking; which would be 20,000 leagues under the sea if they were forced to write off their multi-billion dollar portfolios of stretched out, non-performing foreign loans, and which are hiding and/or digging out from a decade of bad, greed-driven, domestic credit judgments, especially in energy, real estate, and high tech, which were touted as the quick route to easy revenues and riches.

Many of these same big banks — and I can cite chapter and verse — routinely shrug off and do an abominable job of helping, servicing, and responding to the legitimate credit needs of smaller and mid-sized companies.

Why? they're too busy tending their own needs and greeds, fending off regulators, lobbying for broader powers and tax breaks, battling a welter of problems they brought on themselves, attending seminars, long luncheons, and civic affairs.

It takes a lot less brains and sweat and smarts to make a billion-dollar loan than a million-dollar loan.

IMAGINE, IF YOU WILL, what $3.5 billion could do to create jobs and stimulate the economy if parcelled out wisely and well.

Let's say a consortium of big banks made available an average of only $500,000 to each of 7,000 deserving companies with an average payroll of 75 employees each. This is where the working capital crunch at times is most desperate.

That dispersal of credit would create and sustain a total of 525,000 jobs in an environment of growth and expansion. By comparison, Beatrice presently employs fewer than 100,-000 worldwide.

That same $3.5 billion, if it goes to buy Beatrice, will be dispersed mainly among the shareholders of Beatrice.

That massive sum won't create a single new job, and almost certainly will result in a net loss of jobs as the new owners come in with axes honed and under pressure to pare their choking debt load.

NO NEW TAXES will be paid, no operational efficiencies will result. This is nothing more or less than a swapping of many dollars to enrich a few.

The disruption will be staggering and depressing for hundreds of families and communities. Jobs will be lost, children will be uprooted from schools. There will be tears and trauma for many, as the fortunate few count their blessings and their buyout-generated bonanzas.

Benefits will flow freely to some:

• Certainly the takeover bunch and their backers.

• Probably the shareholders in most such deals, where the frenzy bids the stock up.

263

• Clearly those big lenders, who pad their near-term earnings by ladling out huge sums with much the same greedy myopia that got them entangled in so many shaky loans.

• Certainly the hovering lawyers, accountants, investment bankers, consultants, and other fee merchants who claim outrageous stipends for their overblown counsel and clucking midwifery.

WHAT IS THE upshot of all this, the impact, the import, the net effect?

The nation is subtly, surely weakened by the termites in its timbers, by the shifting of wealth from one small band of financial adventurers to another.

Integrity and economy of product are lost in the mad scramble for near-term bucks. Plants are closed. Jobs go off to Korea, Brazil, and other eager, ascendant economies around the globe. America, losing its manufacturing underpinnings, proceeds toward second-class status.

The finite pool of credit dwindles, making it even tougher for smaller companies to obtain capital needed for their daily operations, growth, even survival.

The big banks grovel before and scrimmage brutally for the business of the corporate Goliaths, the Fortune 500 and such, whose combined job count shrinks steadily. Too often they turn aside those small, maneuverable, entrepreneurial Davids, firms which created four of every five new jobs in the U. S. over the past 15 years and are our last, best hope for continued national well-being.

ANTI-TRUST enforcement is all but a memory, and the Reagan Administration seems to define deregulation as letting the biggest do anything they damn please.

The massive federal deficit builds beyond all comprehension. We become a debtor nation, with an ever-escalating deficit trade balance. We trade and break up and destroy manufacturing companies, substituting what we have come to call "service" companies, which produce no tangible products but soak up an increasing share of the nation's wealth.

All this is why I fear for America's future greatness and longer-term prosperity.

• • •

SINCE I DON'T want you to finish this column in a wrist-slitting or otherwise totally downcast mood, I offer this foolproof bit of advice for getting around the system which may otherwise shut you out.

If you're stymied in getting a modest loan from your downtown bank to add a family room, buy $150,000 of Christmas inventory, or beef up working capital, simply take an entirely different approach with your bank officer.

Tell him you're contemplating a takeover of Quaker Oats, Motorola, or Gould. His eyes will glaze, he'll ask you how much you need, and within minutes, he'll instruct an Assistant Vice President to start loading money into the trunk of your car.

It beats any other means of obtaining funds. And you'll pay less than the prime interest rate.

May 31, 1984

Hard questions, strong feelings on the bailout of Continental

There are some hard, critical questions which haven't been answered yet—maybe not even asked—as the gray-faced dowager of LaSalle Street claws for survival in the tempestuous seas of international banking.

This much we know: Chicago's Continental Bank already has been accorded the most lavish emergency revival (translation: bailout!) in banking history in a desperate maneuver to obscure the truth about the precarious fiscal condition of the highest echelon of U. S. banking, as well as the mismanagement, misjudgement, and sheer dereliction of both bankers and bank regulators.

These questions spring to mind, and while I don't profess to have final answers, I do have some very strong feelings:

 • **Where was Continental Bank's glittering, heavyweight Board of Directors during the lengthy period of decline and profuse bleeding?**

Big bank boards traditionally are festooned with the Chief Executive Officers of big, prestigious *Fortune 500* companies. Such a directorship is a juicy plum, an ultimate status symbol for those tapped. Presumably, however, such CEOs are busy running their own sprawling companies, consumed by the demands of their main job.

The Fall '83 American Bank Directory listed among the directors of Continental these names: James F. Beré, Weston R. Christopherson, Robert A Hanson, William B. Johnson, Vernon R. Loucks, Jr., Frank W. Luerssen, Robert H. Malott, John M. Richman, Thomas H. Roberts, Jr., and William L. Weiss. They are CEOs, respectively, of Borg-Warner Corporation; Jewel Companies, Inc.; Deere & Company; IC Industries, Inc.; Baxter Travenol Laboratories, Inc.; Inland Steel Company; FMC Corporation; Dart & Kraft, Inc.; DeKalb AgResearch, Inc., and Illinois Bell Telephone Company — a roster which surely includes some of the Chicago area's and nation's most prestigious firms and their chiefs.

How could these incredibly busy executives possibly give adequate attention to oversee in their spare time the running of a complex financial colossus like Continental Bank? They probably couldn't.

YET THEIR fiduciary responsibilities as directors are wide-ranging and quite explict.

Note this warning in the May newsletter of Third National Corporation, a large Tennessee-based holding company:

"Don't be a dummy director. It used to be if you saw no evil, you couldn't be held responsible. No more! If you accept the responsibility of being a director, you may be personally liable for corporate acts, even if you were absent from a director's meeting. Don't lend your good name to a corporation as a director unless you plan to actually participate in corporate affairs . . . If you object to a corporate action, your dissent should be carefully noted in the corporate minutes. To minimize your liability, you should continue to exert influence on the corporation to change its course."

It would seem pretty clear the 10 directors listed above, who represented more than 50 percent of Continental's Board, did not consistently exercise that sort of role, or at least didn't do so until the ship was listing dangerously.

Another question: Can the directors of such a huge institution really ever know much more than the bank's top officers choose to share with them? Probably not.

Case in point: Continental's high command, the executives who presided over the shipwreck, weren't forced out by the Board until after a failed attempt to pin the blame on subordinates, and well after the situation had deteriorated to a point of extreme crisis.

Which may explain in large part why many of America's top banks are in such sad shape and badly overextended.

• **In attempting to solve the Continental problem, how can the Illinois legislature, Congress, state and federal banking authorities, the Federal Reserve Board, and the Reagan administration even seriously consider allowing the creation of**

an Illinois megabank nearly 10 times larger than its nearest local competitor?

Only if they are moved by sheer panic. For that would be the situation if First Chicago Corp. were to acquire the Continental. The result: a blatant, obvious, and indefensible violation of U. S. antitrust laws and even principles. First National recently acquired Illinois' fifth largest bank, American National of Chicago, leaving Harris Trust, about to be acquired by the Bank of Montreal, and Northern Trust, recovering from energy loan woes similar to those of Continental, as the next largest banks in Illinois. A First Chicago/Continental combination would have assets near $80 billion, while the Harris shows only $7.6 billion and the Northern $6.1 billion, with no other Illinois bank group's assets totalling anywhere near those numbers.

Such a disparity would seem unacceptable. It is clear a takeover by First Chicago would greatly restrict competition in Illinois.

Yet First Chicago, which went through its own bloodletting a few years back, is now in the catbird seat, and, using its considerable clout in Springfield and Washington, seems bent on extracting something major for itself from the trauma of its arch-rival.

If First Chicago's ambitious chairman, Barry Sullivan, formerly a high officer of Chase Manhattan Bank, can't pick up the pieces of Continental, he apparently wants concessions that would allow him to acquire a bank in New York. There's no reason why First Chicago necessarily should benefit from Continental's travail, but the tough, savvy Sullivan clearly senses opportunity in the bloody waters and means to capitalize.

One wonders who's looking after the interests of the smaller banks, which can't count on any such sweeping bailout if they get into trouble.

• Why should serious consideration be given at this time to breaking down the barriers against interstate banking to salvage a failing big bank like Continental?

Decisions as serious as the fate of interstate banking should not be decided in a panic atmosphere, nor should basic principles be overturned to bail out a single institution.

Some say Continental actually "failed" during those "seven days in May" when a massive "run" on its deposits put the big bank perilously close to the edge, and only a massive infusion of working funds by federal "paramedics" and a consortium of big banks staved off ultimate disaster.

"I think the Continental did in fact fail and is being kept alive with embalming fluid," said bank consultant David Cates, quoted by the *Wall Street Journal* in its May 23 edition.

It would be patently unfair to the people of Illinois, who surely count for something, if bank regulators, or the Illinois General Assembly, or Congress, or the Fed were to let down the bars and permit Continental's acquisition by an out-of-state banking colossus, like New York's Citicorp, Chemical Bank, or Morgan Guaranty, or California's Security Pacific, all of which have been mentioned as possible acquirers, or, just as bad, by a foreign giant.

Peeling away several coats of bankerly veneer, the only real interest of the big national and international banks in Illinois is what they can take out of our state to their bottom lines. There is no deep-rooted concern, no history, no tradition, no stimulus to create jobs here, no relationship with our state and its commerce, its industry, its people. It would be an unjustified tragedy, and those who further any such scheme should be earmarked for punishment at the polls or otherwise.

269

- **Moreover, why is a merger the only plausible solution, except as a quick fix to "paper over" the incredible ineptitude of the regulatory agencies and the maladministration of the bank itself?**

Why the need for a shotgun marriage arranged by self-serving brokers whose interests usually are contrary to those of the citizenry and possibly even to the ultimate *stability* of the U. S. banking system?

Far better the federal government provide funds and/or guarantees for the bailout, and maintain airtight scrutiny and control over the Continental as an independent bank, than create a competitive disaster in the Chicago/Illinois financial marketplace. One horrendous scenario would pit a single local megabank against a pack of big foreign banks with no local loyalties or commitments, and a host of giant domestic predators from the two coasts, all battling each other for what they can scoop up in the way of big bucks, major corporate accounts, and easy loans while giving low priority to the urgent financial needs of a great city and state, its people and businesses. Among the big losers inevitably would be most of the rest of Illinois' 1,250 banks.

Continental's road back might be long and tortuous, and its shareholders might be largely wiped out, but why shouldn't its risk be similar to that of Chrysler Corporation, which has rebounded handsomely under the bold, charismatic leadership and vision of Lee Iacocca? Why shouldn't Continental go out and scratch for new investor dollars, just as its customers are obliged to do when Continental calls their loans?

Why should the whole structure of U. S. banking undergo wrenching, painful change and disruption merely to accommodate the "failure" of one large bank? And is it appropriate for government regulators, the Fed, and the Reagan administration to try to hoodwink a skeptical but naïve public into believing all's well with the rickety, overextended U. S. banking establishment?

270

• Finally, how can our government, in decency and fairness, even consider the bailout of a huge bank falling under the weight of its own catastrophic mismanagement and misjudgement while thousands of small, essentially sound companies, for want of a small injection of cash or modest line of credit, fail and merely disappear quietly and permanently into the quicksand of oblivion?

Is this fair? Is it tolerable? Where are the voices of those politicians whose rhetoric makes them sound at election time like passionate backers of the little guy, small business people, the common man?

Politicians like these are standing quietly aside right now, frozen into silence and immobility by the demands of the big banks and regulators.

We are at the point of making far-reaching decisions — mostly bad, even unconscionable decisions, I fear — which will change not just the banking *status quo* for the wrose, but the very character of this nation. The sound of the almighty buck is heard in the land, and it is likely once more to dominate in the legislative corridors and probably all the way to the White House.

The revolutionary restructuring of the banking system, sought so avidly by the giant banks and hastened by the Continental fiasco, seems likely to hand over the reins to a greedy, insensitive plutocracy with the ideals of "so many glorified pawnbrokers," as Theodore Roosevelt put it, thus creating a monster of limitless financial power, a quasi-government with the resources to dictate policy.

The big banks, plumping up their earnings and covering their multitude of bad loans with an artificially high prime interest rate, bid fair, unless checked, by the end of this decade to force thousands of small companies out of business or into the arms of big predators, creating finally an invironment where only the bureaucratic corporate monoliths thrive and smaller companies survive at their whim.

The potential danger is very real, closer than we think, and frightening.

Who will suffer most from whatever scenario is laid on us all as the "answer" to the Continental's woes? Small business. Small to mid-sized, independent banks. Start-up companies. Entrepreneurs. Mr. and Mrs. John Q. Citizen, the American consumer.

Chicago already is considered among the least responsive and creative financial markets in the U. S. It is a bleak and miserable financial environment for small companies, new companies seeking fertile soil to locate within our boundaries. This is an indictment of our biggest banks, the Continental and First Chicago, whose troubles came from imprudent energy and real estate loans made outside Illinois.

Last August, at a meeting of Chicago's Economic Development Council, the guest speaker, Bob E. Sample, an investment banker, stunned the gathering with his blunt comments about the local financial community's negative attitudes toward business expansion in Chicago. He described Chicago's big banks as "very slow and unresponsive to requests for acquisition or expansion financing." His viewpoint has national credence among the knowledgeable.

Most big banks, here and elsewhere, who throw billions at corrupt, insolvent foreign governments and *Fortune 500* companies, pale visibly at the thought of making a $200,000 loan to a guy willing to work his fingers to the bone to build a great company — perhaps a latter-day Henry Ford or Juan Trippe, an Arthur Nielsen or Paul Galvin.

Given more leeway, the big banks will destroy the entrepreneurial spark which made America great. To give them *carte blanche* is akin to insanity.

Far better we establish a national policy to keep alive the smaller, independent banks with deep-etched concern for their communities and the small, private enterprises which create most new jobs and new ideas.

We must not let a greedy band of banking buccaneers use the woes of the Continental Bank to secure their own selfish ends at the expense of the public.

272

A jar full of pennies and a big bank

What, pray tell, is more humble these days than a penny? By itself, it does nothing at all.

It helps pay the sales tax, the uneven tail-end of a $9.98 purchase, maybe 10 minutes of parking in a small-town meter. Some romantics among you still may offer "a penny for your thoughts."

Enough pennies, of course, amount to something.

You may keep a penny jar at home, where you deposit stray pennies when you empty your purse or pockets. We do.

SO DOES A GOOD friend of ours, a northside Chicagoan, who told me this tale worth repeating.

Her penny jar was filled to the brim, and she decided it was time to turn the proceeds into spendable money, five or ten dollars or so, she guessed.

Quite naturally, she took her penny hoard to the nearest neighborhood financial institution.

It turned out to be Citicorp Savings, the world's mightiest, most domineering banking colossus, which has been pressing relentlessly in Washington and Springfield for interstate banking to give themselves an even more lucrative foothold in Illinois and all across the nation.

Our friend placed her penny jar in front of a teller.

"Would you be good enough to count my pennies?" she asked politely."

"Do you have an account with us?"

"No, but I've heard there's a shortage of pennies, and I thought..."

Now our friend didn't expect the teller to count her pennies laboriously one by one. She thought the teller would dump the coins into one of those counting machines which spins and whirrs and gives an accurate total in seconds.

273

BUT THE TELLER was unblinking and unmoved.

"Sorry, we just don't have the time . . ."

"It'll only take a minute or so."

"It's our policy. You'll have to take your pennies some-where else. Next, please."

Our friend was both irritated and nonplussed by her abrupt dismissal.

So she phoned her Loop bank, LaSalle National, to ascertain their penny policy.

"Oh, sure, we'll be glad to take your pennies," she was told.

She took her jar downtown and offered to show the teller her account book

"Oh, no, that won't be necessary," he said. "If you took the trouble to come down here, we'll be glad to help you. We're happy to count pennies for anyone." Which is nice — and human.

HE POURED HER PENNIES into his counting machine, and in a minute or so, gave her a crisp $20 bill plus some change in return for her 2,039 — that was the surprising total — pennies.

"I might have gone to Citicorp in the future," she told me. "It's right in the neighborhood, but not now . . ."

Is there a moral to the story?

Perhaps.

In most cases, big isn't best unless you're reasonably big, too. In fact, the bigger and richer the better. No question about that, as we proceed inexorably toward an ever more impersonal society, where the users of goods and services are further and further removed from the decision makers.

Generally, you're going to be treated more personally and with greater consideration by a company or financial institution with deep roots in your community than by a giant outlander seeking to skim the cream.

It's true, a penny may not be worth much anymore, but one jarful we knew of yielded $20.39 and this column.

Part Three

Of daffodils and smokestacks in England

I wandered lonely as a cloud
that floats on high o'er vales and hills,
When all at once I saw a crowd,
A host, of golden daffodils;
Beside the lake, beneath the trees,
Fluttering and dancing in the breeze.

— William Wordsworth, 1804

All over England last week, from gaudy, gritty London to the industrial heartland, we saw "hosts" of daffodils, including uncountable thousands in the Midlands where Wordsworth lived and wrote.

When I marvelled aloud at the masses of those beckoning yellow blooms, nearly as common to our North Shore as to England, a British friend, whom I know as a no-nonsense, tough-minded managing director, delivered to me shortly a copy of Wordsworth's memorable poem, which I treated too lightly as a schoolboy.

275

A CHARMING, SLIGHTLY boisterous chap with booming voice and shock of thick, black hair, Paul Eckersley has been unfailingly on his best behavior when I've encountered him. Still, I'd pegged him less as a fancier of poetry, than as a bit of a rowdy who could kick up his heels and quaff ale with the best of them, which only shows each of us can misread character.

It was a memorable trip. My business associate, Gene McGuire, and I encountered those daffodils from the windows of our Park Lane hotel rooms, in the endless parks of London, and dotting the fields and hills as we sped by train to Liverpool and back from Birmingham, where the Industrial Revolution took root some 200 years ago.

Along the way, the ewes were dropping their lambs, blackfaced and wobbly, in fields of emerald green as spring made its bow despite weather better suited to our northern Illinois lakeshore in March.

I was told we were two weeks too soon to drink in the full riot of color from the flowering fruit trees and the rest of an English spring, but I was not saddened much, for I knew I would have that opportunity soon in our own backyard.

London is full of incongruity. Scaffolds are up all over that ancient city as workmen labor to restore centuries-old buildings encrusted with the scale of history. Others labor to take down flimsy, badly-built, 30-year old high rises which have failed in mere adolescence to stand the test of time.

THE ARAB INFLUENCE is encompassing. Arab banks, Arab restaurants, Arab potentates, and Arab business types abound. They swarm at the Ritz in Piccadilly, and at the emporiums where Mercedes, Jaguars, and Rolls Royces are "customized" at astronomical — to me, obscene — prices.

Liverpool and Birmingham, on a much more massive scale, reminded me of the Ohio milltown where I grew up. Not all that pretty, perhaps, but solid and more reassuring than the glitzy, often sterile, cities of glass and steel.

In Liverpool and Birmingham, we toured old but serviceable factories — as in Wisconsin or Illinois, even Mississippi, and Georgia — where sheet steel is cut and shaped and painted. These are the smokestack industries, throwbacks to an earlier time, over which the futurists, consultants, journalists, and bankers often wring their hands, and which have seen recent hard times. But they endure to make the ordinary things on which all of us depend every day of our lives.

Our hosts told us of the diverse personalities of their own plants in the two English cities, as different as the one brother who became a priest, the other a gambler. At Liverpool, the workers were cocky and macho, mercurial, sometimes undependable, living for today, products of an environment where work was traditionally unsteady, a kind of day-to-day lottery. There was more stability, a somewhat different pattern, in Birmingham, with higher morale the result. It wasn't all that hard to perceive the difference as we walked through those now-busy factories.

The food in England can be overwhelming. I'm not used to those sumptuous lunches of beef-and-kidney pie, or slice after slice of veal with a sauce of onions and olives, topped off by "trifles," a rich confection of fruit, chocolate, whipped cream, and other assorted treats. The schedule didn't permit, but such midday fare set me up for a nap. On our last evening, in a fit of daring, I chanced cream of Jerusalem artichoke soup and Scotch salmon. Both were worthy of my risk-taking.

THE AMERICAN INFLUENCE is strong, too. There was a full-fledged, U. S.-style McDonald's in Solihull, a quaint, veddy British suburb of Birmingham. Names like Ovaltine, Kodak, and IBM kept popping up as we rolled along by train.

The British spruce up their row houses with "bow"—which we call "bay" — windows, lace curtains, and planting wherever there is a tiny patch of earth. Because the United Kingdom is hardly celebrated for central heating, they set the world standard in gas room heaters and fireplaces, with Valor, whose plants we toured, leading the way.

The much-maligned British newspapers combine a Chicago-like disdain for local pols with graphic samples of British nubility. One government official was raked over the coals on page one last week for buying himself, with tax monies, an expensive Swedish-made Volvo despite a strong "buy British" campaign. With unerring eye, I spotted dozens of "typos," including far too many in the venerable *Times* of London, now a Rupert Murdoch property operated under government strictures.

For pleasant diversion, we visited with old Chicago friends, Gerald and Audrey Marks, onetime Wilmette residents, he a commercial attaché for the U. S. Embassy, and Walter Henry Nelson, celebrated author and head of his own public relations firm in London.

People we encountered were intrigued by the unfolding, confusing political canvas in our country. Most seem to think well of Reagan the Human Being, but to question his aides and policies.

A young Swiss businessman of Italian ancestry, who lives in London, said of the president, "He makes you Americans feel good about yourselves. He stands up and tells it straight."

OUR DRIVER IN Birmingham was impressed by the showing so far of Jesse Jackson but wondered if any one of the present Democrats will be chosen finally to go against Reagan.

It was indeed a memorable trip — productive, too. There is an unfailing grace and warmth about the British. I picture still the symmetry of row houses and bungalows, the elegance of Piccadilly, stately, historic buildings, ancient cemeteries and quaint churches, the proliferation of soccer and rugby fields, meandering streams and ponds with swans, lush parks — and the daffodils.

For oft, when on my couch I lie
In vacant or in pensive mood,
They flash upon that inward eye
Which is the bliss of solitude;
And then my heart with pleasure fills,
And dances with the daffodils.

Reducing crime, saving billions

There is a positive way to attack the grim and worsening scandal of crime and punishment in America. It is simple but not simplistic. It will work. That is clear from many small samples of success, including some in Illinois. Its impact will be felt immediately. And it will save billions of tax dollars.

What I am proposing is simply this:

• Release from prison to parole, supervised probation, work release, halfway houses, restitution programs, and other alternatives to incarceration approximately 100,000 carefully screened *nonviolent* offenders, representing less than 20 percent of the total U. S. prison population.

• Cut down substantially from this point forward on the number of *nonviolent* offenders sentenced to prison, sentencing them instead to a wide range of alternative forms of punishment.

THE IMMEDIATE EFFECTS OF this seemingly revolutionary but thoroughly rational, workable initiative would be to:

• End overcrowding in U. S. prisons and thus eliminate a major element in the violence and inhumanity of prison existence.

• Reduce the staggering cost of corrections by billions of tax dollars.

• Reduce, in some cases sharply, the recidivism rates — based on solid, compelling evidence — of inmates released early from prison.

• Restore to society and reunite with their families thousands of nondangerous prisoners, many first offenders, who would be imprisoned briefly or not at all if they lived in most European countries.

What instantly springs to mind is the question of our safety if 100,000 convicted criminals are suddenly released into the society. But the adverse impact, if any, would be barely noticeable. Prisons breed crime rather than stem it, and there is no solid evidence that prisons have had much impact in controlling and reducing the rate of crime in this country.

DESPITE OUR VAST LAW-ENFORCEMENT apparatus, few dangerous criminals are — or ever will be — locked up. The rest are either not caught, not prosecuted, not convicted, or not jailed. They live among us. Now. Those in prison represent but a small fraction of those who actually have committed violent crimes.

Statistics show, too, that more murders are committed by spouses, children, parents, siblings, other family members, friends, and business associates than by vicious killers roaming the streets and preying on the unwary. In Chicago, for example, more homicides generally are attributed to domestic disputes than to armed robberies.

Is my proposal, flying in the face of all we are fed and swallow whole, irrational and unworkable?

Quite the contrary, "It may be our only salvation," says Michael J. Mahoney, executive director of Chicago's John Howard Association, the nationally renowned prison reform group.

"Anything that reduces the horrendous excesses of U. S. prison sentences is bound to improve a bad situation," he states flatly. "All the research at our disposal supports the concept of early release. Invariably, prisoners released ahead of schedule are less likely to return to prison than those forced to serve every last day."

MAHONEY NOTES THAT THE Illinois Department of Corrections, faced with critical overcrowding, has made effective use of early release until the State Supreme Court ruled against the practice on technical grounds.

Another outspoken advocate of "alternatives" is Milton G. Rector, former president of the National Council on Crime and Delinquency, who called on the 7,500 criminal courts judges nationwide to "strike a powerful blow for justice" by moving the country away from its dependence on incarceration. In a remarkable letter to the judges, he wrote in part:

"You know from firsthand experience that those we confine are mainly the poor, the young, and disproportionately, members of minorities . . . We must recognize, while there is time, that the continued caging of blacks and other minorities is the tinder of revolutionary fires . . . The time has come to change the way the nation responds to crime . . . Judges can put to work a wide range of alternatives for offenders who are not dangerous . . . Offenders sentenced to alternatives have recidivism rates as low or lower than those who are incarcerated. The public is equally well protected . . . Community-based sentences cost the public one-fourth to one-tenth as much as imprisonment. . . ."

Note well what Mr. Rector stresses: the public, he says, would be "equally well protected" and the dollar savings to overburdened taxpayers would be substantial. Neither he nor I propose that a band of savages be loosed on a defenseless public, but only a carefully chosen segment of those certified nonviolent and nondangerous would be released.

"It would be a relatively easy matter," Mahoney told me, "to use present classification systems to screen inmates nationally for early release as you propose."

WHY, THEN, DO WE persist in our folly? When will we heed the hard lessons of our failure to slow the advance of crime? When will our political 'leaders' choose rational, money-saving good sense over vote-grubbing demagogy? When will the people of this nation put their fears in perspective and demand not mere retribution but approaches to crime that will work? Must we simply proceed from an Attica to a New Mexico to the next bloodbath — perhaps at Pontiac or Stateville — without demanding radical change?

Thursday, May 8, 1986

Bill's 10 rules for staying fit and well

• •

*"Preserving the health by too severe a rule
is a wearisome malady."*

— *La Rochefoucauld, 1665*

• •

Are you beset with "wellness" advice from well-meaning friends, relatives, and self-styled experts? Baffled by contradictory counsel in countless diet/fitness books and articles? So torn, tormented, frazzled by your own indecision, uncertainty, and befuddlement that you're on the verge of total breakdown?

Well, relax. Right here, in the next few minutes, let me dispel your doubts with this simple, straightforward, ultimate "last word" guide to being fit and well.

Buckle up and pay attention.

THESE 10 "COMMANDMENTS" of fitness are guaranteed to make you feel better for at least 72 hours, maybe for years. They've gotten me this far.

1. Never feel guilt for not doing what all the health books tell you. Why should you be intimidated by Jane Fonda? Guilt is the sworn enemy of wellness. Guilt will kill you sooner than breaking a few rules.

2. Have fun exercising or don't bother. You don't have to run eight miles a day on hard pavements in cold rain to stay well. Whatever you do to stay fit, make it something to enjoy. Expect this to earn you the undying disdain of true fitness fanatics.

3. Don't adhere religiously to a dumb diet which leaves you starving or unsatisfied. Sneak a hot fudge sundae every so often.

4. Don't feel you have to eat everything on your plate. Leave little piles of food if you're full. There are plenty of starving people in the world, as your mother told you, but they won't get to eat what you leave.

5. Stay as far away as possible from such barely edible "edibles" as rat-tailed plantain, turnip roots, goat glands, bee wings, rutabaga sprouts, llama milk, and so-called health foods recommended by pop nutritional experts. You might catch some infectious disease on the roof of your mouth or develop fear of eating altogether.

6. Drink a daily six-pack of beer. Don't smirk. That's the

283

urging of at least one prominent, allegedly objective wellness disciple. His name is William K. Coors. Honest. I heard him proffer such advice recently with a straight face to a thousand cheering newspaper publishers. If none of that truly wholesome, brand-name brew is available, Mr. Coors says it's all right to take a nip or two of something stronger from your hip flask.

7. If you're serious about exercise, outfit yourself proudly. There's nothing wrong with paying $200 or so for a pair of gravy boat-shaped running shoes or buying yourself a specially-engineered running bra. You shouldn't waste your time exercising until you've run up a bill in low four figures for your designer exercise ensemble and membership in a health club where sports celebrities, starlets, and other notables are said to work out.

8. Don't think fun games like tennis and racquetball will keep you fit. Fun is out. Grim is in. Bear pain. True fitness buffs eschew all joy and lightness in meeting their exercise-for-good-health regimen.

9. If you swim, don't just paddle around in the shallow end. Swim laps, preferably at least 200 or until you drown, whichever comes first.

10. Don't brood about your health. "If you mean to keep as well as possible," wrote Oliver Wendell Holmes, Sr., in 1891, "the less you think about your health the better." G. K. Chesterton added, "The trouble with always trying to preserve the health of the body is that it is so difficult to do without destroying the health of the mind." Which may explain why some of the health advice you get seems so downright wacko.

• • •

Finally, if all else fails, consider heeding the fitness formula espoused by Robert Maynard Hutchins, late president of the University of Chicago, who is credited with saying, "When the urge to exercise comes upon me, I sit quietly until it passes away."

Thursday, October 25, 1984

The conscience of a lifelong Repuglican

The trouble with Reagan . . .

Even the rankest partisan must at times consult his conscience.

For me, one of those hard, even agonizing, moments is at hand.

It is not enough to play the indiscriminate cheerleader, or one loses self-respect, and, ultimately, influence.

I am indeed a lifelong Republican who has labored countless hours in the Republican vineyards over many years to support and encourage better candidates with vision, integrity, and a certain selflessness. I have a vision of a party, as I have said often, that is more "open, responsive and responsible" than today's version.

I AM A STAUNCH and devoted, if sometimes contrary, party member.

It is comfortable, in a way, to pipe the party line and march shoulder to shoulder with one's fellows.

Yet there are some in either party who would embrace Rasputin, Benito Mussolini, or W. C. Fields in the "right" uniform.

There are also the "access hounds," who, for reasons of ego and/or economics, go along with whomever occupies the White House or Governor's mansion.

285

Count me out. For me, that is not possible where principle is at stake or judgment intrudes. I am nobody's rubber stamp, certainly no knee-jerk follower, no strident ideologue.

WHAT I AM GETTING at is that I am increasingly uneasy about Ronald Reagan, about his fitness to lead, about the direction he will take this nation over the next four years. Most of this column was written *before* the two debates, while Mr. Reagan was still the overwhelming favorite. The state of the race, its closeness or otherwise, did not move me then, nor does it now.

What I am saying is that I shall find it difficult, if not impossible, to vote for Reagan in 1984 as I did in 1980.

Let the thunder rumble, let a thousand curses rain down upon my head, and let me explain rationally and quietly without bombast, bluster, or cant.

As a Republican, it would be far easier to go along with Reagan or simply to shut up. Anyone who knows me knows that is not my way, for better or worse.

AS AN EDITOR, I see a different role and responsibility. I see an obligation to look beyond mere partisanship. Our readers expect and deserve something more. I intend to keep faith with them, with those who expect a certain balance, candor, and honesty, and to express my views on the basis of my very best judgment. Conscience must be a guide in such decisions as these.

Everyone knows and says that President Reagan is a brilliant, perhaps matchless, communicator. But it troubles me, and I think others, that he is far better in a tightly-controlled setting buttressed by his 3 x 5 cards than alone under fire and tough questioning, as in a press conference or debate, where his performance often is mediocre and at times downright embarrassing.

• Out on the campaign trail, Reagan rarely communicates much of great substance or specificity, and he rarely delves

286

into the complexities of urgent issues. The people are entitled to more. He preaches a grand scheme built on a rickety foundation of generalities, and his earnest, Fourth of July oratory seems to lull many into a drowsy rut of non-think.

• While he talks triumphantly of the glorious salvation of Grenada, which has been compared to liberating Martha's Vineyard in midwinter, he seems to shrug off the sheer dereliction which led three times to the terrorist massacre of unprotected, defenseless Americans and other civilians in Lebanon.

"What private enterprise would keep on the job a manager who presided over three disasters of the same kind in succession?" asks Anthony Lewis of the *New York Times.*

"America's humiliation in Lebanon is a product of Reaganism in its purest form . . . some strong sounding generalities with no follow-through, no attention to detail, to the hard facts. . . . Policy *is* detail. But this President is unwilling or unable to grasp detail. He does not do the work. He does not learn. . . . What we see in Lebanon, then, is the consequence of an absentee President. . . ."

An editorial in the *Wall Street Journal,* normally supportive of Reagan, was highly critical: ". . . This raises fundamental questions about the management of our national security and foreign affairs. . . . Weren't any lessons learned from the Marine massacre and earlier car bombings. . . . ? . . . . Unless someone is held accountable this time, no one will be accountable next time and another avoidable tragedy will doubtless follow."

GOP columnist William Safire, a former Nixon aide, took an even stronger stand: "Americans are coming to the realization that the Reagan response to these continued outrages will be even more pusillanimous than Jimmy Carter's protracted hand-wringing at the seizure of hostages in Teheran. . . . All we have seen so far is impotence and incompetence, posture posing as policy. . . ."

287

• Reagan proudly takes full credit for a magical economic recovery, but totally ignores Reagan policies which deepened and prolonged the recession, and interest rates which for the small businessman and consumer stand today at 16 percent and up, the highest "real" interest rates in this nation's history when measured against the 4 percent rate of inflation.

• He has made a career of blasting the "budget-busters" who "would mortgage our children's and grandchildren's futures," while he, as the nation's leader, has yet to propose deep, painful, fair, and across-the-board cuts in the budgets he submits to Congress. This should be an affront to every staunch conservative who has made balanced budgets a sacred mission. Yet Reagan presides over the largest budget deficits ever, stretching as far forward as any of us can imagine, and does little except blame everybody but himself for their immensity. His evasion of the need for some form of increased taxation to bring down the deficit shows an unwillingness to risk politically dangerous, bitter medicine if he can get away with sugar pills.

HE HAD THE audacity, in his first debate with Walter Mondale, to state flatly and erroneously that deficits have nothing to do with high interest rates, which suggests he has yet to master the rudiments of Economics 101.

We know, the President must know — even though economists can't tell us exactly when or how — that the massive deficits will be devastating to the U. S. economy. To pretend otherwise is either sadly naïve or downright dishonest.

It is not enough to blame escalating deficits on the Congress and the other party. Who is our leader? Where is our leadership? Who draws and submits the budget to Congress?

• He waits until a few weeks before the election to meet with the Soviets' Gromyko, the first such initiative in four years, which falls far short of a legitimate "summit" session, and then, with straight face, denies political implications in

288

the carefully-staged encounter. I can only wonder, as I'm sure many others do, why such a meeting couldn't have been held two years sooner or six weeks later — *after* the election.

The media, naturally, was invited to the infertile Reagan-Gromyko encounter in the White House under tightly-controlled circumstances. With the tape rolling, the President was heard to mutter something like, "No questions, please, this is a photo opportunity." *Mon Dieu!*

• Then there is the matter of "liberty and justice for all," which seems to have limited meaning in the Reagan Justice Department. A top official at Justice, in a recent speech, called for far tougher, longer sentences for convicted criminals and the abolition of parole. Afterwards, a somewhat skeptical friend of mine in the audience asked the Justice aide how we can afford the huge amount of additional prison space required to incarcerate thousands more.

The Justice official shot back coldly, "We ought to be executing more criminals."

I DO NOT SUGGEST for a second that this is the position espoused by President Reagan, but it is not all that uncharacteristic of the Stone Age mentality prevailing at Justice.

"Which candidate," asks syndicated *Sun-Times* columnist Carl Rowan, "understands the qualities of justice that he will not use his appointive powers to turn the nation's judicial system into a rubber stamp for a draconian nightmare?"

Will Reagan, for example, adhere to a far-out plank of the GOP platform and require that potential judges submit in advance of their appointment to a litmus test on abortion? GOP Sen. Charles H. Percy, whom we already have endorsed, has shown the good sense to reject out of hand this outrageous shackle which would rule out judges of independent, Socratic bent. There are too few even now.

• A majority of Americans are staunch advocates of national security, of a formidable defense as a prime safeguard of peace. But I for one cannot automatically support every wild-eyed, far out, Star Wars-type weapons system which the President demands, nor do I favor the neutron bomb or a continued escalation of the nuclear arms race. This does not make me an advocate of unilateral disarmament or anything close to it, as Reagan is fond of calling many who seek a prudent, rational, cost-effective, affordable, waste-resistant national defense policy.

If Reagan Defense Secretary Caspar Weinberger were indeed "Cap the Knife," as legend has it, he would have brought into balance by now rampaging, uncontrolled military expenditures which have helped boost the federal deficit into outer space.

• The problem, it may be, are the people around Reagan, whose credentials and character become especially vital in view of what *Fortune*'s Peter W. Bernstein describes as "his chairman-of-the-board style, banker's hours, and penchant for vacations at the Santa Barbara ranch, plus catnaps during Cabinet meetings. . . ."

Evenhanded syndicated columnist David Broder appraises the Reagan Cabinet as "barely competent." Half its members fall short of that faint praise.

THE FACT IS, SAYS the incumbent dean of pundits, James Reston, that Reagan "tends to choose his aides from among his narrow circle of friends and ideological buddies. . . . He wants so many of his old California country-club set, who are less qualified than other Republicans who could serve him better. . . . It's clear that when he has a decision to make about his Cabinet or his White House staff, President Reagan looks not to the wide scope of the nation or his party but to the friends in California he knows best. . . ."

A striking exception is Vice President George Bush, decent and able, who has been confined to the shadows over most of the last four years, but whose role is reassuring as understudy to our oldest President.

Secretary Donald Regan brings to the Treasury Department a Wall Street mentality far removed from the earthy reality of Main Street and the thousands of small, private companies that are the spine and sinew of the U. S. economy.

James Watt, bless his soul, is gone. Attorney General William French Smith is a proper, naïve, grey-flannel sheep, fair game among the wolves of the Justice Department.

IN A SECOND REAGAN TERM, Smith would be replaced, if the Senate consents, by California crony Edwin Meese, a smalltime prosecutor, who was exonerated only last month of criminal wrongdoing despite arranging federal jobs for no fewer than seven people who loaned him or his family money.

Former Watergate special prosecutor Archibald Cox, now chairman of Common Cause, offers this harsh appraisal: "His stonewall defense of his initial bad judgment together with his failure to recognize the appearance of serious impropriety shows him utterly insensitive to ethical standards crucial to confidence in Government. These standards become all the more significant when applied to the Attorney General, who does more to strengthen or erode confidence in law and justice than any other official. . . ."

Loyalty is an admirable trait, but misguided loyalty of the sort Reagan often shows demeans his high office.

The Reagan entourage has not been distinguished by its probity. "Thanks to Ulysses S. Grant and his friends," Jon Margolis of the *Chicago Tribune* recently wrote, "The Reagan administration probably does not hold the all-time record for resignations under fire. But it's close. And as it turns out, those who have left the administration under a cloud are outnumbered by those who have stayed, equally clouded."

• There is a widespread notion that, under Reagan, the rich get richer, the poor poorer.

291

No nation, this or any other, can claim greatness for itself which treats its poor, its ailing and infirm, its unfortunate, as second-class citizens.

You've heard all the old, stale chestnuts about welfare queens and welfare ripoffs, jobs going begging, shiftless ne'er-do-wells, and all the rest. Well, they are absolutely irrelevant to the genuine needs of those who are hurting and bleeding, hungry and homeless, this very day. Such stories are generally a rationale for neglect, even cruelty.

There is no question that hundreds of thousands have slipped below the poverty line while the Reagan administration was fashioning its "miraculous" recovery. To me, something is badly out of kilter.

I CLIPPED OUT OF THE January '83 newsletter of the Church of the Holy Spirit, Lake Forest, these words of The Most Rev. Robert Runcie, Archbishop of Canterbury:

"Put at its simplest, what I believe to be the greatest ethical problem of the day is this: The rich and powerful of the world are too self-centered; the poor of the world are in growing despair. The gap between them is widening. It is a recipe for violence of an increasingly horrifying dimension."

If the Republican Party becomes the party of greed, selfish interest, the almighty buck, and disregard for the less fortunate and dispossessed, we will wither and die and lose our opportunity to lead and create a better, fairer America, free from the possible "violence" which the Archbishop fears.

• With consummate crust, Reagan invokes at every opportunity the names of hallowed Democrats like Franklin Delano Roosevelt, Harry S. Truman, John F. Kennedy, and Hubert H. Humphrey. Such posturing is more than a little tasteless and obviously infuriates their heirs and apostles. JFK's brother, Senator Ted, rightly blasted Reagan for pre-empting his late brother's name for political ends. Truman, according to former U. S. Information Chief Leonard Marks, railed at Reagan in 1948 as an undependable "left-wing Democrat."

In an exclusive *News/Voice* interview last week, Anne Roosevelt Johnston of Wilmette, granddaughter of FDR and Eleanor, said "there's no question" her grandmother would have "vigorously hit the campaign trail for Walter Mondale if she were alive today."

Obviously, Reagan hasn't had much to say lately about Richard Nixon and Herbert Hoover, but he's given equally short shrift to Presidents Ike and Jerry Ford, legitimate Republican models.

THERE ARE GRAVE, GNAWING issues to be confronted in a thoughtful, rational manner, and we Americans hunger for straight answers, yet the President, kept under tight control by a cadre of aides, has campaigned in a cocoon, emerging briefly to give his patented Fourth of July speech and pose for TV cameras in controlled, contrived settings.

His lighthearted challenge to "arm-wrestle" Mondale after the first debate was puerile and has nothing to do with his ability to grapple with demanding mental challenges over the next 50 months.

Ronald Reagan is a gracious, engaging man who symbolizes much that we Americans find wholesome, reassuring, and appealing. His optimism is contagious, but often has no more substance than a puff of smoke. He skillfully manages to escape accountability.

Much of Reagan's support today is coming from those who don't understand the difference between what he is saying and what he has done and is seeking to do. His agenda is often sharply at odds with his utterances. What he says often runs sharply counter to what he does. This may be unrealism, or it may be a certain duplicity. He uses all the right words — compassion, security, family, freedom — but many of his policies and actions fly in the face of his oratory. He repeatedly serves up dollops of whipped cream on hot fudge sundaes without getting to the core of critical issues.

ALL OF THIS, AS I SAID earlier, makes me distinctly uneasy about a second Reagan term, about his course if the restraints of a campaign are lifted.

I have nothing to gain from this litany of concerns unless it is self-respect and the release of feelings I am compelled to share.

The polls, so often untrustworthy, say Ronald Reagan will be the overwhelming victor on November 6.

But what if by some miracle Walter Mondale is elected?

It will not be the end of all we hold dear.

AMERICA, AFTER ALL, survived Harry Truman after the demigod Roosevelt.

Hear this assessment two weeks ago by George Will, the staunchly conservative columnist and close Reagan friend, in a speech to the Economic Club of Chicago:

Walter Mondale has endured "the acid rain of ridicule. He is a fine, moderate, intelligent, professional politician who is not to be patronized or ignored."

Thursday, February 27, 1986

Great Lakes: a place for 'uplift and inspiration'

Gloom and doom, toil and trouble, snakes and spiders, drugs, corruption, meanness, hypocrisy, venom and violence, pestilence and perfidy.

We are force-fed daily a steady diet of such poison pie in the metro press and on the pervasive tube — but we can only suffer so much.

Every so often, each of us needs a cleansing, purifying experience. We need to breathe fresh air. We crave a stiff dose of uplift and inspiration.

Aha. Martha and I were treated earlier this month to just that, the sweet nectar of the upbeat at a place which might surprise you: Great Lakes. The North Shore's Naval Training Center.

IT CAME ABOUT because I was invited to be guest of honor at the Navy's weekly Recruit Training graduation ceremonies, that is, the formal passage of so-called "boots" into the ranks of legitimate sailors, members of the U. S. fleet.

There was all the spit and polish, pageantry and pomp, associated with the military.

But there was much more, something I could see in the eyes of the young seamen as they came forward to receive honors, as they passed close by in review, straining for a certain perfection.

I could see and feel how discipline and routine and predictable pattern, the Navy way, had molded these callow kids from the cornfields and the concrete, some raggedy and rousting, others awed and timid, into good sailors, and, hopefully, one day, into better citizens.

As I reviewed the troops, shoulder to shoulder with Admiral Thomas Robert Fox, commander of the Navy's Training Center at Orlando, there was for me a gauzy veil of memories over the stirring proceedings. Around 40 years ago, I went through much the same experience at Great Lakes as a boot in wartime.

IT WAS A TRIFLE eerie. So little has changed superficially at the sprawling base. Most of the historic buildings, hallowed even then, remain largely the same. I guess back then I did my share of grousing, chased North Shore girls, and took it all with less than total gravity. But some of it rubbed off. I'm glad of that and feel genuine good came of the experience.

Many who live on the North Shore take Great Lakes for granted, barely aware of its existence or its dimensions, or the jobs it provides, or the youth it shapes. Yet it may be the world's premiere, and certainly largest, facility for training young people. It is a "community" of more than 30,000, if you count its permanent command, Navy retirees, civilian employees, and the thousands of recruits who flow through its gates.

It is commanded today by what would have been unthinkable four decades ago: a woman who is a Rear Admiral. A remarkable woman, too, is Admiral Roberta Hazard, who introduces herself as "Bobbie," who seems to stimulate, even command, respect from one and all, who is a rare combination of skill, devotion, toughness, sensitivity and charm. Her top aide, Captain Angus MacDonald, one of the nicest people you could meet inside or outside the Navy, keeps things running her way.

AT A BRIEF reception before the ceremonies, I watched the admiral pull herself away from the brass and dignitaries to talk intently for a full five or six minutes with a "Mutt-and-Jeff" tandem of sailors, a tall blond youth and a tiny Latino, both of whom would be honored later in the day.

Later I asked Admiral Hazard, what, if I wasn't being too nosy, they were talking about.

"I asked them," she told me, "as I often do, 'Why do you think you achieved such success here?' They almost all tell me their parents expected them to do well and they didn't want to disappoint their parents."

The whole base has responded to her touch and surely is the better for it.

Captain Norman Lord, I suppose, is the schoolmaster, the principal, the one who oversees the training of the recruits. Amiable, soft-spoken, erect, he and his staff do a quite remarkable job. When those new straggly inductees stagger off the bus and pass through the portals of Great Lakes, the task must seem hopeless to accomplish in just eight weeks.

WE WERE MIGHTILY impressed by the precision of the recruit drill team, whose bayonets would inflict serious injury if they slipped an inch or two; by the powerful choral rendition of "I am the American sailor," anchored by a young black man whose basso profundo shivered the huge Quonset-type drill hall, and by the stirring martial music of the recruit band.

What astounded Martha and me is that each of these recruit "teams" came together brilliantly in just eight weeks of boot camp rather than several years of working together.

If we have a female Admiral these days, where are all the female recruits? They're trained in Orlando under Admiral Tom Fox's command. He's a Rear Admiral with an engaging way, bright, rugged, upbeat, anything but crusty, doubtless a first-rate role model, and I'm guessing about half the lady sailors at Orlando have a secret crush on him.

The U. S. military takes hard knocks today. The climate is much different than in World War II, when everybody in uniform was something of a hero.

But a few hours at Great Lakes earlier this month gave Martha and me a very good feeling. They're clearly doing something right up there. It was an inspiring, uplifting respite from a workaday world fraught with a mass media diet of malice and mayhem.

The Navy is still working a certain magic in turning uncertain kids into good sailors and good citizens.

Thursday, February 6, 1986

Thoughts on the perils of space, the limits of our powers and resources, 'the fragility' of humans

Men are still men and women are women. We are all human beings, small and imperfect and very fragile in an awe-

297

some universe. At any moment, life may end unexpectedly for any one of us.

I was boarding a plane for New York in the late morning of Tuesday, Jan. 28, when the flight attendant who took my boarding pass told me grimly the space shuttle had exploded a minute or so after liftoff. Aghast, I went to my seat and for most of the two hour flight, without knowing anything more, pondered and wrote of the implications of both this unspeakable tragedy and our bold attempts to conquer space.

My first thought beyond the assumption that all aboard the shuttle had perished is that I can't name a single crew member or passenger on this space flight. I seem to recall that "a school teacher," a woman, is among them. But to me at least, all at this moment are anonymous. I think back to the early space flights and the vivid images of heroic astronauts like John Glenn and Neil Armstrong, Cernan and Gus Grissom and Slayton, who became household names attached to real people.

BUT NOW, IT SEEMS, our successes have turned recent space flights into non-events, rendered trivial and routine, spawning the assumption that probing space is nearly as safe and ordinary as flying on a commercial airliner.

I am "hoping" as I proceed to New York that the teacher is single rather than married and a mother. The pain for her husband and children, if they exist, surely will be excruciating. And I am wondering, too, how much truly is gained by firing people into space entombed in metallic capsules from which there is no escape.

I can picture how President Reagan will react. Somehow his finest hours come in the aftermath of a tragedy. He will anoint each of the dead space group as heroes, which they surely are, and he will call for a time of national mourning, which is only right. He will say with certainty and clenched jaw that we must "press on" with our space program and not let the Russians surpass us in this area of critical strategic importance. The people of America will support him, as they

298

seem wont to do, whenever he addresses them in the wake of any national tragedy.

I am less certain that we must pursue with untempered zeal our incredibly-expensive, still-perilous space program at a time when tax dollars are a precious resource and our federal deficit soars out of control. The space effort, despite its glamour and the national pride it engenders, must not become a sacred cow beyond hard scrutiny.

ON EARTH, AFTER ALL, there are other pressing matters at least as deserving of our attention and our money.

Admittedly, there is a tantalizing mystique about space, the wonders of the heavens, and the remote planets, which beguiles many of us. Such emotions are exploited effectively by all who have a stake in our multibillion dollar space programs, including huge companies, politicians, and space scientists, but this tragedy should cause us to look hard and long at what we are doing in space and what our ambitious agenda is doing for all Americans and all humankind.

With abundant arrogance, we assume at times we have mastered technology and even nature. This failure proves we have not done so in space, just as a commercial plane crash caused by wind shear violence proves we have not harnessed the forces of nature.

It is exhilarating to take on great challenges. Such is the mission of a bold people. But our powers and our resources are finite. That may be the most profitable lesson to emerge from this wrenching disaster.

● ● ●

Within a few hours after landing in New York, I learned from media accounts the grim details of the space ship Challenger's demise. The names and faces of seven dead heroes, and confirmation of the age-old truth that we humans are indeed frail, imperfect, and mortal.

299

Old age: We hope to 'reach' it and 'triumph' over it

> Old places and old persons in their turn,
> when spirit dwells in them, have an intrinsic
> vitality of which youth is incapable; precisely
> the balance and wisdom that comes from long
> perspectives and broad foundations.
>
> — GEORGE SANTAYANA

How sad and wasteful that we chew up and spit out so many people fortunate enough to live past, let's say, 55 and 60 and continue in robust good health!

A distinguished-looking man came to my office the other day to keep an appointment. His resumé told me he'd been a trust officer for a major bank.

Despite his background, he was responding to an ad we ran in *News/Voice* for advertising salesmen. Curious, I thought at the time.

He seemed ill at ease and squirmed on the couch. His story began to unfold. His bank got into serious trouble 18 months ago and lost a lot of business. The need for his special expertise declined sharply.

THEY DANGLED an early retirement deal, and "I foolishly took it," he said ruefully. It was a lump sum payoff, and most of it was gone now, some lost on a townhouse scam, much of the rest frittered away "mainly because it was there."

"I really need a job. The money's pretty well run out. I've never sold advertising, but your ad appealed to me and *News/Voice* sounds like an exciting place to work. I'll do anything."

"But why," I wanted to know, "can't you find something more in your field, a bank job, some sort of financial role?"

300

He paused, gulped, and seemed near breaking.

"I've got 135 resumés out. I've had six or seven interviews, Mr. Rentschler. Nobody wants me. All the big companies say I'm overpriced, overqualified, and over-age. Too old. They've all got policies on age, and I'm too old."

How old are you?

FIFTY-SEVEN.

Good God. What have we come to? What mindless idiocy. Here's a man like countless others, with exceptional experience and a good record, who's literally been cast aside by our youth-obsessed society. Is there no premium on loyalty, judgment, stability, competence?

"I remember," he told me, "when George Bush was running for President in the winter of 1980. He kept saying he was in 'the prime of life, ready to take on anything.' He was 56 then. I'm 57 now . . ." His voice trailed off and he stared past me numbly.

He was not looking for an outlandish salary or cushy job. He offered maturity and seasoning, which come with years of doing a job well, living a life well.

The system is rigged against the steady, loyal, competent performer. Thousands of this sort, who have devoted their lives to big corporations, fall through the cracks in today's frenzy of massive takeovers, megamergers, plant closings, and "redeployment of assets." They must move over and out to accommodate hotshot MBAs and driven yuppies, whose focus on the next quarter and the fast buck has eroded America's manufacturing base and our onetime industrial dominance.

WE PROFESS TO respect age, but how many share the cynicism of Edgar Watson Howe, who wrote: "How good we all are, in theory, to the old; and how in fact we wish them to wander off like old dogs, die without bothering us, and bury themselves"?

Age, I am convinced, is more than anything a state of mind.

You have known boys of 10 who were little old men. I have known those of 35 whose juices had ceased to flow and who had become stodgy ancients.

At the same time, you and I have known men and women of 75 and 80 with the zest and verve of vibrant youth. John Donne wrote of these: "No spring, nor summer beauty hath such grace, as I have seen in one autumnal face."

Bernard Baruch, financier and park-bench philosopher, said at 85, "To me, old age is always 15 years older than I am." He died a vigorous 95.

Some old men become known as oracles of wisdom and founts of goodness, mainly because they have acquired vast storehouses of money. Ours is a society which often equates wealth with wisdom and virtue, even though there is no earthly link between the two.

THE SAGE BION, who lived in the second century B.C., warned against "heaping reproaches on old age, seeing that we all hope to reach it."

And so we do.

Age is a mystery none of us fully comprehends, but most of us nonetheless wish to achieve.

Thomas Baily Aldrich offered at the turn of the century this prescription for living well in later years: "To keep the heart unwrinkled, to be hopeful, kindly, cheerful, reverent — That is to triumph over old age."

Finally, Robert Browning puts growing old in a perspective which makes it palatable, companionable, maybe even desirable, more so when we ponder the alternative:

Grow old along with me,
the best is yet to be,
The last of life, for which the first was made:
Our times are in His hand
Who saith "A whole I planned,
Youth shows but half;
Trust God: see all nor be afraid!

The question remains, as our nation and its people grow older: How can we tap this enormous resource of age and experience for our benefit rather than treating it as a heavy burden to be discarded prematurely?

Abe Lincoln's 20 years that might have been

It is not unreasonable to assume Abe Lincoln might have shared with his countrymen another 20 years or so of his matchless wit and wisdom if he hadn't been *handgunned* down by an assassin at age 56.

It is unlikely John Wilkes Booth could have performed his dastardly act with a knife or club.

Handguns.

Their sole purpose from that infamous day in 1865, and long before, to the bloody days of 1985 is to kill — not pheasants or squirrels or deer — but people. Human beings. Any one of us, our children, our friends, our Presidents, at any moment.

AWFUL THOUGHT, awful prospect, but a very real prospect. Every 52 minutes, someone in America is murdered with a handgun. Last year, 23,000 Americans died from handgun wounds.

• There was the gnomish little man, barely five feet tall, disgruntled by a routine reprimand on the job last week, who went home, got his .32 caliber handgun, returned to the Skokie foundry where he worked, and allegedly shot at point-blank range two of his bosses and a third man who tried to disarm him.

• There was the tall, graceful black youth, a virtuoso on the basketball court sought by colleges from coast to coast, who was felled recently by gang bullets on a Chicago street.

• There were the Kennedy brothers, Martin Luther King, the Pope, President Reagan, Jim Brady. The list goes on and on to eternity.

IT IS ALL TOO GRIM and grisly to grasp easily.

Handgun deaths, Joseph Cardinal Bernardin has said, are "a continuing tragic story in our society."

Many Americans, syndicated columnist Roger Simon observed last week in Chicago, have a "strange emotional attachment" to their weapons, especially their guns. It seems a kind of throwback to long-gone frontier days.

Simon, speaking to the annual Lincoln Day dinner of the Illinois Council Against Handgun Violence, noted that our language is peppered with gun-related symbols:

Good guys, for example, are "straight shooters" who "bite the bullet" . . . "keep their powder dry" . . . "make every shot count" — you know the type. On the other hand, there are others who are "gun-shy" and go off "half cocked" — you might call them "wimps."

DESPITE THE MYRIAD shortcomings of our criminal justice system, it is a little sickening to me to hear some people hail Bernhard Hugo Goetz, New York's subway vigilante, as a modern American hero. Granted our frustration, but there must be a limit.

Simon pointed out that Goetz, rather than merely protecting himself, as he alleges and his fans rationalize, may have been "out hunting" the night he shot four black kids who approached him on a subway. Goetz, Simon reported, was wearing a "quick draw" holster and had in his handgun some dum-

304

dum bullets, which expand on impact, literally tearing gaping wounds in the flesh, and which have been banned by the Geneva Convention as too brutal to use even in war.

The police report, Simon said, showed the four did not "threaten" Goetz, but "asked" for five dollars and some cigarettes. Several were found later to be carrying sharpened screwdrivers. Two were shot in the back while fleeing.

I don't want some self-anointed psycho with a gun shooting at my children or my friends' children or anybody else on the assumption that they pose some kind of vague threat for whatever paranoid reason. That's why I think nobody should be permitted to carry or even own handguns which aren't registered for some very good reason.

THE EVIDENCE IS overwhelming, it seems to me, that handguns would best be banned in this nation. Most people who keep one stashed in a bedside drawer or bureau are far more likely to shoot themselves in the foot or shoot an innocent child by accident in the dark than a dangerous intruder.

Let's leave the heroics for the local police, who do a yeoman job and keep our North Shore largely free from violent crime.

Consider the rich legacy of Abe Lincoln's 20 "extra" years. Or the continuing crusade of Martin Luther King for black pride and progress and brotherhood. Or John F. Kennedy's further imprint on his country and even his young children.

Must we be subjected forever to the tyranny of all who carry the small, easily concealed, deadly handgun, whether that person be a maddened drunk, stealthy killer, jealous spouse, or armed robber?

Let us ban the handgun.

What is the worth of a nurse compared to an injured quarterback or big-time executive?

I've told my wife she has no choice but to hire a top agent for her next contract negotiations.

Martha is a Registered Nurse with two degrees. She and her "fellows" in the nursing profession generally make anywhere from $10 to $13 an hour for ministering to the needs of the ill, easing pain, attending patients in life-threatening situations. Average hourly pay in the Midwest is $11.60.

Martha is balking at my advice, saying it's unseemly for a Registered Nurse at a North Shore hospital to concern herself about money when the critical need is for devoted and caring attention to the needs of her patients.

BUT I TURNED her head the other day with a few telling points.

I asked her if she was aware that a sawed-off quarterback out of Boston College was signed last winter to a pro contract that paid him — take a deep breath! — $25,926 per hour.

Some of you will remember Doug Flutie, who became a legend in 20 seconds when he uncorked a desperation "Hail Mary" touchdown pass to win a big game on the last play. After a few lacklustre games as quarterback for the New Jersey Generals, Flutie's collecting that obscene salary while sidelined with an injury and earning still more bucks doing TV commentary on the side.

Nobody else I'm aware of matches Flutie's hourly take, but some genuine superstars, which Flutie is not, do pretty well, too. The hourly pay of Larry Bird, the brilliant basketball magician of the Boston Celtics, is $10,439, and matchless hockey wizard Wayne Gretzky of the Edmonton Oilers makes $5,000 per hour.

BUT A COUPLE of genuine 1985 disappointments, Joe Montana of the San Francisco '49ers, and George Foster of the New York Mets, haul in a ridiculous $17,708 and $4,938 per hour, respectively.

Unless you are a certified, deep-dyed baseball fan, it's probable you never heard of Johnnie LeMaster, Shane Rawley, and Bruce Berenyi.

Well, these three, who are on the rosters of the Pittsburgh Pirates, Philadelphia Phillies, and Mets, were paid, respectively, annual salaries for the past season of $500,000, $700,-000, and $325,000. Two of the three were on the disabled list most of the year.

You Cub fans, of course, know Rick Sutcliffe, a scintillating pitcher for the 1984 Eastern Division champs of the National League. All he "earned" in 1985 was a cool $1,260,-000, mainly for lolling on the bench with injuries.

IF MARTHA PULLED a hamstring, I have no doubt she'd crawl out of bed and hobble to the hospital for a full eight-hour shift. Just for the record, she is *not* a strapping 6 foot, three inch, 210-pound 23-year-old.

I shall restrain here my normal inclination to rail against the outlandish level of legal fees. But how would you like to be part of this scenario: You're laid up in the hospital with shingles or gout or some other painful infirmity, you ring for the nurse, that blessed angel of mercy, and a lawyer in pin stripes suddenly appears in your room, sputtering legalistic jargon and unable to tell a bedpan from a spittoon? Wouldn't that be enough to induce a relapse? And remember, he's probably drawing down $150 an hour, while she's collecting her paltry $11.60 or thereabouts. Please, nurse, help me, help, help!

I have one last comment on rip-offs of great magnitude: The so-called "Golden Parachute." If my sources are right, the all-time classic was recently worked out for his benefit by the outgoing chairman of the Beatrice Companies, who cut for himself a $7 million deal in severance benefits when he leaves and the new owners take over. The astounding part of William Granger's unprecedented "diamond/platinum" goodie is that he came out of retirement and assumed a caretaker role just four months ago, when predecessor James Dutt was sacked.

Presumably, Granger had been well compensated when he retired as Vice Chairman after a long career with Beatrice.

WITH THE COMPANY'S takeover in an unprecedented $6.1 billion leveraged buyout deal, Granger has arranged a payout amounting to *$1.75 million per month* for *each* of those four months. And his Board of Directors, supposedly watchdogs over the corporate treasury and the interests of stockholders, went along with the outrageous payoff.

How much in fact is $1.75 million per *month?* Well, if a Registered Nurse wanted to make that amount *in an entire career,* she'd have to work an impossible *70 years* or *840 months.* An executive averaging $50,000 a year for 40 years would earn $2 million for a lifetime of service.

According to reports filtering out, the Beatrice board didn't agree to the Kohlberg Kravis Roberts buyout offer until some 60 top Beatrice executives nailed down for themselves some $60 to $80 million in total benefits.

One executive named Lipson, who joined Beatrice in April, is supposed to receive $4.5 million for his brief sojourn. This self-enrichment ripoff is being challenged in court.

By the way, the word is that thousands of middle- and lower-echelon Beatrice employees won't reap any such bonanzas, even on a modest scale, though many are likely to be squeezed out as the new owners strive to pare down their monstrous debt.

Do you get the picture? Do you see why U. S. manufacturers can't compete with foreign companies?

ANY WONDER THERE are deep divisions in the country?
Have we lost our senses entirely in the greedy stampede
for unjust riches?

What is one nurse or laborer, clerk or teacher, worth in a
society with such values as these?

Thursday, October 17, 1985

'The Great Mentioner' picks a president

Mentions are the prime beef of politics, the life blood of
the political animal.

There are incumbent or aspiring public servants who would
run down their grandmothers for the *right* mention in the
right place at the *right* time. Such mentions have been known
to launch political unknowns, ignite flagging careers, and trigger the ascent of Presidential hopefuls.

Some mentions are both natural and obvious. These started
long ago as mere seedlings and have flowered to the point
where they are now implanted in the national consciousness
and assumed to be unassailable truth.

Let me cite an example: Former U. S. Senate majority
leader Howard H. Baker, Vice President George Bush, incumbent Senate leader Bob Dole, and Congressman Jack
Kemp are endlessly mentioned by the *right* political pundits
as credible candidates for the Republican presidential nomination. Their names have been mentiond often enough and
long enough to be accepted by the public as serious contenders.

OTHER, LESS OBVIOUS GOP names — a kind of second
tier — likewise are mentioned as White House possibles. Mentions are sought and treasured by the likes of former Delaware

Gov. Pierre DuPont IV, retiring U. S. Senator and Reagan pal Paul Laxalt of Nevada, and Gov. Richard Thornburgh of Pennsylvania.

Any day now, the name of Donald Rumsfeld, former Defense secretary and CEO of G. D. Searle & Co., will begin to surface as a mentionable Presidential candidate.

Some political meteors, once the object of innumerable mentions, flame out. Ohio Sen. John Glenn is getting the silent treatment after his abortive run in '84. The longer he serves, the less Gov. Big Jim Thompson of Illinois is being mentioned in connection with The Brass Ring on Pennsylvania Avenue.

Mentions are critically important to upward political mobility.

The typical Congressman — probably around 430 out of 435 members — yearns to be mentioned as a likely Senator. The state rep seeks mention as a possible candidate for statewide office. Such speculation in the form of mentions enhances an office-holder's stature even if it comes to naught.

TWO VISIBLE Illinoisans are reveling in recent mentions. Former federal prosecutor Dan Webb and business tycoon Bill Farley, both relentless self-promoters, are being mentioned widely, with their blessing, as candidates for just about every available lofty office, but especially Mayor of Chicago and GOP Senate nominee to oppose senior U. S. Sen. Alan Dixon.

Chrysler's miracle man and bestselling author, Lee Iacocca, is getting mentions everywhere as the Democrats' best presidential hope, and, of course, Senators Ted Kennedy and Gary Hart are mentioned frequently by the national press corps.

Nationally-syndicated columnist George Will went beyond mere mention in a recent piece lauding the aforementioned Pete DuPont, which is likely to stimulate many more mentions for this smart, articulate bearer of a household name who wants to be President.

310

WHAT GOOD DO mentions do?

• They lend credibility.

• They are essential in raising money, which is about 80 percent of what it takes to get elected in the '80s. If a candidate doesn't have his own money — made or inherited — he/she must raise it. Get enough mentions where it counts, and the lobbyists come a-swarming with open pocketbooks. Sad, but true.

• Mentions get a candidate entered in the polling sweepstakes. Polls these days may be more important than elections. It's all decided in early October by the pollsters, and then the voters go back to their normal pursuits, tune out the escalating political rhetoric, and assume the election is indeed all wrapped up. When the polls show one candidate far ahead, he and his handlers pooh-pooh the opponent as a sure loser, the media rely on *their* polls to brand No. 2 as an also-ran, and, more often than not, the public accepts as gospel the verdict of 600 or so "guinea pigs" selected "scientifically" by some high-priced polling outfit.

THE OUTCOME THUS becomes a self-fulfilling prophecy, and our democratic process is undermined.

This is why every crafty politician cultivates, cherishes, and literally "kills" for mentions.

Take the case of Geraldine Ferraro, a comparative nobody toiling in Congress until a few mentions crept into her life. The trickle became a torrent. From anonymity, she became the Democratic vice presidential nominee, a hot literary/talk show property, an instant household word. It all started with those mentions. True, she didn't make it, nor did her running mate, but she can't blame her mentions.

You may be wondering how mentions get started. According to legend, there is The Great Mentioner in the Sky, who combines all the finest qualities — the wisdom and perception

311

and mental acuity — of the most revered pundits of our past. He is the ghost of legendary pundits like Walter Lippman, H. L. Mencken, and Edward R. Murrow. He scans literally thousands of press clippings and inflated resumés before sitting down at his heavenly Smith-Corona — manual, of course — and pecks out a long list of potential mentionees, discarding the vast majority as unmentionable.

AT THE CONCLUSION of The Great Mentioner's exhaustive research, the hallowed list is dispatched via heavenly post (the supernatural answer to Federal Express) to a select cadre of pundits, most of whom work the NewYork/Washington corridor, such as James Reston, David Broder, Vermont Royster, and occasionally, the likes of Evans & Novak and William F. Buckley.

These senior pundits are empowered to cull the list at their discretion, and share their erudition with local political savants, that is, their more parochial, unwashed press brethren in the hinterlands (rough translation: Midwest), where we live. Thus is the "mention" structure established all across the nation. It works with surprising precision.

So, finally, one among the select choices of The Great Mentioner in the Sky is elected to the highest office in the Free World.

The Mentioner smiles a smile of satisfaction and knows He has not labored in vain.

Conversation with Otto Kerner: a prison interview

In an exclusive prison interview shortly before his death in 1975, the respected former Illinois governor and federal appellate judge tells *News/Voice* Editor Bill Rentschler of his ordeal and the 'fervent conviction of his innocence.'

Only the raspy call of distant crows disturbs the quiet of the hazy late October morning. We drive slowly, Martha and I, up the long, straight blacktop driveway to the yellow brick-and-stone administration building at the center of the cluster of buildings, a dreadnaught floating in a gently-rolling sea of Kentucky bluegrass, an architectural monstrosity as ungainly and forbidding and impractical as a turn-of-century railroad terminal.

This doesn't look much like a prison. There are no high walls or gun turrets, no heavy gates or steel bars, no uniforms or obvious security. It looks even less like a country club, which is how some reporters have described it. We have come to the Federal Correctional Institution at Lexington, Kentucky, to visit Otto Kerner.

Otto Kerner, governor, general, judge at three levels, United States Attorney, legal scholar, staunch fighter for civil rights and prison reform, graduate of Brown and Northwestern, student at Cambridge.

Now Otto Kerner, prison inmate. It is less than easy to grasp and accept that status for this man as we walk up the stone steps and into the sterile front lobby, which is large enough to house two or three giant construction cranes. I envision a Piper Cub buzzing around up near the ceiling.

WE HAVE MADE NO advance arrangements and have no idea what to expect. I simply tell the girl at the front desk that "Mr." Kerner is a friend, which he is, and we are here to see him. We have no assurance we'll get in or how much red tape will be involved. There is none. When she finally looks up, she tells me in the rich accent of the border-state mountaineer to sign in on a ruled sheet.

"Let me see some identification."

I fish out my driver's license. She glances at it, nods and without asking Martha for anything at all, directs us through a door behind her and down some stairs to a basement room, where she tells us to find a seat and wait.

The low-ceilinged room with peeling yellow walls reminds me of a small-town "greasy spoon" cafe in downstate Illinois. We sit on straight-backed plastic-and-chrome chairs at a square table for four with chrome legs and black plastic top, one of a dozen such tables in the room. There is a beanbag ashtray half full of cigarette butts in the center of the table. A bank of vending machines lines one wall. A middle-aged man with grey brush cut, who looks like a Marine colonel, talks earnestly with a woman, possibly his mother, obviously strained, at one table.

Two towhead, look-alike boys, about four and six, crayon quietly at another table while their parents stare blankly at each other, occasionally mumbling a few words. This is the visiting area of the Federal Correctional Institution, a prison.

MARTHA NUDGES MY ARM. "There he is," she whispers. Otto Kerner is in the doorway. He spots us and walks briskly across the room.

"Hello, Bill, it's so good of you to come. My, this is a surprise."

"Hello, Governor. Good to see you. You remember Martha."

"Of course. I'm so glad to see you, Martha. Won't you sit down?"

Otto Kerner is an innately gracious man, and he greets us

314

with the same warmth and hostly cordiality I recall from past encounters. We might as well have been coming for dinner at the Governor's mansion in Springfield.

BUT THERE ARE differences. Once Martha and I are seated, he picks up the bean-bag ashtray, carries it across the room, and empties it into a trash can.

"I can't stand a mess," he says over his shoulder. "I'm getting used to doing this sort of thing." He smiles and sits down. There is no self-consciousness.

He is not dressed like an inmate, a judge, or a governor. His clothes are casual, a blue knit sport shirt, darker blue, checked cardigan sweater, gray trousers, and black loafers. As ever, he looks impeccable, a little gaunter than when I last saw him seven months earlier, but still erect, a mark of his military training, his blue-gray eyes clear and alert.

"You look as if you've lost some weight," I tell him.

"Oh, about 10 pounds, that's all, most of it after Mrs. Kerner died and before I came down here."

"You're feeling well?"

"Generally I'm doing all right," he responds, but Martha and I sense there is more to it, so I press a little further.

"Yes, I have my bad days. My heart acts up from time to time. I've had two attacks since I've been here, one bad one, the worst ever." He is reluctant to talk about this sort of thing. He is a disciplined man who doesn't want to seem the complainer.

"BUT I THOUGHT the judge at your trial said you were supposed to be released the minute there was any evidence of a threat to your health. How bad were those attacks?" I press on.

"Considerable pain, shortness of breath. That's about all. I carry nitroglycerine tablets with me at all times." Kerner pulls a small bottle out of his pocket and holds it up. "The doctors here are surprisingly good, but the emergency facilities are inadequate. I don't know what would happen if I had

315

a severe coronary. I don't know the exact status of my health. I've never had an EKG (electrocardiogram) since I've been here."

Martha, who works at the hospital in Lake Forest, where we live, looks a little shaken. "How can they possibly know your condition, how serious it really is, if they don't give you EKGs every so often?" she wants to know.

"I really don't know. I wonder myself." Otto Kerner smiles. "I'd like to find out for myself, but I haven't seen the front gate since I came here last July. All those stories about this place being a country club . . . well, there's a lady present, so let's just say they're so much fiction. Some of the reporters get carried away. You know how it is, Bill."

I ask, "How are they treating you down here, Governor?"

"I'd say I get special treatment." Long pause, as he watches our expressions. Then: "Yes, special treatment — *in reverse,*" he says wryly.

HE EXPLAINS. Even though furloughs for inmates are routine and granted frequently and almost casually to most non-violent inmates, that does not hold true for Kerner. He was invited to teach a college course in Lexington, something he would have found rewarding, but permission was denied. After nearly five weeks of waiting, he was granted a furlough to testify at a tax hearing in Chicago, but he was required to sign a paper saying he would grant no press interviews, a seeming denial of his Constitutional rights. Additionally, I have since learned he was one of only 22 inmates turned down for a Thanksgiving pass. Kerner also was denied a furlough over Christmas. His two children, Tony and Helena, both in their mid-20s, visited him at the prison in Lexington, but his 89-year old mother was unable to make the trip.

I get the feeling prison and law enforcement authorities think of Otto Kerner as a time bomb which may go off in their hands. They concern themselves mainly with possible bad publicity.

I change the subject. I wonder how Kerner feels about

316

President Ford's pardon of the resigned and exiled Richard Nixon, long an antagonist of Kerner's, whom the former governor's friends still blame bitterly at least in part for Kerner's prosecution by Nixon-appointed U. S. Attorney James R. Thompson.

"Would you seek a Presidential pardon?" I ask.

Kerner, proud and doughty, is quick to respond.

"I wouldn't accept it. It would be an acknowledgment of guilt. I am innocent."

A SIMPLE DECLARATIVE statement: I am innocent. One can see he believes deeply that he has been wronged. It is evident he will carry with him to the end of his life that fervent conviction of his innocence.

Otto Kerner seems for the moment to be seeking to restrain himself. There is a period of silence as Martha and I wait, expectantly. We can tell he has more to say.

"I hate to say this, Bill, but I've become convinced the criminal justice system isn't working in this country today. The poor man can't afford a decent lawyer. So he often goes to jail and sits and rots whether he's innocent or guilty. He's one victim of the system.

"The hardened criminal, the repeater, the one who represents a real threat to society, the killer, the rapist, the professional, seems to get easy treatment and often second and third and fourth chances.

"At the same time, it is nearly impossible for the public figure to be tried fairly in court and to be judged fairly in public. Juries today seem almost indiscriminate in hanging public figures. The prosecutors are out for blood. There is a powerful anti-politician syndrome working today, which may be understandable especially after Watergate, but this prevailing attitude imposes an even greater measure of responsibility for balance and restraint on judges and prosecutors, who, after all, are responsible for a just society.

"I know what I'm telling you, Bill. After all, I served as a prosecutor and judge myself at various levels for many years.

The trend today is to get the conviction at all costs, even at the expense of justice, and that is very wrong. Prosecutorial restraint is out the window."

Kerner is highly critical of the Omnibus Crime Bill, which he says "was sold (in 1970) to Congress by Nixon and Mitchell as the only way to stamp out organized crime. What an outrageous farce!" A bitter, short laugh.

THE MAIN TROUBLE with the Nixon-Mitchell thesis, Kerner says, is that the tough provisions of the bill have had no appreciable impact on organized crime or the hardened criminal, but are being "misused for political and white-collar prosecutions, which have maximum publicity value for ambitious prosecutors."

"It's ironic," he adds, a twinkle replacing the grim expression, "that John Mitchell (former U. S. Attorney General) is likely to be a victim of his own bad bill." Then the shift again to gravity.

"I am appalled and sick at heart as I see the abuse of some of these legal tools. The misuse of immunity is the worst offense of all. The widespread granting of immunity inevitably leads to a certain amount of perjury. After all, the prosecutor is in the position of bartering a man's freedom for his testimony, and what is more precious to a man than his freedom? What happens is that some people lie — I suppose you can't blame them — and some innocent people are convicted. This is the height of injustice."

Kerner admits to deep depression about the state of the criminal justice system.

"You know, when I talk like this, I suppose some people say he's bitter and just lashing out against his accusers. But I have been expressing my concern about the state of the criminal justice system for many years and I've proposed many reforms and I've spoken out against some of the more repressive legislation advanced in the name of 'law and order.'

"The purpose of the grand jury has been distorted, too. Its role today is to return indictments at the whim of the

318

prosecutor — not to protect the rights of the accused, as was originally intended under the English system. Any prosecutor can get an indictment from any grand jury. He can get whatever he wants, and that fact should impose on the prosecutor an immense burden of responsibility and restraint. This is the era of the prosecutor. It's easy to get an indictment and conviction against the politician or businessman, anybody who seems to be rich or powerful or prominent, and too many prosecutors, especially in Chicago right now under (James R.) Thompson (then U. S. Attorney, now Governor of Illinois), are taking advantage of that situation. It hurts everybody in the long run. It compromises freedom. Let's hope to God the pendulum swings the other way."

"Unfortunately," Kerner continues, "most people today presume that a man who is indicted is guilty on the theory that where there's smoke, there must be fire. This means the presumption of innocence has become a casualty. There's a presumption of guilt instead, and the accused is put in the ghastly position of being obliged to prove he's not guilty. That, of course, is a direct contradiction of what our system of justice intends."

KERNER BELIEVES the typical jury, no matter how conscientious, often is not equipped to make valid judgments in highly-technical cases, where subtle distinctions and specialized knowledge are involved.

"How can a stonemason or elevator starter, a short order cook or bus driver or housewife or store-clerk — all good, well-meaning people — how can they possibly comprehend and pass judgment on some of the complex matters that come before the courts today? A clever prosecutor can oversimplify and tie them in knots."

"I ask you," and Otto Kerner looks directly at Martha, "is it better to let five guilty men go free than to convict one innocent man? I don't know if anybody much cares these days, but that's a question that used to trouble conscientious lawyers and prosecutors and judges."

"How are things going for you, Bill? I guess you're learning what it's all about, and that's no fun these days." He seems genuinely concerned.

"Oh, I'm surviving. I guess you could say I'm bloody but unbowed. Martha and the children have been great. Unbelievable. They believe in me. So do my friends and lots of people I barely know. I'm a fighter by nature. But it's tough. The money thing is awful. Defense lawyers cost a fortune, and the government can keep sending in fresh troops without regard for money."

Otto Kerner nods, smiles, then sets off in a new direction.

"You know, I don't like what they're doing to Nelson Rockefeller (former four-term Governor of New York, during Senate confirmation hearings for Vice President under Gerald Ford). He's a fine public servant. I have great respect for him. If they cut him down, for whatever reason, who of any stature will we ever be able to get into public life? Who will qualify?" His questions are rhetorical, and he goes on.

"I used to think maybe you had to be rich to be in public life. Now, after seeing the treatment Governor Rockefeller is getting, I think we may be reaching the point where we'll be governed by the unsuccessful, the mediocre, people who have nothing to explain because they've never done much or accomplished much.

"The Governor's a good man. My high regard for him dropped just a little when he pushed through that extremely harsh drug law in New York to deal with minor users and small-fry. That was ill-advised. He'd make a splendid President, I think, but he's too liberal and humane and independent for the kingmakers and the Establishment, so I doubt he'll ever be nominated for President."

I ASK THE GOVERNOR how he spends his days in prison.

"Oh, I keep busy. I do some clerical work with prison records, and I'm teaching reading to several inmates. I do a good deal of writing, putting my thoughts down and writing letters, 10 or 15 a day."

Then he chuckles.

"Saxbe ought to be glad to get rid of me since he's paying the postage."

He is referring to U. S. Attorney General William B. Saxbe, and he explains that inmates are not permitted to have stamps, but that the prison system supplies postage for all outgoing mail.

Incoming letters, he says, must be opened in the presence of prison authorities.

"I guess so somebody doesn't send me stamps, money, needles, drugs like heroin or strychnine, or something else I'm not supposed to have." Wry smile.

Kerner says he delivers his outgoing letters unsealed as required but nonetheless believes they are not censored or even read.

HE MENTIONS THAT four letters from his attorneys were delivered to him opened — contrary to prison regulations — early in his prison term. He complained to the warden and "it hasn't happened since."

I tell him of a mutual friend, a restaurant captain in Chicago, who gathered in a week more than 1,000 signatures on a petition for leniency shortly before Kerner's sentencing. Some of Chicago's most prominent citizens, men and women of widely-varying political persuasions, practically fought to sign their names. I remind Kerner a great many people "still believe in you and continue to have great respect for you."

"I know," Otto Kerner replies quietly without a suggestion of arrogance. "That's what keeps me going down here."

Everything considered, Otto Kerner is bearing up well in prison. His mental state is positive and he looks to the future. He is resigned to serve at least until January 1975. He had hoped to be paroled prior to Christmas, and was disappointed when the Federal Parole Board met in October and took no action on his case. But he is philosophical about the setback.

321

He feels he is, as the Reverend Andrew Greeley has described him, "a political prisoner."

The Nixon Administration and U. S. Attorney Jim Thompson "set out to get me and they got me," he says with emphasis. "I am clearly a victim of selective prosecution. My conviction was the price of prominence. Others have paid it and will pay it. You're a classic example yourself."

Kerner makes clear his belief that other public figures "far more deeply and directly involved than I" in Illinois racing matters have escaped prosecution for various reasons.

Kerner wonders aloud, his skepticism obvious, whether the hearings conducted by the Illinois Racing Board under Chairman Anthony Scariano will result in indictments.

"I'm the fish they wanted to catch," he sighs resignedly.

OF THE FEDERAL Correctional Institution at Lexington, Kerner says flatly, "There is nothing correctional about it. It's a prison — period. I keep a low profile here. That's best. I made a few suggestions at first. They weren't rejected. They just died. When I get out, I plan to continue to work for prison reform. The system is so dehumanizing."

It is good to hear Otto Kerner talk of "getting out." The blue-gray eyes are alive. The spirit is unbroken despite the humiliation. He is clearly a man with much yet to do and to give.

I can't help thinking, as I study his still-ruddy, patrician face, of the incredible twist of fate that has made Otto Kerner-the-Reformer a prime victim of the prison system he deplored and sought to improve. Life, as playwright James Barrie once wrote, is "a long lesson in humility."

It is when Kerner contemplates the federal law enforcement apparatus in Chicago that his mouth tightens into a thin line and his eyes take on a glacial hardness.

"That office in the Dirksen Federal Building . . . there's a Nazi youth-cult mentality . . . it simply drips with arrogance," he says, shaking his head in disbelief. "Everything is hyperbole, exaggeration. They can make a baptism sound like a drowning. They're smart and clever and innovative over there, but they're unethical, too, and they're cry-babies. They can't stand criticism.

"You know, I was U. S. Attorney for eight years. We thought we ran a pretty good office. I know how that office ought to be run. They bought (race-track owner) Bill Miller's testimony against me, literally bought it. He got off scot-free, and now he's living high off the hog in Florida with all his millions. And our U. S. Attorney (Thompson) himself went so far as to vouch for the good character of Marje Everett (another race-track owner who testified against Kerner under a grant of immunity) when she wanted to get into racing in California. Wouldn't you say that's going pretty far?

"I was convicted by perjured testimony."

I THINK HIS EYES are misting. Then he proceeds.

"I'd like to see that office pay some attention to organized crime, the sort of crime that adversely affects the lives of people, that really hurts people. When was the last time you saw the U. S. Attorney in Chicago hold one of his many press conferences to announce the indictment of a confirmed criminal or major racketeer? When? There's much less mileage in that than in indicting big-name politicians."

We talk for a while longer. Then it is time to leave. Otto Kerner is still the courtly host as he escorts us up the stairs to the capacious lobby.

"You must leave before I do — presumably so you won't give me anything I'm not supposed to have. You know, like hacksaw blades or heroin." Wry smile.

"It was good of you to come, Bill. Martha, so nice to see you again. Thank you both so much. I hope I'll see you again soon."

We walk out and down the steps to our car in the parking lot. We sit there for five minutes or so. It seems far longer. We say nothing to each other. We are oddly exhausted and depressed. Then we move slowly down that long driveway with Martha at the wheel. I am scratching on a yellow pad as she turns into I-75 toward Cincinnati en route to Chicago and home.

I finally interrupt the quiet to say what both are thinking.

"Isn't it incredible to be visiting Otto Kerner in prison? One of the best men Illinois ever produced, a fine human being."

Martha nods sadly.

Part Four

Truly free press must 'police' itself

Polls and other indicators tell us a majority of the American public is dissatisfied with the balance and performance of the more influential daily newspapers.

Publisher Harold Andersen of the *Omaha World-Herald,* former president of the American Newspaper Publishers Association, has said, "Some reporters almost joyously cast themselves in the role of an adversary. In seeming to take the extreme position that no one in government is really to be trusted, (they) thereby encourage a backlash which casts doubt on our own trustworthiness."

SOME PEOPLE, SOME high public officials seem convinced the only answer is to restrict freedom of the press, to choke off or filter the flow of information. They are dead wrong; this is a thoughtless, narrow, self-defeating approach.

Every citizen concerned with his own and his family's freedom ought to be willing to fight to his last breath for the sacred right of the press to pursue the truth with unrelenting vigor. A press that is unshackled and responsible is the one dependable bulwark against encroachment on our freedoms.

325

The prime burden for assuring that the free press is also responsible must fall on the press itself. The responsible free press must look at itself with an eye at least as critical and objective as that which it trains on others. It must "investigate" itself with a zeal that would reflect credit on its best investigative reporters. It must reform itself and change with the times. It must listen and respond to constructive outside influences. It must freely offer redress to those who believe they have been wronged or unfairly defamed.

THE QUESTION THEN becomes: how and where can the press do better? Let me offer these few thoughts:

(1) Much of the media today appears to operate on the premise that the public figure is guilty until and unless proven innocent. Watergate gave some credence to that notion, but it *does* conflict with deep-etched concepts of justice, and it does, I am convinced, keep many of our very best people out of the public arena. It also tends to nurture to our detriment the overwhelming cynicism and anti-politician syndrome which pervades the nation today.

(2) Too many reporters today seem far more concerned with achieving superstar status than with covering the news objectively, factually, fairly, with restraint, without sensationalism. Too many reporters seem to be angling for instant status as a Mike Royko or Bob Greene, a James Reston or Jack Anderson, an Evans-Novak or Woodward-Bernstein. Or they're cranking up to write a million-dollar book, join the press staff of an ascendant politician, do almost anything but report the news with care. There was a time when the reporter was a reporter, just that, fairly obscure perhaps, but a careful, dependable craftsman. Perhaps that was as it ought to be.

(3) With some justification, the press today claims to be "intimidated" by government. But intimidation is a two-way street. Government and many public figures feel at least equal-

326

ly intimidated by the press, often with equal justification. For the press, too, has immense power — the power to do good, but also the power to smudge a reputation, to end or at least derail a career, to destroy a life. Many — right or not — feel it is suicidal to take on the press, even to right a glaring wrong. The press has its way of dealing with the complaining politician and the persistent critic. The unfettered press must go to extreme lengths to be fair, to avoid above all the unfair, the unbalanced, the unverified. The press must be as careful as government to avoid any course which might be interpreted as intimidation.

(4) The role of the editor is especially critical. Strong editors of high principles with the courage on occasion to "cross" prima donna reporters are essential to maintaining and ever-implementing the integrity of the press. For a reporter, sometimes green, untrained, unleavened by any real depth of background, at other times seasoned but venal, arrogant, unresponsive to reason or enthusiasm, has influence that may exceed that of all but a handful of individuals across the whole spectrum of our society. To permit a green medic to perform delicate brain surgery could be akin to murder. Yet a green reporter's prejudice or slant or his lack of information or historical perspective can kill a good bill, stall a vital project, elevate a dolt, or blacken a reputation. The first-rate editor must exercise to the utmost his/her influence, discretion, discrimination, and, yes, veto power, even at the risk of offending a prize reporter, if he is to produce finally a fair and balanced product — whether it be a newspaper or a TV news show.

(5) One of the most constructive contributions the media can make is a faithful recounting of the positive performance of most public officials. The almost-unrelieved downgrading of politicians has resulted in a serious erosion of public confidence and respect for those in public life. The public servant has become "fair game" to the extent that many of our most able and qualified citizens are unwilling to subject their fam-

327

ilies and reputations to the abuse they inevitably suffer. The "adversary" relationship between press and government makes good sense except when carried to destructive extremes. The press must continue to investigate and unearth and criticize, but it has at least an equal obligation to add to public understanding of the public sector and its people by factual reporting, backgrounding, explaining, and interpreting in a rational, unsensational manner.

WE ALL HAVE a stake in preserving and nurturing a press that functions without external restraint, without fear, without cause to fear. But to earn more widespread trust among its readers and viewers, the truly free press cannot reject or escape the restraints of conscience and responsibility.

March 22, 1984

Aftermath of defeat: the 'taste of ashes'

Primary elections for me are a trifle bittersweet. I recall clearly the taste of ashes the morning after two very special primaries some years back. The losers last Tuesday are feeling that same emptiness, the wrenching adjustment from the frenetic exhilaration of campaigning to the deadly pace of defeat's aftermath.

Twice, in 1960 and 1970, I ran for the U. S. Senate in Republican primaries. Twice I lost in fairly close races to the "machine" candidate. When there's a GOP governor in Springfield, the Republicans have their machine, too, which is effective mainly in a primary.

I'M A HARD LOSER, and defeat is painful in any case, but I wouldn't trade those campaigns for all the cotton in Mississippi.

People, some I didn't even know, bled for me and truly cared about the outcome. You who read my column know I like to sound off, and the whole, sprawling state of Illinois was my bully pulpit. I met all kinds of fantastic people who are still my friends. I came to appreciate the broad sweep of the Illinois prairie and its special greatness as I never would have under any other circumstances.

I was in my early 30s in the first campaign, and my opponent in the fall was to be a genuine titan of the Senate, Paul H. Douglas, a lumbering polar bear of a man with a sense of decency and compassion.

How I came to run is a small story in itself. My political "career" started as chairman of the then-dormant Lake County Young Republicans, which a small group of us were able to revitalize. The state YR organization was equally dead in the water, and I guess I seemed less so than the rest, so I became its president. I thus began to develop a modest statewide "profile."

Even that was pretty heady stuff for a young buck arrived in Illinois only six years earlier.

One evening in 1958, at a Republican reception in a fancy Chicago high-rise, I stood respectfully in a circle of eminent senior Republicans talking of the near-impossible task of defeating Douglas in 1960.

AFTER A WHILE, two of them beckoned me away from the circle and led me down a corridor to an empty room where the beds were piled high with coats, ranging from Republican cloth to mink.

The elder of the two was R. Douglas Stuart of Lake Forest, whom I then knew only slightly, the chairman of Quaker Oats, former U. S. Ambassador to Canada and treasurer of the Republican National Committee. He became one of my heroes, a man of unbending integrity and earthy wisdom, a rare and splendid human being. The other was Stanley Guyer, a canny, affable, cherubic lawyer from Rockford, state GOP chairman for Illinois.

"We've been watching you, Bill," Mr. Stuart started in his quiet way. "We need somebody like you with energy and ideas to run for the Senate."

Stan Guyer was nodding assent. I was slow to catch on. Maybe Mr. Stuart was talking about the Illinois Senate, a lofty thought for a greenhorn like me.

He continued.

"We won't beat Douglas with the same old faces. We need a new face and new ideas. Would you consider it? We could help you."

I was completely bowled over.

I did run — with everything I could muster. Gov. William G. Stratton came up with his own candidate, a good, gray GOP lawyer Mr. Stuart predicted would lose in November by a half-million votes, which he did.

POLLS WERE NOT as sophisticated then, but there was evidence I had a slight edge three weeks before the primary. Unthinkable, grumbled the pros. Damn whippersnapper, muttered Bill Stratton and his powerful ally, *Chicago Tribune* political editor George Tagge.

Their strategy was simple. Tell the voters Bill Rentschler doesn't have a prayer, which is what they did, with Tagge's daily think-piece relegating me to also-ran status in a six-man field. It was atrocious journalism, but it worked. I lost by a 5-4 margin.

My total campaign kitty was a paltry $125,000 to spread the story of a political unknown to 11 million Illinoisans. I think back and gag when I read of long-shot challenger Tom Corcoran spending well in excess of a million dollars in his race against Chuck Percy, and Alex Seith using more than $800,000 of his own money in the Democratic primary.

I ran again 10 years later when the death of legendary Everett McKinley Dirksen left a gaping hole in the U. S. Senate. In 1968, I had chaired the successful Nixon "back-from-the-political-dead" campaign in Illinois and thus was primed for combat in 1970.

GOVERNOR RICHARD OGILVIE had other ideas he meant to enforce. He paid off an old campaign promise by appointing to the seat an early supporter, former Illinois House majority leader Ralph Tyler Smith of deep downstate Alton. The dour Ogilvie was enraged when I decided to take on Smith, an almost certain loser to then State Treasurer Adlai E. Stevenson III in November. Ogilvie threatened me ominously with "political and financial destruction," called out an armada of payrollers to work for Smith, and effectively turned off the vital money tap. I didn't accept it at the time, but the outcome was inevitable. I carried big downstate counties like Winnebago and Peoria, but didn't have the resources to compete in Chicago. Stevenson went on to annihilate Smith.

I guess what saddens me most about primaries is that they are largely ignored by the people. Only around 800,000 Republicans cared enough to vote in those two primaries in which I bled, battled, and lost. It was much the same as the majority stayed home last Tuesday.

October 27, 1983

Let's ban forever the deadly handgun

It is a sad, senseless litany of death.

• Oscar Gerber of Lake Forest, a casual friend for 20 years and the respected head of a successful family firm, is gunned down by a distraught employee in a Lincolnwood hotel room.

• A business associate who accompanied him, Bruno Spiewak of Glenview, is slain by the same handgun-wielding attacker.

• Then the murderer extinguishes his own life with a second handgun.

• A Cook County judge, who believes violence is "a tool of ignorance," is murdered on the bench by an ex-policeman during a divorce hearing, who draws a concealed handgun and fells the jurist with a fatal bullet.

• A young lawyer, so staunch a believer in gun control he won't allow his children to have toy guns or even pretend to play with guns, is shot in that same courtroom, where he represents the killer's wife, and dies two hours later.

Five human beings dead in a grisly 24-hour span last week, five more victims of handguns.

WHEN WILL IT end, all the horror and heartbreak, all the senseless killing in what we call a civilized society? When will it end, this bitter script of violence and tears?

Only when We the People demand it and stop it forever in this bloodstained land of ours. Only when handguns are absolutely forbidden (for all but collectors and exhibitors) and their mere illegal possession made a felony.

We've all suffered the endless gibberish dished out by the handgun apologists. We've read their bumper stickers: "Guns don't kill people. People kill people."

Hogwash. Handguns are made to shoot people, kill people. Nothing else. The Saturday night special is not for sport. Nobody hunts ducks or pheasants or deer with handguns.

The purpose of target practice with handguns is mainly to become more proficient in the deadly game of shooting people.

Only handguns really lend themselves to shooting people at close range, because they can be easily, and usually are, concealed.

DO YOU THINK the judge's murderer could have carried a rifle, shotgun, or even ball bat into the courtroom he soon bloodied? Or that the killer could have risen from his wheelchair, clambered over the bench, and killed the judge with a knife? Or that he could have snuffed out not one, but two, human lives in that courtroom with anything but a hidden handgun?

Emphatically, unequivocally, no, no, and no!

The two men who squeezed those triggers in Lincolnwood and Chicago last week were not hardened killers or professional outlaws. They were men tormented by the demons of divorce, failure, what they perceived as the unfairness of life, emotions which for a terrible, pressure-packed moment could grip many among us. There are thousands like them, time bombs waiting to explode in fury. With handguns in their possession, people like these become lethal weapons.

Consider for a moment the handgun kept at home for family "protection." How many times have you read of the child who stumbles onto an "unloaded" gun that fires accidentally and kills him or a sibling or playmate? How often have you been horrified by the story of the gun-owner who kills a friend while proudly showing off a newly-acquired weapon?

WE KNOW A grieving father, heart forever broken, who heard a "prowler" downstairs in the pre-dawn, fired at a shadow figure in the darkness, and killed his daughter unexpectedly sneaking in after a late date.

Police warn fairly routinely that if you shoot a housebreaker, you'd better kill him, or he may return to seek revenge. Would you really rather take a life than surrender a TV set and some silverware?

Most burglars are unarmed and scared stiff. Despite misguided macho tendencies, you'll generally do far better to stay in bed and call the police rather than confront an intruder with your gun blazing.

Handguns are a terrible curse in our society, whether in the hands of violent lawbreakers or well-meaning citizens.

THE PRESSURE TO allow their use is powerful and organized. More than two million are sold each year. That's tens of millions of dollars in blood money.

If we're serious about reducing violent crime, as well as tragic accidental deaths, the first and most important step is to ban outright the most convenient, deadly, easy-to-get, easy-to-use murder weapon ever devised.

The handgun. We *must* ban the handgun. I argued that very same case in February, 1981, in a commentary on National Public Radio — before the handgun attacks on President Reagan and Pope John Paul II. Even those devastating episodes did not sway the handgun clique.

The spinelessness of many public officials on this issue can only be classed as criminal negligence.

Where do our "tough-on-crime" politicians, including the Governor, really stand on this issue? How about our state and national legislators? We must insist on hard, unequivocal answers, and must seek our satisfaction at the polls. The fact is that many quavering politicians are frozen into immobility on this critical issue.

In the face of such inaction, the Morton Grove city council, which voted a handgun ban (since upheld by the U. S. Supreme Court through its refusal to hear a challenge to the law), seems heroic in its courage and vision.

AS A FIRST step, I am convinced other North Shore communities must take similar action to reflect the clear sentiment of a majority of their residents. Ultimately, Congress must show more steel than simper and pass a national law forbidding the manufacturer, import, sale, use, and possession of handguns.

I hope I may be present when a vast mountain of handguns is dumped into a bubbling cauldron, melted down, and sculptured into a monument dedicated to sanity.

Idealistic lawyers like Tad can make a difference

My stepson, Tad, graduated from law school in late May, and, after weeks of burning the midnight oil, recently completed his bar exams, a gruelling three-day obstacle course, which only 41 percent pass on the first try in California.

By way of encouragement, I've told him with some regularity, "If there's one thing this country doesn't need, it's one more lawyer."

But I always add, "Tad, if we're forced to endure one more lawyer, I'm glad it's you."

TAD CARES.

He cares about the poor and the black and the hurting, who are routinely denied a fair shake in our courts.

He cares about the sacred mission of our judicial system to deliver fair and equal justice. He has something of the clown about him and he enjoys a rollicking good time, but I sense fire in his belly.

He is not alone among lawyers in caring about the values and ethics of his profession, but he won't find himself jostled in a crowd or even a majority who worry deep down about such things.

I SUPPOSE MOST fledgling barristers start out concerned and caring, but too many quickly shed their idealism and sense of commitment. They turn too soon jaded, cynical, money-hungry, willing to compromise principle.

This nation has too many lawyers. On that score, there is little disagreement, even among most lawyers. This surfeit of legal "availability" raises the volume of litigation to the point where the courts are impossibly overburdened. Justice suffers. People are denied their Constitutional right to a speedy trial. The process becomes cold, slipshod, unfeeling, uncaring. It

335

misfires to the detriment of both plaintiff and defendant, and of respect for a vital institution.

Lawyers, scratching to maintain sometimes unreasonably high incomes, string out cases interminably, in effect "padding" their bills. The cost of decent legal services has soared beyond the reach of all but a few. The big prestigious law firms hire themselves out mainly to giant corporations and the very wealthy.

This is wrong and it is damaging to our society.

CHICAGO ALONE HAS 21 times as many attorneys as all of Japan. This fact alone gives Japan a distinct competitive advantage over the U. S. Our lawyers slow the introduction of new products and new techniques and set up legal thickets that impede progress and increase costs.

The Japanese simply don't get bogged down in the excesses of litigation and the resulting complexity, legal caterwauling, and cautionary advice which plague and paralyze American companies.

"We train engineers," Sony chairman Akio Morita has said, "while you breed lawyers."

In today's environment, if a small to mid-sized manufacturing company can manage even to obtain product liability insurance, the rates are astronomical, up three to ten or more times over a year or so ago, even in cases where claims were minimal or even non-existent.

This is due in part to the greed and inept performance of some insurers, but mainly results from the accelerating rash of damage suits and often outlandish judgments awarded by sympathetic juries to plaintiffs who misused otherwise safe products.

THE SELF-STYLED FUTURISTS these days predict that our prosperity depends largely on the growth of "service" industries, prominent among which is the legal profession.

If this be true, if indeed service industries dominate the U. S. economy, I fear for the future greatness and economic well-being of America. What will they have left to "serve" if the producers have withered or fled these shores?

Much of our public policy and proposed tax reforms are geared toward driving manufacturing jobs overseas and encouraging a society of "non-producers," which create few jobs, build no tangible products, and merely minister to the wants, needs, and appetites of a populace whose standard of living in such circumstances will steadily decline.

These are fateful — possibly fatal — decisions, and we could end up saddled largely with imported goods, foreign investment, massive unemployment, and a wealthy elite separated widely from the vast majority of Americans in terms of power and privilege.

THAT MAY BE AN ACCEPTABLE way of life in Latin America and the Middle East. But it is a distant and doleful departure from the sort of land our forefathers carved from the North American wilderness and envisioned for those of us who inherited their dream.

It isn't fair to blame this bleak scenario entirely or even mainly on lawyers, nor do I, but they surely deserve a fair share of the dubious credit.

I wish Tad well in his new profession. He knows I do so with love and respect.

I expect him to grow, but not to forsake his ideals.

Lawyers like Tad can make a difference.

November 24, 1983

Man from Greece: Such gratitude !

We give thanks, each in his own way, some silently, some outwardly, still others in clearly tangible ways.

Most native Americans, I suspect, who have not known the

iron boot of oppression, seldom give more than a passing thought to their gift of freedom, rarely thank God that they live in this "land of the free."

OFTEN IT IS those from other lands who understand and truly prize freedom and opportunity, which so many of us take for granted and assume will continue forever even without constant nurturing and vigilance.

Let me tell you about John Psihos of Gurnee, who came to Illinois from Greece on July 22, 1976, and who, he recounts proudly, ever since has "worked 12, 15 hours a day, seven days a week, to build a future."

John Psihos and his brother, Spiros, own and operate the Full Moon Restaurant at the extreme north end of Lake Bluff, a little south of Buckley Road on the east side of Route 41.

John is a shaggy man with bushy mustache, soft voice, thick accent, and outsized heart. His wife is expecting their first child on Christmas Day. We talked last Friday over coffee at his immaculate roadside restaurant with Tiffany lamps hanging over the booths and old-fashioned brass ceiling fans.

TWO NIGHTS EARLIER — eight days before Thanksgiving — he started cooking the first of 150 or so 30-pound turkeys he will serve on Thanksgiving Day from 11 A.M. to 9 P.M. *absolutely free to all comers.*

He expects to welcome at least 1,500 dinner guests for a meal that will include lots of turkey — "We'll pile it high" — with stuffing, cranberry sauce, mashed potatoes, corn, French bread, and rolls.

Who's invited? I asked him.

Everybody.

No restrictions. Rich, poor, young, old, families, singles. No demeaning poverty test, no discrimination or separation by class or color, religion or how much money in the bank. Just come on in, John says.

338

WHY DO you do it, John?

"For the people, to thank everybody."

What do you mean, John?

"I appreciate my patrons, the people who come here. They come from all around, the offices, the navy base, all around here. Many are lonely, the sailors from Great Lakes, old people, singles, people with no families. They lonelier on Thanksgiving. I share with them, see them smile and feel good.

"I appreciate the opportunity I have in America. We do well here. I want to do something for the people.

"I cook the turkeys myself. I don't have to work so hard, so long hours, but I want it to be right, that's the way I am."

John Psihos is proud. He is building a new dining room at the south end of this long, narrow restaurant.

"I have a nice place for meetings and parties, for all the people from the offices around here."

MY INTRODUCTION to the Full Moon came last year when my friend Steve Ramsey, and his daughter, Sarah, 10, invited me and her pal, Hope, to join them there for Sunday breakfast.

Steve called it a first-rate "truck-stop." It is common knowledge that truck drivers go where the food is good and bountiful. It was both at the Full Moon.

John told me his "truck" business is down from 40 to 20 percent because the Illinois Department of Transportation put in two "unnecessary islands" which make it hard for the drivers to maneuver their big rigs into the Full Moon's newly-blacktopped parking lot.

But business is brisk anyway and growing all the time, John says.

Think of it.

FIFTEEN HUNDRED or so guests for Thanksgiving Dinner — a sailor from faraway Montana with peach fuzz on his cheeks, an old couple struggling to get by on a meager social security check, a young woman recently divorced and alone, a college kid with no fare money to get home for the holiday, a still out-of-work machinist with his wife and three youngsters — all compliments of a Greek immigrant who, in his special way, only wants to express his thanks.

Such gratitude! If his ways would only spread, we might turn the whole world around.

Thursday, March 14, 1985

Will Lester Crown and General Dynamics be done in by a dog?

It is beyond debate that Lester Crown and his family have been notable contributors to good causes here and across the country. For that, they merit cheers and gratitude.

But no amount of generosity or civic benevolence precludes a relentless, hardnosed investigation and continued tough scrutiny of Crown-controlled General Dynamics, which has come under heavy, richly-deserved, and not exactly new fire for alleged huge cost overruns, systematic underbidding, scandalous personnel irregularities, and other taxpayer gouges which have ballooned our defense outlays beyond all rational limits and surely beyond what is necsssary for national security.

General Dynamics is hardly alone among the giant defense contractors in ripping off the citizenry, but General Dynamics is the biggest and possibly the most blatant and unyielding in its excesses.

A focus of heated controversy in the ongoing Congressional hearings has been the role of Lester Crown in a highly-publicized political scandal involving payoffs of members of the Illinois General Assembly in 1976.

THESE AND OTHER DISCLOSURES threaten, at least momentarily while the iron is at white-hot intensity, Crown's security clearance, his position on the Board of Directors as overseer of his family's multi-billion dollar interest, and even General Dynamics' preeminent posture as No. 1 purveyor to the Pentagon.

In the 1976 episode, five Illinois legislators were sent to prison for three to five years each on the basis of Crown's testimony, under an eye-opening grant of immunity from prosecution, that he had bribed them. Crown was named in the indictment as an "unindicted co-conspirator."

The so-called "bribes" were in the petty range of $300 to $700. The legislators and their lawyers protested vigorously that the "bribes" were nothing more than routine political contributions.

They had a point. It is scarcely conceivable that a part-time legislator with an income of $30,000 to $50,000 or more would be corrupted by a few hundred dollars.

YET CROWN TESTIFIED THAT he kept in an office safe tens of thousands of dollars in cash, which he used to "influence legislation." Not too surprising when one considers that Lester's father, Colonel Henry Crown, made countless millions in the "sand and gravel" business in Chicago, where corruption has been akin to religion. If those legislators were in fact bribed, that would make Lester Crown a briber, even though the more typical bribers, through their ever-elastic and endlessly innovative lawyers, invariably claim in a crunch that the bribes were "extorted" by the recipients.

The prosecutorial decision to prosecute the penny ante legislators while allowing the rich corrupter to escape a stiff jail term is a classic example of selective prosecution and the inequities of what we call "justice." It is also depressing evidence that the super-rich live by different rules.

What the visionary Plato said nearly 2,000 years ago holds true today: "Everywhere there is one principle of justice, which is the interest of the stronger."

341

Such was the pattern in the mid-1970s when Big Jim Thompson ran the federal prosecutorial "net" in Chicago and gleaned the gaudy publicity that propelled him from obscurity to the Governor's mansion. Thompson and his right-hand aide, Sam (then known as "The Hammer") Skinner, who succeeded him in 1975, repeatedly made outrageous deals with a host of rich corrupters bargaining to avoid jail and willing to testify against prominent public officials.

LESTER CROWN WAS a prime beneficiary. The Crown family's longtime lawyer, shrewd and well-connected Albert E. Jenner, Jr., marched into Thompson's office and cut an immunity deal for his most lucrative client which is said to be as broad in its scope as any ever approved in U. S. District Court.

Lawyers who read it have told me the document would have protected Crown if he had shot a neighbor and saved the company if it had been charged with a bald anti-trust or securities violation.

With Thompson plotting a political career at the time, he doubtless assumed it wouldn't hurt to be on the good side of Bert Jenner and Lester Crown, so he gave them the moon with a fence around it. Surely Jenner would go to almost any lengths for Crown, whose companies have paid the Jenner & Block law firm millions in legal fees over the years, and substantially more than $2,000,000 in the past year.

Beyond the Crowns and General Dynamics, it becomes obvious somebody — Congress may be our last, best hope — must rein in what President Dwight D. Eisenhower labelled "the military/industrial complex," a force he saw as threatening to our national solvency and perhaps even our liberties.

IT RAMPAGES OUT OF HAND today. Secretary of Defense Weinberger, a zealot once known as "Cap the Knife," has fallen under its spell and has been mesmerized to the point of irrationality and unbalance. The President of the United States is the staunchest among his waning band of

342

supporters. It took an executive's dog boarded at Pentagon expense and a $200 hotel suite for Lester Crown to get Weinberger's attention for an instant. In a laughable gesture of futility, he has ordered withheld $40 million in payments to General Dynamics, which extracts more than $500 million monthly in tax dollars through its cozy Pentagon ties.

A runaway deficit threatens the American future. Unless we want a painful tax increase, which we may get anyway, we'd best demand of our Senators and Congressmen sharp slashes in the rate of defense spending, where waste, excess, and apparently corruption force our government to cut back on school lunches, plow under farmers, and sacrifice the "have-nots" for exotic, unproven weaponry.

March 8, 1984

Selecting a president or a prom queen?

Why all the fuss about New Hampshire?

Why have we let Gary Hart's margin of less than 10,000 votes over Walter Mondale shiver the ramparts of civilization and take on such towering political significance?

WHY DO WE take so seriously the stubborn assertion by a small band of cantankerous Yankees that they prefer Hart to Mondale by about as many votes as it takes to elect a prom queen at a big state university?

"Live free or die" — New Hampshire's defiant state slogan — mirrors the prickly, singular nature of its people, who in 1776 became the first of the 13 American colonies to declare formally their freedom from Great Britain and adopt their own Constitution six months before this small, struggling nation ratified the Constitution we cherish to this day as the touchstone of our society.

343

It is this strain of stiff-backed independence which manifested itself when that clutch of New Hampshire Democrats opted last month to give the Kennedyesque, "new" politics of Hart an edge over the machine-powered, "old" politics of Mondale.

Both images, of course, were largely the contrivance of the major media, which, as it invariably does, inflated the first primary to larger-than-life proportions and touted it as the crucial and decisive event in the long and tortuous Presidential selection process.

HOW MUCH OF this, I ask myself, was a matter of reporting legitimate news and how much was sheer hoopla, hype, the calculated *creation* of a glitzy-yet-folksy media event, designed to benefit chiefly the TV ringmasters, but also the national print media?

To what extent did the massive coverage bend and influence enough of those crusty New Englanders to affect the New Hampshire outcome and then spill over across the border to help "rig" the result last Sunday of the Maine caucuses?

Does this obvious media overkill mock truly responsible standards of journalism? Can it be described as a rank "commercial" departure which despoils the image of the media for those who expect adherence to a rigid code of balance and objectivity?

The results in New Hampshire and Maine may not be critical in and of themselves, but their enormous psychological impact and the vast importance ascribed to them by the media — and thus by many voters nationwide — combine to produce an aura of inevitability, a bandwagon psychology, the momentum of a giant snowball.

THIS MAY PRODUCE a dangerous distortion of reality. Surely it elevates the role of the media from faithful observer and chronicler of events to maker and shaper of news.

It is a hell of a way to decide who is the fittest to lead us.

Let lawyers pay for their own 'playing field'

Of all the great private "industries" in America, only one — perhaps relatively the most lucrative of all — has its "playing field" and operating structure largely underwritten by government, and so by tax dollars extracted from the citizenry.

THUS EVERY taxpayer supports this particular industry while also contributing its huge "profits" in the form of service fees.

This "industry" is the sprawling legal profession, one of the great growth industries of our time, its tentacles spreading richly in all directions even as many of its clients continue their struggle to emerge from recession-induced red ink and barely make ends meet.

Lawyers generate their often bloated fees through their free use of an enormously expensive judicial structure — consisting of courts, judges, and all the costly trappings — which is subsidized almost totally by the beleaguered taxpayer. More than three-fourths of the multi-million dollar budget of Cook County, for example, goes to support its courts, judicial, criminal justice, and penal apparatus.

Lawyers pay virtually nothing — only filing fees and other outlays of petty cash proportions — for their use, and misuse, of this elaborate and complex mechanism. The clever stratagems of some lawyers, who skillfully employ tactics of delay, procrastination, and obfuscation, and the growing lust for litigation, are the prime causes of bulging court calendars, the tortoise-like movement of cases through an overloaded system, and the pell-mell escalation of legal fees.

Most Americans literally are denied access to adequate legal representation because they simply can't afford it. Increasingly, few but big corporations can pay the tab.

LAWYERS' INCOMES have soared out of sight, out of line with most other commercial compensation. In big cities, like Chicago, New York, Los Angeles, Washington, and Houston, summer law interns and full-time recruits, fresh out of law school, green as grass, callow, inexperienced, launch their careers at salaries ranging from $33,000 to more than $40,000 a year. These rookie barristers can't possibly be worth that kind of money except in an environment where remuneration generally is utterly out of whack with reality.

In big, prestigious law firms, top partner incomes often soar above $200,000 a year. The national average for all lawyers everywhere is said to exceed $50,000 annually.

Many skilled, savvy, experienced executives and owners/operators of successful smaller companies who actually add something tangible to the gross national product — as practicing lawyers do not — never ascend to such levels of compensation during long and successful careers.

Lawyers create and contribute to much of the complexity they offer to unravel for top dollars. Lawyers constitute a huge net drain on public coffers. Lawyers, as a profession, probably contribute relatively more to inflation than any other segment of American society.

Because there are so many more lawyers in the U. S. than anywhere else in the world — two and one-half times as many in Chicago as in all of Japan — and because they add indisputably to complexity and inefficiency, the American legal profession likely has contributed measurably to the devastating decline in U. S. corporate productivity over the past decade.

AKIO MORITA, chairman and co-founder of the $5 billion Sony Corporation, believes this is so, noting there are 21 times more law school graduates in the U. S. than in Japan.

"That's your trouble," he says. "Too many legal problems and not enough engineering problems. Because we have few lawyers, we have few legal problems."

346

Lawyers have reached the point where many seem to believe the world owes them not merely a living, but a way of life. The first class sections of major airlines overflow with lawyers (CPAs, professional athletes, and rock stars, too) riding on their clients' expense accounts. Most business travelers, who know the value of a buck and are gauged on bottom-line performance, ride coach.

I have a suggestion that would weight the scales a bit in favor of all America's "clients" — that is, all of us great unwashed non-lawyers.

I propose that lawyers be required to pay, let's call it a "court tax" or "reverse legal fee," to offset the huge tax burden required at all levels of government to support the vast judicial system which, if it does nothing else especially well, enriches lawyers.

SUCH A TAX would be based on a percentage of each law firm's total revenues, or an individual lawyer's gross income from legal fees. What could be fairer? What could do more to right a frightful imbalance?

To the first legislator in any of the 50 states, or the first Congressman, or the first U. S. Senator, who proposes and pushes such a measure, I pledge the first $100 to erect a bronze statue in his/her honor outside The American Bar Association's Chicago headquarters.

If that sainted legislator happens also to be a lawyer, the statue should be of pure gold and the good barrister guaranteed early admission to heaven.

Unsigned News / Voice *editorials by the author*

Thursday, April 17, 1986

Spring again: God's time of year

If ever you doubt the existence of God, of a supreme being, Spring is the season to erase those doubts.

If human beings decorated the tulips and dandelions, paint surely would be slopped on the grass and ground.

If human beings scheduled the arrival of the bulbs and blossoms, many would miss the deadline and be born, only to die, not in the gentleness of Spring but in the harshness of winter.

If human beings composed the melodies of birds, half the sounds would be garish and grating and offensive to our ears.

IF HUMAN BEINGS designed the leaves, they would be dull and identical and made of plastic, instead of delicate, translucent, and endlessly graceful and unique.

Where human beings have touched the waters and skies, they have created muck and murk and fouled the air, and only God can set them right again.

Who else but God would have thought to drape in snow this April week the yellow forsythia blooms and tender green leaves.

In many ways, we have conquered our environment and turned nature to our use in positive ways. But the pageantry of renewal each Spring, this Spring, is far beyond mere man's capacity to create or reproduce.

February 2, 1984

Attack the 'Great Deficit Dragon'

We don't recall if it was Mark Twain, Will Rogers, or some other homespun philosopher who warned that the people are not safe as long as the "legislature" is in session.

Well, Congress is back from the hinterlands and assembled once again on Capitol Hill, so the public presumably is in danger.

THIS TIME, WE worry about what Congress (and the White House) *won't* be doing, because 1984 is an election year, which normally brings with it much raucous rhetoric and scant constructive action.

But the agenda — global and national — is urgent, and we citizens shouldn't tolerate preening, posturing, and foot-dragging at the expense of pressing needs. It is dereliction of the worst sort for our legislators to let things drift and fritter away the critical months between now and November.

Take the budget deficit. It's out of hand, yet almost everybody, including President Reagan, who's made a pretty good living blasting the "budget-busters," is looking the other way. No question there's scads of fat in the defense budget, yet the administration is seeking a multi-billion dollar increase. Many other programs likewise need a good whacking, but we assuredly can't balance the budget on the backs of hungry children and the impoverished elderly. Unconscionable medicare payments and early retirement bonanzas for military and government personnel would be a good place to start.

The Grace Commission has offered some good ideas for budget-cutting. Chrysler's Lee Iacocca proposed $60 billion in cuts which made sense to the Economic Club of Chicago. Let's have at it!

OTHERWISE, THE GREAT Deficit Dragon surely will rise up to send interest rates out of sight, rekindle inflation, and choke off the recovery (probably soon after the '84 election).

News/Voice will support no one for the Presidency, Congress, or the U. S. Senate who in 1984 does not give genuine, vigorous, and deadly-serious support to meaningful budget reduction.

We'll be watching.

February 9, 1984

A judicial setback for our right to know

Those omnipotent judges who sit in our courts — from local courthouse to U. S. Supreme Court — have far greater influence over our daily lives than most of us realize.

A case in point:

Freedom of information — the right of us citizens to know about the actions of our government — has been dealt a severe and mysterious setback by the U. S. Seventh Circuit Court of Appeals in Chicago which affects North Shore residents and, in fact, all of Illinois.

IN AN ODD, unexplained, and in our view dubious, decision, the federal appellate court last month ordered *sealed* all documents and records relating to giant Citicorp's federally-

351

engineered takeover of First Federal Savings of Chicago, a move vigorously opposed by Illinois Attorney General Hartigan, Senators Percy and Dixon, and other responsible voices here.

No matter of national security is involved. No subversive or terrorist activity is suspected. We see no justifiable reason for denying access to those records. Yet the court has clamped a lid of secrecy on the chain of events that led to the "rescue" of First Federal, which Citicorp testified was a "drowning" institution.

Perhaps the decision relates in some way to the character of the Seventh Circuit. One lawyer who specializes in appeals told *News/Voice* that body has a reputation for "extreme conservatism." Another said the court leans heavily to the "progovernment" and "pro-establishment" side, rarely sustaining either a criminal or civil appeal against the federal system.

Citicorp's resources and influence are so great that it can be likened to a shadowy arm of government wielding enormous power worldwide. Citicorp Chairman Walter Wriston is considered the nation's most powerful financier, with ready access to the White House, Congress, Fortune 500 boardrooms and foreign governments.

Even the suggestion of Citicorp's failure or vincibility would cause tremors of global magnitude; thus our government must step in to assist when Citicorp's huge portfolio of questionable loans to insolvent foreign nations threatens to go sour.

Citicorp's foray into Illinois affects not only the public and local financial institutions in myriad important ways, now and in the future, but also the structure of our national banking apparatus.

The sealing of records by the court has about it the stench of cover-up. The people are entitled to know exactly what kind of deal was struck.

WHY EVEN SUSPICION of a cover-up? Did somebody bend to Citicorp's clout? Was the deal a rape of taxpayers?

352

Why were local bidders given short shrift? Were the judges protecting federal regulatory agencies from charges of bungling or worse?

Are these questions far-fetched?

We think not. We think they cry out to be answered. The sealing of these records is a serious stain on the credibility of the court, which seems in this instance a virtual handmaiden of government. We feel the court's order is the very sort that undermines the confidence of the people in our judicial system. We believe the court has a sacred obligation to protect, rather than deny, such rights as these.

The people have a right to know.

Thursday, August 29, 1985

'Our leaders are failing us . . .'

At a perilous moment in U. S. history, our elected leaders are failing us.

Yes, failing.

Congress and the President.

Both are demonstrating an inability to cope with grave problems, a failure of nerve and judgment in time of crisis, an absence of true courage and a surplus of macho bombast.

THE SUMMER is ending.

The President, returning from California, will pause on the steps of the helicopter with Nancy beside him, give us a cheery grin and reassuring wave. His rhetoric will be polished and the autumn battle plan agreed on.

The Congress — 435 members of the House and 100 from the Senate — will return from the hinterlands, full of quotable quotes, solemn promises, and no more guts than they displayed in July.

It is all so much hokum. Depressing.
They're letting us down deplorably, dismally.

NORTH SHORE Congressman John E. Porter (R., 10th) is one of a handful of stars in a sea of disappointment.

Porter's word for the Great Deficit Compromise is "phony." It is just that. Far too little, much too late.

It will yield a miniscule budget reduction, far less than advertised, nowhere near enough to make a genuine dent in the mountain of debt which is more a threat to bury us than the Soviet Union.

Is this the best we can expect?

WHERE IS OUR leadership?

It's not emerging from the White House. President Reagan, who for years has castigated the budget-busters, has been positively lackadaisical about the deficit. A flurry of symbolic vetoes won't get to the heart of the matter.

During September and thereafter, the President can be depended on to heap shovelfuls of dirt and blame on Congress, which deserves everything he dishes out.

But he's the top dog. He's the nation's leader. The nation looks to him for leadership.

In a situation that calls for drastic measures, the President continues to shield military spending and Social Security as untouchable sacred cows, and stonewalls against a tax increase, which has become just about as inevitable as tomorrow morning.

EVERYWHERE WE TURN, there are unsolved problems of a serious nature: the huge trade deficit, the flood of imports, the export of U. S. jobs, mounting farm woes, high unemployment, U. S. involvement in messy situations around the world, and, yes, that unchecked federal budget deficit.

These are not partisan issues. They're American issues, matters which affect each of us. We have elected a Congress and a President to tackle them with courage, clear-sighted vision, and some measure of wisdom.

OUR LEADERS ARE failing us.

If we had the option, we'd turn out the whole wretched bunch and start afresh.

Almost anything would be better than what we're getting now.

Let's consider a single 6-year term for our Presidents

What if we elected the President of the United States to a single six-year term?

• No reelection hassles and distractions.

• A more coherent, less political approach to nagging national problems.

• The assurance that Presidential decisions would not be influenced by reelection considerations.

• The reduced impact of campaign contributions — which increase sharply when a President seeks a second term — on the political process.

These are some of the benefits claimed by supporters of the single-term concept, which was debated nearly two centuries ago in the Constitutional Convention.

IN 1830, PRESIDENT Andrew Jackson urged a single term, saying the office should "be placed beyond the reach of any improper influences."

355

It's unlikely many of our readers up to now have thought much about the idea, which would require a Constitutional amendment.

Yet this very moment, a high-powered committee of influential Americans, including many who have served in the Cabinet and other high government posts, is seeking a consensus for such a signal change in the way we elect our Presidents.

A leading Chicagoan, Philip M. Klutznick, Secretary of Commerce under Jimmy Carter, recently assembled a small group of prominent citizens downtown to hear former Senator William B. Saxbe (R., Ohio) and U. S. Attorney General under Presidents Nixon and Ford, make a compelling case for the single six-year term, which to some seems somewhat contrary to American tradition.

But the crusty, plain-spoken Saxbe, a son of Mechanicsburg, Ohio, is all for it.

PRESIDENTS, HE SAYS, "get to think they're indispensable and omnipotent, like the 80-year-old who got married and bought a house near a school."

The single term, Saxbe maintains, would give the President an opportunity to be "more deliberative, free of much pressure, above the electoral battle. He'd be spared all that second-term maneuvering."

Klutznick feels strongly a President "can put together a better government with the assurance of six years in office. It would reduce the uncertainties and resulting instability."

Reelection concerns worry incumbent Presidents and clearly affect their decisions, often to the nation's detriment. In 1963, for example, John F. Kennedy told Sen. Mike Mansfield he knew the perils of Vietnam, but could not win reelection in 1964 if he pulled out. Lyndon B. Johnson acknowledged our Presidents, including himself, postponed the hard decisions until the second term, which may never come.

Support for a single six-year term spans the ideological spectrum, from Sen. Strom Thurmond (R., S. C.) on the ex-

356

treme right to Congressman John Conyers, a black Democrat from Detroit, on the far left, from Carter's liberal Secretary of State Cyrus Vance to Ford's conservative Secretary of the Treasury William E. Simon.

We like the single-term idea. It deserves a hard look.

Wednesday, March 26, 1986

With 'nothing to prove,' a time for caution

This nation pulls together in moments of crisis, and it is no different now.

In tense times, such as those off the coast of Libya, our leaders — in this case, President Reagan — ask us to support their actions. This we do as a matter of trust and patriotism.

Our President, the ultimate communicator, is hard to resist, and the public response, at least for now, is near unanimous.

Many of us, however, Republicans and Democrats alike, have doubts about the increasing tendency of President Reagan, egged on, it would seem, by the likes of Messrs. Weinberger, Regan, and Buchanan, to engage in what seems "gunboat diplomacy."

We are fearful of an escalation, possibly unintended, that could trigger an unwanted, unnecessary war and provoke terrorist retaliation — a chilling thought — in this country.

America has nothing to prove. We should resist actions which may be interpreted as unnecessarily provocative. This is surely a time for caution and a cool, evenhanded demeanor in the Libyan crisis and elsewhere around the world.

357

Chicago is part of us:
Its Mayor and people need our help
in attacking 'a welter of woes'

At last, it appears Mayor Harold Washington may have a chance to provide the brand of leadership and reform he pledged to bring to Chicago three long years ago.

Denied a majority and tormented by obstructionists in the City Council, the Mayor has performed remarkably against long odds. Somehow, he has held the city together. Now, with an opportunity himself to cast the tie-breaking vote on key matters, it seems likely — despite a court challenge — he'll be in position for the next year to show his stuff and mettle before the 1987 mayoral election.

If you think Chicago's woes are too remote to affect us suburbanites, you're removed from reality. If you think we can live in relative luxury and calm far from the grimy, littered streets of the metropolis, you'd be well advised to think again. If you think we can pull up the drawbridge and ignore the distress of our urban neighbors, you may be in for rude shocks far beyond your expectations.

Our well-being and prosperity are inextricably linked to the central city. We cannot in good conscience or enlightened self-interest shrug off the despair, the poverty, hunger, and homelessness which grip so much of Chicago. We cannot ignore or casually tolerate the joblessness, illiteracy, and festering crime, which are a veritable plague.

THE SUBURBS, after all, did not spawn Chicago. They derive their grace and beauty, their tranquility and opulence from the economic wellsprings of the city. If these wither, so shall we.

Each of us who lives in the green ring outside the city proper must do what we can, in ways great and small, to ease the

358

pain of so many whose future seems bleak and hopeless, to volunteer in city projects, to contribute time and money, to assume some role in making our city livable and safe. Chicago's greatness is not concentrated in the glittering high rises, the opulent downtown hotels, the Gold Coast and Magnificent Mile, but rather more in the hearts and souls, the muscle and determination of its people, whose colors vary and who speak many languages, but whose yearnings for their futures and families are every bit as real and deep-felt as yours and mine.

Chicago, we know, is beset by a welter of woes. Mayor Washington seeks to untangle them and move the city ahead. Let us recognize his devotion and give him what support we can.

A gentler side

A small Christmas miracle

She had not been her vibrant self for months. Her family sensed it and worried.

A brilliant student, gifted writer, superb swimmer, pretty and normally outgoing, she felt alienated for no special reason.

She was suffused with an anger she couldn't explain, a hostility and depression that drained away much of life's joy. Despite her honors, she questioned her worth. She found it hard, close to impossible, to love herself, to acknowledge her virtues.

Last week, she sat alone at a small table in a New England coffee shop.

AS IF BY SOMETHING more than mere chance, he guided his wheelchair directly to her table and stopped next to her. "How's your Christmas going?" he asked in a matter of fact way.

She said without enthusiasm she guessed "all right."

He seemed instantly to understand all was not well with her, that she was "bummed out," but he didn't press it. He would talk instead about himself.

An athlete who won a football scholarship to the Univer-

361

sity of New Hampshire, he told her he'd led a wild life in his college years and for a while thereafter. Then, on a visit to Hawaii, he fell from a banyan tree and suffered the injuries that left him a paraplegic, paralyzed from the neck down, with only limited vertical movement of his arms.

The Lord came to him, he told her, and said he could serve best by spreading the Gospel and the word of the Lord. The young woman, groping, trying to find herself, was transfixed, eyes riveted on his, as he spoke.

Those eyes, she related, were luminous, a brilliant cobalt blue, radiating an inner light. His features were those of a strong, vital, athletic man, his body withered by disuse.

HE SPOKE WITH quiet passion directly to her. He seemed to perceive clearly without prompting her mental state.

He spoke of faith and God's love, which had enabled him to endure his debilitating injury and maintain good spirits, and a positive outlook most of the time. He told her his closeness to the Lord was all that had kept him going, and now he had a mission.

He had learned to paint by clutching a brush and moving his arms up and down. Schools in the area were inviting him to tell young students how his faith had helped him overcome his crippling handicap and to teach them painting, which he did with relish.

Sitting there in the coffee shop with the inspiring stranger, she lost all track of time. She was nearly two hours late for her job at the bookstore.

She will not forget their meeting. It seems to have turned her life around. She has returned. She is soaring now, alive again, looking ahead with hope and anticipation. She knows the road is studded with obstacles and sharp turns, as it is for each of us, but she feels more able to cope. She is cautiously pondering a relationship with the Lord.

A state of euphoria is not constant, which she understands, but for her, this encounter, perhaps not merely by chance, is a Christmas miracle.

Where has our compassion gone?

Where has our compassion gone? There is a cold wind blowing through our land, a strange and callous mood abroad in much of the civilized world.

It seems in some respects a throwback to those days of supreme righteousness when the "good people" of New England in their wisdom burned at the stake those they "knew" to be "witches." Former U. S. Sen. J. W. Fulbright calls it "that Puritan self-righteousness which is never very far below the surface of American life. . . ." It is by no means confined to this nation.

IN THIS SAME SPIRIT of arrogance, the Italian government steadfastly refused to negotiate to spare the life of Aldo Moro, surely one of the greatest of their 20th Century countrymen. The world condemned the terrorists who kidnapped him, which took no special perception or courage, but there was only small outcry against the almost casual decision of the ruling Social Democrats to sacrifice the elder statesman of their own party.

Here was a disquieting absence of compassion for a single human being and for his family, and a sort of easy certainty that there is in fact no other rational way to deal with terrorists.

IN ANOTHER INSTANCE, Patty Hearst was returned to jail with scarcely a murmur of protest. We live, after all, in a nation ruled by laws, not men, so the old chestnut goes, and therefore it is perfectly all right to toss the rich heiress back into the clink for another 14 months of her young life. It doesn't seem to matter that she was kidnapped, terrorized, brutalized, and incredibly lucky to survive her ordeal.

How ironic that she should be convicted as a bank robber when she obviously entered the bank with her captors' guns threatening her life at any moment! But, after all, Patty Hearst is rich and prominent and fair game for a hungry prosecutor and a lot of green-eyed, mean-minded people. And what judge would risk their wrath in setting her free?

Once again, where is our sense of compassion for a fellow human being, even our sense of fairness and balance? Who suffered so much as a scratch or the loss of a single dollar as a result of Patty Hearst's "infamous crime"? Will our streets be a little safer while Patty Hearst is tucked away in what one reporter gratuitously described as a "campus-like" prison setting? Will any future kidnap victim be deterred from permitting herself to be kidnapped, or will Patty herself be cleansed of all evil?

FINALLY, DOES ANYBODY really care about the slaughter of hundreds of thousands of Cambodians over the past several years by the Khmer Rouge? We are sickened and depressed some 35 years after the fact by Hitler's atrocities during World War II, but for all our outrage, we raise neither our voices nor our hands to decry atrocities of comparable scope which are continuing this very day.

The UN's peacekeepers have declined to investigate. The U. S. government has remained largely silent. The way of the civilized world is merely to look away, just as we did nothing to condemn or prevent the holocaust of the 1940s.

We demonstrate anew our worth and nobility as human beings by the extent to which we rise above the primitive instincts of vengeance and vindictiveness and show our concern and love for every other human being.

THE WORLD TODAY — and our society, even our own neighborhood — needs less phony thumping of the hairy chest and more sensitivity and compassion for each individual, be he weak or powerful, rich or poor, friend or stranger.

Each of us would be the gainer.

Things undone leave a burden of shame

I still feel rotten about two things I didn't do when I was in New York a few months ago.

Just don't have the time, I said to myself.

I was rushing down Fifth Avenue for one of those oh-so-important meetings.

It doesn't seem all that important now, and an extra minute or so wouldn't have mattered a lick.

WALKING WITH LONG STRIDES, I whipped past a slight woman who stood motionless at the curb. Halfway across the street, I turned, almost by reflex, and looked back. She held a white cane. She was obviously blind, confused, afraid to venture further into the maelstrom of traffic.

I thought I should go back and help her.

But I didn't.

I hurried on, driven to get wherever I was going on time.

From the far side of the street, I peered back again and saw a black man helping her to cross.

I CHEERED HIM SILENTLY and felt a bit ashamed of myself.

That was not all.

Later that day, my important meeting behind me, I had yet another "crucial" appointment on my calendar. The pace hadn't slowed, and I was still running late.

It was cold and drear as I sought to hail a scarce cab. Dozens, driven by unblinking zombies, sped past. I was wearing a lightweight suit, and the chill wind cut straight to my bones.

Suddenly, out of the whirlpool of darting, weaving vehicles, a Checker heeded my frantic wave and veered toward me. I shivered and felt a small burst of relief.

AS THE CAB SLOWED, 1 spotted a man a short way down the street pushing a woman in a wheelchair. He, too, was signalling urgently for a taxi, and "mine" had gunned past him.

My first instinct was to step aside in a gallant gesture and surrender "my" cab.

I didn't. After all, I had a pressing engagement and couldn't for the world be later than I was.

Why in hell not?

I CLIMBED INTO THAT precious cab and made my meeting. Big deal.

To this day, I feel like a rotter of sorts for my callous indifference to that "wounded" pair.

I'm not normally given to self-flagellation. Like Harry Truman, I get a good night's sleep after making a hard decision.

But this was different. It has stayed with me.

This was sheer self-indulgence accompanied by an overdose of self-importance. I'm lucky to have a patch of turf like this to cleanse my conscience.

THE NEXT DAY, still in New York, I passed a blind man slumped against a building.

He held a cup, and beside him was a dirty, dog-eared sign crudely lettered, "THERE BUT FOR THE GRACE OF GOD GO I."

I put a dollar bill and four quarters into his cup.

I guess you could call it a guilt offering.

Tale of a canny, lovable old cat

Around our household, I've never been known as a cat-lover. Cats know it, and they seek me out, sidle up, rub, and do all the creepy, sneaky things that make my flesh crawl. Even if they mean well.

SHIVER, OUR PRESENT CAT, is the exception. Shiver is a 15-year old, black and white, garden-variety cat one of our children bought for $1.50 as a tiny ball of fluff at the Church of the Holy Spirit's annual spring fair in Lake Forest.

Shiver is different. Shiver defies all my ingrained notions and prejudices about cats. Everyone else in our family — my wife and nine older children — has been fond of Shiver in varying degrees. But Hope, now 10, positively adores her. Shiver is equally enamored of Hope.

Most cats I've known were spooky or irritable or damnably aloof or a threat at any moment and for no good reason to rake a hand or arm with needle-sharp claws. I never before encountered a cat I thought loved anybody but itself. Shiver loves Hope.

All her life, Hope has been able to do anything to and with Shiver and get away with it: kiss her on the mouth, pick her up from the wrong end, carry her upside-down like a sack of oats, dress her like a baby, sleep with her. Shiver seems to enjoy every minute of it — and always comes back for more. I've concluded that any cat with the good sense to feel that way about *my* beloved daughter can't be all bad. And thereby hangs a summer tale which harks back to a fierce winter.

You'll recall with a shudder that our unlamented winter of 1979 was probably the worst in history. One February night during The Great Snow that year, when the mercury was hovering around zero, when the wind chill must have been at least 30-below, when three feet of snow still covered the

367

ground, and drifted mounds of the stuff reached nine or ten feet outside our front door, I stayed up late wrestling with some paperwork at the dining room table. Thus it fell to me before I came to bed to "put out" Shiver and Blarney, our late, great Irish setter. That was less a chore than usual during The Great Snow because neither domestic beast could make it more than about 15 feet beyond the drift-banked door, and almost instantly they were scratching to return to warmth.

ON THIS NIGHT, Blarney was ready in less than two minutes. Usually, Shiver scurried in between her legs. This time, Blarney hurried in alone. I held the door open for a bit, peering out as the wind howled. No sign of Shiver. Damn.

How do you call a cat? I grumped to myself. All children know, I thought. So do most wives, but I'm damned if I have the vaguest idea. So I called Shiver the way you call a dog. No Shiver. It was freezing cold out there, so I slammed the door, a little unsettled.

Damn cat doesn't have enough brains to hustle herself back inside even on a bitter night like this. I opened the door again and gave my dog-call for Shiver. Nothing. Perfect silence and the eerie look of the frozen tundra.

I could feel concern creeping over me. Plenty cold out there for a house-cat.

STANDING THERE IN MY WOOLLY SLIPPERS and flannel pajamas, I had no idea what to do next. I walked through the house to the back door and turned on the floodlights. Not a creature was stirring. What to do? Call the police? Or the fire department? They'd laugh, I concluded. Get dressed and tramp the vast wasteland? Instead I attempted to wake up Martha.

"Darling, Shiver's not in."

"Glump, wub, wassat, erp."

"Darling, Shiver's still out and I'm afraid she'll freeze."

"Why'd you let her out? There's a litter pan in the basement."

I had visions of that poor, affectionate cat, who loved Hope with a passion, lying somewhere under a bush, frozen stiff as a board.

I could see Hope's crumpled face when I told her, the unending flow of tears, the disbelieving, accusatory look.

My daddy the cat-killer.

I felt desolate. Helpless. Downright awful. I turned on every light outside the house and kept moving from window to window hoping to catch a glimpse of our suddenly precious cat. No Shiver.

FINALLY, I WENT TO BED, wide awake. Once I leapt up, thinking I heard something. It must have been the roof groaning under the mass of snow. As she often does, Hope crawled in between us. It was around 4:30 A.M. Shiver had been out there five hours. She had to be dead. Hope would never forgive me. Why hadn't I locked Shiver in the basement with the kitty litter?

I slept fitfully until six. Then I got up and made the rounds again, hoping to find that funny face — black mustache and notched ear — peering up at me when I opened the door. No cat. Nothing.

This was it. I was grim now, a little panicky, certain I was party to, uh, felicide, er, cat murder.

I retreated to the bedroom. Martha opened one eye. I started to whisper the gloomy news. I was plainly agitated. Hope looked up, too. I started to spell "S-H-" — then realized that wouldn't fox Hope.

Martha, when she caught my message, was maddeningly casual.

"Oh, she'll probably be fine."

Hope was blissfully unaware of the impending tragedy.

SOON THE HOUSE started to wake. Lights, coffee, running water, bustle. In the light of dawn, our street looked

369

almost as cold and forbidding as at night. Poor Shiver. Soon I was ready to leave, dreading the inevitable, my stomach in a knot.

"She couldn't possibly survive a night like that," I said to Martha.

"Maybe she found a warm spot somewhere."

"Yeah, like where?"

I kissed the two ladies, pulled open the door — and there ... there was Shiver!

She padded jauntily past me into the house without even so much as a "by your leave, sir," looking the picture of good health and high spirits. Hope pounced on her, oblivious of the high drama. I was almost pathetically glad to see that splendid cat.

CANNY, LOVABLE OLD SHIVER had made it through the frigid night, just as my knowing wife said she would.

And Shiver, I must say, seemed in considerably better shape after her ordeal, such as it was, than I after mine.

Thursday, September 20, 1984

A 'great' life, a sad parting

We *do* come to love our animal friends.

Often they become a part of the family.

Sometimes they're nicer, less trouble, and more dependable than relatives.

More than a year ago, I wrote in this space about Shiver, our lovable black-and-white cat with funny face and notched ear, who turned me from a confirmed cat-hater into a great fan of hers, if not necessarily the whole worldwide feline community.

We acquired Shiver at a church fair long ago when she was

little more than a ball of fluff with watchful eyes and fetching pink nose. That same day, we also brought home her sister, Calico (Callie, we called her), who disappeared into the mists eight or nine years ago and never again was seen, at least by us.

Shiver was special.

She won the devotion of every last member of our sizeable clan, and she's been a steadfast household fixture, outlasting a menagerie of other pets, as well as our nine older children, who sprouted wings and soared off to slay dragons, scale mountain-tops and wait tables.

EXCEPT, THAT IS, FOR HOPE, who's 11 and has her own special rapport with Shiver. During Hope's "baby" days, Shiver tolerated with style and true catlike stoicism virtually every indignity known to and inflicted on cats. Yet those two became fast and affectionate soulmates, and there existed between them a bond of happy understanding.

For the record, it should be noted here, however, that Hope's mother, through sunlight and storm, has handled with only minimal complaint the feeding, litter pan, shots, and other such mundane details.

This summer, we calculated that Shiver, in human terms, had reached the ripe old age of 105 or thereabouts. She was walking a little more stiffly, moving a bit more slowly, looking ever more bony and straggly. She nonetheless was able to leap from floor to counter, which she did whenever she sensed the presence up there of unguarded food. A natural-born chowhound ("chowcat," if you wish), she hovered close by at mealtime, hoping to snatch a treat if anyone left the table for any reason.

One early morning last week, as I was shaving, I peered out by dawn's early light and saw Shiver gingerly picking her way along the garden's edge to the far reaches of our backyard. I smiled to myself, letting my mind drift back

371

through the years and thinking vaguely of Shiver's seeming "permanence" in our lives.

LITTLE DID I realize that would be my last glimpse of her.

Ninety minutes later, some teen-age neighbors en route to school found Shiver lying helplessly and painfully in the grassy circle at the end of Holland Court, the cul-de-sac which runs along the east boundary of our lot. Apparently, she had been struck by a city truck or paper delivery jeep as she continued her dawn "constitutional" a few hundred feet from our back door.

Those kindly youngsters, who knew Shiver fondly as a beggar seeking handouts, raced her by car to an emergency pet shelter, which was closed, and then to another where the quick diagnosis was grim.

Our vets, where Martha took her later in the morning, tried gamely to save her by wiring her pelvis where it was broken in two places, and stimulating her heart with drugs, all to no avail. The damage was too extensive, the trauma too much for a very dear old lady.

As cats go, I'd judge Shiver had a great life. How can you ask for more than all that love and a warm house?

We'll miss her.